Grade Aid

for

Butcher, Mineka, and Hooley

Abnormal Psychology

Thirteenth Edition

prepared by

Mary McNaughton-Cassill
University of Texas at San Antonio

PEARSON

Boston   New York   San Francisco
Mexico City   Montreal   Toronto   London   Madrid   Munich   Paris
Hong Kong   Singapore   Tokyo   Cape Town   Sydney

ISBN   0-205-48900-1

Printed in the United States of America

10 9 8 7 6 5 4 3 2 1   10 09 08 07 06

TABLE OF CONTENTS

PREFACE

HOW TO USE THIS GRADE AID

This book is an aide, a tool that will help you understand the concepts presented in the textbook. It is meant to give you a comprehensive, but concise, overview of the important aspects of each chapter.

The various sections of the Grade Aid are designed to give you a variety of learning experiences and test-taking practice. The answers to the questions are provided in the back of each chapter. However, page numbers also follow each question or exercise, giving you optimum availability to check your answers.

The following is a more detailed description of the sections provided in the Grade Aid.

BEFORE YOU READ

This section provides a brief overview and table of content of the chapter. Its purpose is to introduce you to the chapter before you begin to answer the questions in the Grade Aid. The table of content comes directly from the corresponding chapter in the textbook.

OBJECTIVES

These are goals you are expected to achieve after reading the chapter. They can be used as a measuring stick to determine your mastery of the subject.

AS YOU READ

The exercises in this section are meant to provide you with a variety of ways to remember the material. Given that not all people learn the same way, the selection of exercises hopefully will provide something for everyone. These sections include:

• Key words: use this part to define the important words identified by the authors. The page number that the word appears on is provided so that you may check your work. These are not in the answer section of your book.

• Who's Who and What's What—Matching: A matching section gives you the opportunity to become familiar with some important people, places, things, and ideas which are presented in each chapter. Again, it allows you to test your memory for important aspects of the chapter.

• Short answers: Writing is an important part of any class. This exercise is designed to see how well you can put your thoughts onto paper in a concise manner.

• The Doctor Is In: If you are taking an abnormal psychology class, perhaps you have aspirations of becoming a therapist. This section gives you an opportunity to test you diagnostic skill. Scenarios of disorders represented in the chapter are given, and you are asked to act as a "therapist" by diagnosing and treating the patient.

AFTER YOU READ

This section contains three practice tests. They are designed to give you experience test taking, roughly dividing the chapter into thirds—each test asking questions from a third of the text. Again, the page numbers are provided at the end of each question. Take these tests and see how well you do. Then go back and correct your answers. These tests are to prepare you for the comprehensive test coming up next.

COMPREHENSIVE PRACTICE TEST
There are three types of test in this section, multiple choice, true/false, and essay. They cover the entire chapter and give you an opportunity to see how well you understand the concepts. Because there are several testing methods provided, you will have lots of practice before the real thing.

USE IT OR LOSE IT
This section consists of thought questions designed to help you apply what you've learned in the chapter to current issues open for discussion and debate.

WEB LINKS
A few web sites are provided for more information concerning topics covered in each chapter.

CRISS CROSS
Another tool provided is a crossword puzzle that uses key words from the chapter. This comes at the end of each Grade Aid chapter and is a way to see how well you remember the definitions to the key words.

Chapter 1: Abnormal Psychology, An Overview

BEFORE YOU READ

It is likely that you already know someone with a mental disorder, although some disorders are easier to recognize than others. Certainly, we can all remember seeing people talking to themselves in a public setting, hearing about a friend's depression, or seeing a movie about someone struggling with alcoholism. Clearly, the elements of abnormal psychology surround us. This chapter will help you learn to separate the fact from fiction about abnormality, and to understand how scientific research contributes to this understanding. It is the goal of *Chapter 1, Abnormal Psychology: An Overview*, to provide you with a basis for understanding how mental disorders are defined and classified, how they occur in the real world, and how to use psychological research methods to expand our knowledge regarding abnormality. These concepts will give you a solid basis for reading the remainder of this text, and making sense of abnormality.

- **WHAT DO WE MEAN BY ABNORMAL BEHAVIOR?**

    Classification; Definition; Cultural Issues in Abnormality

- **HOW COMMON ARE MENTAL DISORDERS?**

    Prevalence and Incidence Estimates for Mental Disorders

    Treatment, and the Mental Health Team.

- **RESEARCH APPROACHES IN ABNORMAL BEHAVIOR**

    Sources of information

    Forming Hypotheses

    Sampling and Generalization

    Criterion and Comparison Groups

    Retrospective Versus Prospective Strategies

    Manipulating Variables

    Studying Treatment Efficacy

    Single-case designs

Animal Research.

- **THE FOCUS OF THIS BOOK**

- **UNRESOLVED ISSUES**

Are We All Becoming Mentally Ill?

<u>OBJECTIVES</u>

After reading this chapter, you should be able to:

1. Discuss why it is so difficult to define abnormal behavior.
2. Explain the purpose of classifying mental disorders.
3. Explain the DSM-IV definition of mental disorders.
4. Identify how cultural issues can influence the definition of abnormal psychology.
5. Describe what epidemiology tells us about the incidence and occurrence of mental illness.
6. Discuss the differences between inpatient and outpatient treatment for mental illness.
7. Describe the members of a modern mental health team.
8. Compare and contrast research approaches to the study of abnormal psychology.
9. Discuss how researchers can control sources of bias in the study of abnormality.
10. Discuss the issue of generalizing from animal research to human behavior.
11. Summarize the author's 3 principles regarding the study of abnormality.

AS YOU READ

Answers can be found in the Answer Key at the end of the chapter.

KEY WORDS

Each of the words below is important in understanding the concepts presented in this chapter. Write the definition next to each of the words. The page numbers are provided in case you need to refer to the book.

Term	Page		
ABAB design	22		
Abnormal behavior	5		
Acute	14		
Analogue studies	23		
Case study	16		
Chronic	14		
Dependent variable	21		
Direct observation	16		
Double-blind study	4		
Epidemiology	12		
Experimental research	22		
Family aggregation	2		
Incidence	12		
Independent variable	21		
Labeling	8		
Lifetime prevalence	12		
Negative correlation	21		
Nomenclature	6		
Observational research	19		
One-year prevalence	12		
Placebo	4		
Point prevalence	12		
Positive correlation	20		
Prevalence	12		
Prospective strategy	20		
Retrospective strategy	20		
Sampling	18		
Self-report data	16		
Single-case research	22		

design		
Stereotyping	8	
Stigma symptom	8	
Syndrome	8	

MATCHING

Who's Who in the Mental Health Field

Match each of the following people with her/his accomplishment or theory.

__C__ Jerome Wakefield

__F__ Kazdin (1998)

__D__ Emil Kraeplin (1856-1926)

__A__ Eugen Bleuler (1857-1939)

__B__ Alois Alzheimer (1864-1945)

__E__ Sigmund Freud (1856-1939)

A. Swiss psychiatrist who worked with Kraepelin to write about schizophrenia and manic depression

B. described disorder that was to become associated with a disorder common to elderly people

C. proposed idea of mental disorders as being "harmful dysfunctions."

D. German psychiatrist who worked with Bleuler to write about schizophrenia and manic depression

E. founder of psychoanalysis

F. "Methodology is not merely a compilation of practices and procedures. Rather, it is an approach toward problem solving, thinking, and acquiring knowledge."

What's What?

Match each of the following professions with its definition.

_E_ Clinical Psychologist

_A_ Counseling Psychologist

_D_ School Psychologist

_B_ Psychiatrist

_C_ Psychoanalyst

_F_ Psychiatric Social Worker

_H_ Psychiatric Nursing

_I_ Occupational Therapist

_G_ Pastoral Counselor

A. Ph.D. in psychology and internship in mental or student counseling

B. M.D. with residency in psychiatric hospital

C. M.D. or Ph.D. with emphasis on psychoanalysis

D. May or may not have Ph.D., but has extensive training regarding academic or learning problems

E. Ph.D. in psychology with research and clinical skills

F. M.S.W. or Ph.D. with clinical training in mental health settings

G. Ministerial background and training in psychology

H. R.N. certification but could also have M.A. or Ph.D. specializing in care and treatment of psychiatric clients

SHORT ANSWERS

Provide brief answers to the following questions.

1. What is the purpose of classifying mental disorders in a formal way? (p. 6)

2. How do cultural factors impact our definitions of abnormality? (p. 10)

3. Describe what we mean by prevalence and incidence, and how they compare. (p 12)

4. Discuss the strengths and limitations associated with using an experimental

approach to study mental illness. (p. 19)

5. When might a single-case experimental design yield useful clinical
   information?   (p. 21).

THE DOCTOR IS IN...PSYCHIATRIC HELP—5¢

You want to know whether a new treatment for depression is effective. Describe how
you would set up an experiment to answer your question.

<u>AFTER YOU READ</u>

<u>PRACTICE TESTS</u>

*Take the following three multiple-choice tests to see how much you have
comprehended from the chapter. Each represents roughly one-third of the
chapter. As you study the chapter, use these to check your progress.*

PRACTICE TEST NUMBER 1

1. Commonly accepted definitions of abnormality assume that (p. 5)
     a. there are clear elements of abnormality that are sufficient on their own.
     b. culture is not a factor in true abnormality.
     c. movies that deal with mental disorders, such as "A Beautiful Mind" or "As Good
     as it Gets" lend no insight into mental illness.
     d. judgments of abnormality are based on the similarity between a behavior and
     the elements of abnormality.

2. The removal of _____ as a mental disorder from the DSM is an
     example of how the definition of what is termed "abnormal" or "deviant"
     may change over time. (p. 6)
     a. depression
     b. pedophilia

c. homosexuality

d. voyeurism

3. People who work with the mentally ill are trained to classify the disorder, not the person. An example of this is (p. 9)

 a. "The bipolar in room 325."

 b. "Suzie, who has schizophrenia, in Room 627."

 c. "Phobic John in Room 520."

 d. none of the above.

4. The most recent edition of the DSM is (p. 9)

 a. DSM-IV.

 b. DSM-IV-TR.

 c. DSM-V.

 d. DSM-III-R.

5. A problem with classifying mental illness is the fact that it can lead to (p. 8)

 a. stereotyping.

 b. labeling.

 c. stigmas .

 d. all of the above

6. John has been exhibiting the following symptoms: having trouble sleeping, feeling sad, having difficulty concentrating, and losing weight. Together, all of these behaviors are referred to as a (p. 9)

 a. syndrome.

 b. disorder.

 c. symptom.

 d. none of the above

7. Ataque de Nervios, is an example of a psychopathology that is specific to which

culture? (p. 11)

a. Middle Eastern

b. African

c. Asian

d. Hispanic

8. The World Around Us 1.3 "Personnel in Mental Health" describes professional and para-professional persons who work in the area of mental health. Two para-professionals described are (p.15)

a. pastoral counselor and community health worker.

b. occupational therapist and alcohol- or drug-abuse counselor.

c. community mental health worker and alcohol- or drug-abuse counselor.

d. pastoral counselor and occupational therapist.

9. The ECH and NCS epidemiology studies cited in your book found that the most prevalent kind of psychological disorder in the United States is a(n) (p. 13)

a. mood disorder.

b. anxiety disorder.

c. cognitive disorder.

d. sexual disorder.

10. The NCS study found that _____ percent of people with a mild mental disorder also had one or more additional disorders. (p. 1-20)

a. 28

b. 12

c. 7

d. 68

PRACTICE TEST NUMBER 2

1. Hypotheses are generated to (p. 17)

a. explain predict or explore behavior

b. explain unusual or unexpected research findings

c. test the validity of observations

d. all of the above

2. Carol sits in a chair with several electrodes attached to her scalp. She is asked a series of questions. How her brain is processing information is being recorded. The method that is being used to collect information is (p. 16)

a. direct observation.

b. brain-imaging techniques.

c. self-report.

d. case study.

3. Epidemiology is concerned with (p. 12)

a. the distribution of diseases, disorders or health-related behaviors in a given population.

b. gaining control of abnormal behavior.

c. comparing clinical treatment strategies for a particular mental illness.

d. none of the above

4. Although single-case studies can be valuable, these do have drawbacks, one of which is (p. 18)

a. the failure to generate a hypothesis.

b. not yielding enough information to make generalizations.

c. not causing us to think intelligently.

d. a and c.

5. The most important thing to consider when conducting a research study is (p. 18)

a. finding people who mirror the larger population of interest.

b. passing out surveys.

c. limiting your study to a small homogeneous group.

d. none of the above

6. The variable which is measured in a study is the (p. 20)

    a. independent variable.

    b. dependent variable.

    c. manipulative variable.

    d. acute variable.

7. Retrospective research relies on (p. 20)

    a. estimates of information about the future.

    b. the recall of information from the past.

    c. an ABAB design.

    d. b and c.

8. A criterion group is used to (p.19)

    a. compare people with a diagnosis of interest to those who do not have the disorder.

    b. compare people with the same disorder to each other.

    c. control for bias in case study.

    d. control for careless research.

9. The most basic experimental design in single-case research is the (p. 22)

    a. BABA design.

    b. DSM-IV-TR design.

    c. ABAB design.

    d. MINH design.

10. In a single-case research design, the same _____ is studied over time.(p. 18)

    a. population

b. subject

c. treatment

d. all of the above

PRACTICE TEST NUMBER 3

1. A(n) _____ research approach focuses on individuals who have a higher-than-average likelihood of developing a psychological disorder by providing assistance before the disorder develops. (p. 20)

a. prospective

b. retrospective

c. introspective

d. detective

2. Drs. Abby and Normal are conducting experimental research on the effects of sound on student concentration. They will be manipulating the sound level in their experiment. The sound is known as the (p. 20)

a. dependent variable.

b. independent variable.

c. correlational variable.

d. co-existing variable.

3. The outcome of the above experiment is known as the (p. 20)

a. dependent variable.

b. independent variable.

c. correlational variable.

d. co-existing variable.

4. Pat was in a study in which she received a sugar pill instead of the experimental medication. Afterward she reported feeling better. Pat's reaction is a result of what? (p. 4)

a. placebo treatment

b. luck

c. not having anything wrong in the first place

d. being in the wrong group

5. The DSM-IV-TR (p. 9)

    a. focuses heavily on the causes or etiological factors of abnormal behavior.

    b. specifies on theoretical interpretation of a set of symptoms.

    c. is considered to be atheoretical

    d. the final word on the definition of mental disorders

6. There is strong evidence for significant overlap between anxiety and depression.

    Still a patient receives two diagnoses: one for anxiety and one for depression.

    This is an example of (p.14)

    a. synthesis.

    b. concurrence.

    c. convergence.

    d. comorbidity.

7. Which of the following terms refers to a mental condition of relatively short duration?

    (p. 15)

    a. episodic

    b. acute

    c. chronic

    d. factitious

8. In order to make sense of observed behavior, psychologists generate more or less

    plausible ideas called (p. 17)

    a. constructs.

    b. hypotheses.

    c. principles.

d. theories.

9. The purpose of _____ is to ensure, in effect, that each member of the population has an equal chance of being included in the study's sample. (p. 18)
   a. increasing reliability
   b. hypothesis testing
   c. structured set sampling
   d. random selection

10. A psychologist identifies 50 children who have schizophrenic mothers. At adolescence, the researcher compares those who develop schizophrenia with those who don't. This is an example of a _____ study. (p. 20)
   a. clinical case
   b. comparative outcome
   c. prospective
   d. retrospective

COMPREHENSIVE PRACTICE TEST

The following tests are designed to give you an idea of how well you understood the entire chapter. There are three different types of tests: multiple-choice, true-false, and essay.

MULTIPLE-CHOICE

1. A classification system for mental disorders is advantageous because it gives us a way to (p. 6)
   a. structure information.
   b. advance research.
   c. create treatment plans.
   d. all of the above.

2. The DSM is published by the (p. 9)

   a. American Psychological Association

   b. American Medical Association.

   c. American Psychiatric Association.

   d. American Social Work Association.

3. The number of active cases of an illness in a population during any given period of time is referred to as (p. 12)

   a. incidences.

   b. epidemiology.

   c. clinically significant.

   d. prevalence.

4. The number of new cases that occur over a period of time is referred to as (p. 13)

   a. incidences.

   b. epidemiology.

   c. clinically significant.

   d. prevalence.

5. Research in abnormal psychology helps to (p.18)

   a. study the nature of the disorder.

   b. understand the causes.

   c. provide the best care.

   d. all of the above

6. Doing research on shopping behavior for her class, Sally sat on a bench in a busy mall making notes of what she saw. Sally was using what method to gather information? (p. 16)

   a. direct observation

   b. psychophysiological variables

   c. self-report

   d. case study

7. Dr. Casey has what she thinks is a unique client and has done extensive data collection when working with him, including taking photographs of the behavior. She plans to present this client's behavior at a national convention. Dr. Casey is using what method to gather this information? (p. 16)

   a. direct observation

   b. brain-imaging techniques

   c. self-report

   d. case study

8. Stan and Jim are eager to find out if college students at their school are typical with regard to the ever-increasing problem of binge drinking. To gather this information, they create a survey asking a number of questions about student's drinking habits. The method that Stan and Jim are using is (p 17)

   a. direct observation.

   b. brain-imaging techniques.

   c. self-report.

   d. case study.

9. Jennifer is doing research on the effects of violent video games on children's behavior. Her observations have lead her to believe that possibly there is a connection. She wants to test this concept. Jennifer's idea is called a(n) (p. 17)

   a. projection.

   b. case study.

   c. hypothesis.

   d. finding.

10. To test a hypothesis, researchers use _____ of people who don't exhibit the disorder being studied. (p. 19)

a. an interesting group

b. a control group

c. a loosely structured group

d. a variable group

11. Unlike a controlled-research approach, observational or correlational research (p. 19)

a. manipulates variables.

b. uses a control group.

c. does not manipulate variables.

d. all of the above

12. The possible reason(s) two variables are highly correlated is/are (p. 19)

a. variable A causes B (or vice versa).

b. variable A and variable B are both caused by variable C.

c. variables A and B are both involved in a pattern of other variables that influence A and B.

d. all of the above

13. Chris is studying depression in animals. He hopes that his findings may be generalized to humans. Chris's work is referred to as a(n) (p. 23)

a. retrospective study.

b. prospective study.

c. case study.

d. analogue study.

14. Observational research studies things as they (p. 19)

a. want to be.

b. seem to be.

c. are.

d. a and c.

Why do you think the mentally ill have been so poorly treated over the years, and how do you think that future generations will view our treatment of people with mental illness?

CRISS-CROSS

Now that you know all there is to know about this chapter, here's your chance to put that knowledge to work.

CRISS CROSS CLUES

Across

2. occurrence rate of a given disorder

5. the process of selecting a representative subgroup

6. sudden onset of a disorder, usually with intense symptoms

8. patient's subjective description of a physical or mental disorder

9. long-standing or frequent disorder, often with progressing seriousness

11. identifying two or more disorders in a psychologically disordered individual

Down

1. the proportion of active cases that can be identified during a given time period

3. positive effect experienced after an inactive treatment is administered

4. study of the distribution of mental disorders

7. symptoms that occur together and represent the typical picture of a disorder

10. experiment wherein neither participants nor staff knows which group gets the placebo

Puzzle created with Puzzlemaker at DiscoverySchool.com

ANSWERS TO TEST QUESTIONS – CHAPTER ONE

MATCHING
C. Jerome Wakefield
F. Kazdin (1998)
D. Emil Kraeplin (1856-1926)
A. Eugen Bleuler (1857-1939)
B. Alois Alzheimer (1864-1945)
E. Sigmund Freud (1856-1939)

WHAT'S WHAT?
E. Clinical Psychologist
A. Counseling Psychologist
D. School Psychologist
B. Psychiatrist
C. Psychoanalyst
F. Psychiatric Social Worker
H. Psychiatric Nursing
I. Occupational Therapist
G. Pastoral Counselor

SHORT ANSWERS
(Your answer should contain the following points.)

1. Most sciences use classification systems which provide a nomenclature which can be used to structure and organize information in a helpful way. In the mental health field, definitions of pathology assist in defining the range of problems mental health professionals can address, and how their treatment should be reimbursed.

2. Cultural beliefs define how behaviors are accepted, and therefore determine whether a behavior is seen as normal or abnormal by others in that culture.

3. *Prevalence* refers to the number of active cases in a population during any given time period. *Incidence* refers to the number of new cases that occur over a given period of time. Incidence rates are typically lower than prevalence rates because they exclude already existing cases.

4. a. Strengths: Straightforward set-up and design—proposed treatment given to one group of patients and withheld from another similar group of patients. If treated patients improve, compared to the untreated group, the treatment works. Treatment can then be given to the "waiting list" control group.
b. Limitations: Withholding beneficial treatment for a period of time.

5. When you want to study the same person over time, under a variety of conditions (or interventions).

THE DOCTOR IS IN

Your response should indicate that you would either conduct an experimental study with a control group, using random sampling and assignment, and a measurable dependent variable, or that you are trying an ABAB design on a particular depressed patients. Ideally you should also mention the ethical issues involved in providing treatment to some but not all of your subjects, or in starting and stopping the treatment with one patient.

PRACTICE TESTS

Q#	TEST 1	TEST 2	TEST 3
1	D	D	A
2	C	B	B
3	B	A	A
4	B	B	A
5	D	A	C
6	A	B	D
7	D	B	B
8	C	A	B
9	B	C	D
10	C	B	C

COMPREHENSIVE PRACTICE TEST

Q#	M/C	T/F
1	D	T
2	C	F
3	D	T
4	A	T
5	D	F
6	A	F
7	D	T
8	C	F
9	C	F
10	B	T
11	C	T
12	D	F
13	D	T
14	C	
15	A	

ESSAY QUESTIONS
(Your answer should contain the following points.)

1. The elements of suffering must include:

a. Suffering: psychological suffering
b. Maladaptiveness: behavior that interferes with well-being and ability to enjoy work and relationships.
c. Deviancy: statistically rare behavior
d. Violation of the standards of society: failure to follow conventional social and moral rules
e. Social discomfort: discomfort of those around a person who has violated social rules
f. Irrationality and unpredictability: behavior is not expected, and the person is unable to control his or her behavior

2. Steve will set up his research by:

a. Formulating a hypothesis.
b. Finding a representative sampling of depressed people.
c. Creating a control group.
d. Showing each group funny movies.
e. Measuring results-dependent variables.

USE IT OR LOSE IT

Because mentally ill individuals often behave in abnormal ways they make people feel uncomfortable and scared. Consequently, many societies have imprisoned, or tortured the mentally ill in order to try to make them behave in more normal ways. As we improve our understanding of how the brain works it is likely that many of the treatments used to treat mental illness today will seem unusual, unhelpful, or even harmful in the future.

CRISS-CROSS ANSWERS

Across
2. Incidence
5. Sampling
6. Acute
8. Symptoms
9. Chronic
11. Comorbidity

Down
1. Prevalence
3. Placebo
4. Epidemiology
7. Syndrome
10. Double-blind

Chapter 2: Historical and Contemporary Views of Abnormal Behavior

BEFORE YOU READ

For thousands of years, people have been fascinated by why humans behave the way they do. Pictures, songs, and stories dating back of thousands of years indicate attempts to observe and explain both normal and abnormal behavior. Of course these explanations don't occur in a vacuum, but rather are influenced by the culture and environment of the observer. This chapter will review the many ways abnormal behaviors have been described and explained, and how people exhibiting such behavior have been treated from ancient times to the present. Reading this chapter will enable you to see how these viewpoints have evolved, and why we view abnormality the way we do today.

- **HISTORICAL VIEWS OF ABNORMAL BEHAVIOR**

    Demonology, gods, and magic

    Hippocrates' early medical concepts

    Early philosophical conceptions of consciousness and mental discovery

    Later Greek and Roman thought

    Abnormality during the Middle Ages

- **TOWARD HUMANITARIAN APPROACHES**

    Resurgence of scientific questioning

    The establishment of early asylums and shrines

    Humanitarian reform

    19th-Century views of the causes and treatment of mental disorders

    Changing attitudes toward mental health in the 20th century

    Mental hospital care in the 20th century

- **CONTEMPORARY VIEWS**

Establishing the link between the brain and mental disorders

The beginnings of a classification system

The Evolution of the psychological research tradition

Experimental Psychology

• **UNRESOLVED ISSUES**

Interpreting historical events

OBJECTIVES

After reading this chapter, you should be able to:

1. Explain why abnormal behavior was often attributed to possession by a demon or god in ancient times.

2. Describe how exorcism was administered by shamans and priests as the primary type of treatment for demonic possession.

3. Describe the contributions of Hippocrates, Plato, Aristotle, and Galen (460 B.C. to 200 A.D.) to the conceptualization of the nature and causes of abnormal behavior.

4. Discuss how mental disorders were viewed during the Middle Ages.

5. Describe what was meant by *mass madness* or *mass hysteria* and summarize the explanations offered for these phenomena..

6. Outline the arguments of Paracelsus, Teresa of Avila, Johan Weyer, Reginald Scot, and St. Vincent de Paul (late Middle Ages and early Renaissance), all who recommended that those showing abnormal behavior should be seen as mentally ill and treated humanely.

7. Discuss the inhumane ways in which mental patients were treated in the "insane asylums" of Europe and the United States.

8. Describe the humanitarian reforms instigated by Philippe Pinel, William Tuke, Benjamin Rush, and Dorothea Dix regarding the

treatment of mental patients.

9. Explain why the discovery of a biological basis for general paresis and a handful of other disorders (such as, the senile mental disorders, toxic mental disorders, and certain types of mental retardation), contributed to the development of a scientific approach to abnormal psychology, and the emergence of biologically based modern experimental approaches to science.

10. Distinguish between biological and non-biological versions of medical-model thinking about psychopathology.

11. Trace the important events in the development of psychoanalysis and the psychodynamic perspective.

12. Compare and contrast the biological and psychodynamic views of abnormal disorders.

13. Describe how the techniques of free association and dream analysis helped analysts and their patients.

14. List the major features of the behavioral perspective.

15. Discriminate between classical and operant conditioning.

16. Explain the problems associated with interpreting historical events.

AS YOU READ

Answers can be found in the Answer Key at the end of the chapter.

KEY WORDS

Each of the words below is important in understanding the concepts presented in this chapter. Write the definition next to each of the words. The page numbers are provided in case you need to refer to the book.

Term	Page	Definition
Asylum	36	
Behavioral perspective	49	
Behaviorism	49	

Catharsis	48	
Classical conditioning	49	
Deinstitutionalization	42	
Dream analysis	48	
Exorcism	33	
Free association	48	
Insanity	37	
Lycanthropy	33	
Mass madness	32	
Mental hygiene movement	39	
Mesmerism	49	
Moral management	39	
Nancy School	47	
Operant conditioning	50	
Psychoanalysis	46	
Psychoanalytic perspective	46	
Saint Vitus's Dance	32	
Tarantism	32	
Unconscious	48	

SHORT ANSWERS

Provide brief answers to the following questions.

1. Describe the contributions Hippocrates made to the understanding of mental illness. (p.29)

2. The occurrence of mass madness peaked in the 14th and 15th centuries. Why, according to the text, was mass madness so common during these years?

(p. 33-34)

3. Describe the atmosphere and treatment methods at the early asylums. (p. 36-37).

4. Discuss the reasons moral management of the mentally ill had been abandoned by the last part of the 19th century. (p. 39).

5. Explain the important events that lead to the biomedical breakthrough in discovering a cure for general paresis. (p. 45).

WHO'S WHO IN THE HISTORY OF ABNORMAL PSYCHOLOGY

From the list which follows, write the number of the achievement or description on the line next to the corresponding name given below, and list two or three relevant benefits or accomplishments of the era.

THE ANCIENT WORLD

Plato *(429-347 B.C.)*

Galen *(130-200 A.D.)*

Hippocrates *(460-377 B.C.)*

Aristotle *(384-322 B.C.)*

THE MIDDLE AGES

Martin Luther *(1483-1546)*

Teresa of Avila *(1515-1582)*

Avicenna *(980-1037)*

Paracelsus *(1490-1541)*

THE 16th THROUGH THE 18th CENTURIES

Riginald Scot *(1538-1599)*

William Tuke *(1732-1822)*

Johann Weyer *(1515-1588)*

Robert Burton *(1576-1640)*

Philippe Pinel *(1745-1826)*

Dorothea Dix *(1802-1887)*

Benjamin Rush *(1745-1813)*

Clifford Beers *(1876-1943)*

THE 19th AND EARLY 20th CENTURIES

Emil Kraepelin *(1856-1926)*

Franz Anton Mesmer *(1734-1815)*

Sigmund Freud *(1856-1938)*

Wilhelm Wundt *(1832-1920)*

Lightner Witmer *(1867-1956)*

J. McKeen Cattell *(1860-1944)*

William Healy *(1869-1963)*

Ivan Pavlov *(1849-1936)*

John B. Watson *(1878-1958)*

B. F. Skinner *(1904-1990)*

E. L. Thorndike *(1874-1949)*

Descriptions and Achievements

1. German theologian during the Reformation who held the belief, common to his time, that the mentally disturbed were possessed by the devil.

2. Englishman who refuted the notion of demons as the cause of mental disorders and was castigated by King James I.

3. American psychologist who adopted Wundt's methods and studied individual differences in mental processing.

4. American teacher who founded the mental hygiene movement in the United States.

5. Austrian physician who conducted early investigations into hypnosis as a medical treatment.

6. A Greek philosopher who believed that mental patients should be treated humanely.

7. Canonized Spanish nun who argued that mental disorder was an illness of the mind.

8. Islamic Arabian-born physician who adopted principles of humane treatment for the mentally disturbed at a time when Western approaches to mental illness were the opposite.

9. American psychologist who established the Chicago Juvenile Psychopathic Institute.

10. American who campaigned to change public attitudes toward mental patients after his own experiences in mental institutions.

11. English Quaker who established the York Retreat, where mental patients lived in humane surroundings.

12. Swiss physician who rejected demonology as a cause of abnormal behavior.

13. Greek physician who believed that mental disease was the result of natural causes and brain pathology, rather than demonology.

14. American psychologist who established the first psychological clinic in the United States, focusing on problems of mentally deficient children.

15. French physician who pioneered the use of moral management in La Bicétre and La Salpétriére hospitals in France.

16. Known as the father of behaviorism.

17. Oxford scholar who wrote *Anatomy of Melancholia,* in 1621.

18. The founder of the school of psychological therapy known as psychoanalysis.

19. Greek physician and advocate of the Hippocratic tradition who contributed much to our understanding of the nervous system.

20. German psychiatrist who developed the first diagnostic system.

21. German scientist who established the first experimental psychology laboratory in 1879.

22. American physician and founder of American psychiatry.

23. Russian physiologist who published classical studies in the psychology of learning.

24. Developed concept of instrumental conditioning.

25. Studied how consequences of behavior influences behavior operant conditioning.

26. German physician who argued against demonology and was ostracized by his peers and the Church for his progressive views.

27. Greek philosopher and a pupil of Plato who believed in the Hippocratic theory that various agents, or humors, within the body when imbalanced, were responsible for mental disorders.

THE DOCTOR IS IN...PSYCHIATRIC HELP—5¢

Read the following scenarios and diagnose the client. Remember to look carefully at the criteria for the disorder before you make a decision as to the diagnosis. Make a list of other information you might need to help you understand the causal factors.

1. You are an assistant to the great Greek physician, Hippocrates. A patient comes to you and is sad, lacks interest in things he used to enjoy doing, is having trouble sleeping, and feels hopeless about his situation. Hippocrates asks for your opinion on what is wrong with this patient, the cause, and the treatment. What would you say? (p. 29-30)

2. As a psychiatrist in the early 19th century, you have just become affiliated with the local asylum. A young woman comes to the asylum and tells you she is feeling low, lacks energy, and has several physical symptoms: crying, and pain in several areas of her body. How would you diagnose her and what would you consider the cause of her affliction? (p. 41)

3. It's 1912 and you have just been referred to Dr. Sigmund Freud. You have have symptoms of hysteria and he is the leading expert in the field. What would you expect Dr. Freud to tell you about the cause of your disorder and what treatments would he use? (p. 48)

AFTER YOU READ

PRACTICE TESTS

Take the following multiple-choice tests to see how much you have comprehended from the chapter. Once again, if you get stuck, the page numbers are listed at the end of the study aid chapter along with the answers.

PRACTICE TEST NUMBER 1

1. Stone-age cave dwellers treated mental illness by performing a crude operation known as (p. 28)

   a. tripoding.

   b. trephining.

   c. triazing.

   d. catharsis.

2. What did the ancient Chinese, Egyptians, Hebrews, and Greeks believe caused abnormal behavior? (p. 28)

   a. bad genes

   b. disobeying the state

   c. demon or god possessions

   d. bad humor

3. A person who "spoke with a god" in ancient China would have been considered to be (p. 28)

   a. possessed by evil spirits or demons.

   b. not him or her self.

   c. trying to get attention.

   d. possessed by good spirits.

4. If a person were considered possessed by a demon, treatment usually was (p. 28)

    a. confinement to an institution.

    b. dream analysis.

    c. exorcism.

    d. plenty of sleep.

5. Hippocrates and later, Galen, supported an early paradigm that stated that _____ bodily humors were responsible for human behavior. (p. 29)

    a. five

    b. thirty-seven

    c. eight

    d. four

6. The first person to consider dreams an important tool in understanding a patient's problem was (p. 29)

    a. Freud.

    b. Pinel.

    c. Hippocrates.

    d. Galen.

7. The first person to propose that people with mental disorders weren't responsible for their criminal behavior was (p. 29)

    a. Hipprocates.

    b. Galen.

    c. Freud.

    d. Plato.

8. The first to provide descriptions of consciousness and to write extensively on mental disorders was (p. 30)

a. Aristotle.

b. Plato.

c. Galen.

d. Freud.

9. The ancient Roman physician, Galen, maintained a very scientific approach to psychological disorders by dividing their causes into _____ categories. (p. 51)

a. spiritual and demonic

b. practical and impractical

c. known and unknown

d. physical and mental

10. _____, known as the "prince of physicians," wrote *The Canon of Medicine* during the Middle Ages. (p. 32)

a. Aleppo

b. Avicenna

c. Damascus

d. Galen

PRACTICE TEST NUMBER 2

1. During the Middle Ages in Europe, people with mental disorders were (p. 32-34)

a. treated with care and respect.

b. given the most current treatment.

c. studied in the light of scientific thinking.

d. deprived of humane treatment.

2. Johann Weyer, one of the first physicians to specialize in mental disorders, is also know as the founder of (p. 36)

a. modern psychopathology.

b. humanism.

c. psychoanalysis.

d. electrotherapy.

3. Who is considered the first person to begin humane treatment of the mentally ill in French asylums? (p. 31)

a. Benjamin Franklin

b. Philippe Pinel

c. Henry VIII

d. William Tuke

4. This man established the York Retreat, a country house where the mentally ill could live, work, and rest in a religious atmosphere. (p. 39)

a. Philippe Pinel

b. William Tuke

c. Benjamin Rush

d. Benjamin Franklin

5. He is the founder of Clinical Psychology (p. 49)

a. Lightner Witmer

b. James Watson

c. Benjamin Rush

d. Carl Rogers

6. *The Snake Pit* was written in 1946 by _____. It called attention to the need for more humane mental health care in the _____, not overcrowded mental hospitals. (p. 41)

a. Mary Jane Ward; community

b. Sigmund Freud; community

    c. Clifford Beers; private residence

    d. William James; private residence

7. The National Institutes of Mental Health was organized in (p. 42)

    a. 1925.

    b. 1946.

    c. 1950.

    d. 1492.

8. General Paresis, a mental disorder which produces paralysis, insanity and eventual death if untreated, is caused by (p. 45)

    a. syphilis

    b. pneumonia

    c. mesmerism

    d. malaria

9. Emil Kraepelin, in his work to classify mental disorders, distinguished among mental disorders and thought the course of each was (p. 31)

    a. left to chance.

    b. predictable and predetermined.

    c. similar.

    d. at the whim of fate.

10. Freud's method of treatment, psychoanalysis, has its roots in the study of (p. 46)

    a. hypnosis.

    b. brain chemistry.

    c. individuals.

    d. groups.

PRACTICE TEST NUMBER 3

1. Franz Anton Mesmer (1734-1815), in his belief that people possessed magnetic fields that could be used to cure mental disorders, demonstrated most of the phenomena later associated with (p. 46)

    a. dream analysis.

    b. psychoanalysis.

    c. hypnosis.

    d. a and b

2. According to the Nancy School approach to mental illness, hypnotism was related to (p. 48)

    a. hysteria.

    b. hypochondriasis.

    c. hilarity.

    d. syphilis.

3. The approach to abnormal behavior which is based on experimentation and scientific data is called (p. 49).

    a. psychoanalysis

    b. humanism

    c. cognitive

    d. behaviorism

4. Ivan Pavlov (1849-1936) is noted for his work with dogs in which he demonstrated what was to become known as (p. 49-50)

    a. operant conditioning.

    b. generalization.

    c. classical conditioning.

    d. a and c

5. Operant conditioning theory, developed by E. L. Thorndike (1874-1949) and B. F. Skinner (1904-1990), explores how behaviors are influenced by (p. 50-51)

    a. feelings.

    b. thoughts.

    c. family dynamics.

    d. consequences.

6. Mesmer argued that sitting in a tub surrounded by chemicals and iron rods could (p. 46)

    a. alter blood flow.

    b. alter magnetic fluid in the body.

    c. change blood pressure.

    d. alter breathing.

7. Classical and operant conditioning differ primarily with respect to (p. 49-50)

    a. the types of reinforcers involved.

    b. an emphasis on animal versus human subjects.

    c. the number of trials to reach criterion performance.

    d. whether the outcome (reinforcer) is dependent on the animal's behavior.

8. To understand current events in psychology, or any area for that matter, it is important to have an understanding of the _____ developments. (p. 53)

    a. historical

    b. future

    c. concrete

    d. empirical

9. It is often difficult to study historical information and form accurate pictures. Why is this the case? (p. 53)

    a. Events are open to reinterpretation.

    b. Researchers may be biased.

    c. One cannot rely on direct observation.

    d. all of the above

10. Freud believed that the _____ plays a huge role in human behavior (p. 48).

    a. conscious

    b. unconscious

    c. cortex

    d. hypnosis

COMPREHENSIVE PRACTICE TEST

The following tests are designed to give you an idea of how well you understood the entire chapter. There are three different types of tests: multiple-choice, true-false, and essay.

MULTIPLE-CHOICE

1. Information dating back to the 16th century B.C. on the treatment of disease and mental disorders appears on (p. 28)

    a. the Edwin Smith and Ebers papyri.

    b. cave walls.

    c. the Rosetta Stone.

    d. tools used to perform treatment.

2. Early Chinese, Egyptians, Hebrews, and Greeks believed person who became excited or overactive and perhaps exhibited strange behavior to be (p. 28)

a. possessed by evil spirits or demons.

b. not him or herself.

c. trying to get attention.

d. possessed by good spirits.

3. Hippocrates said that mental illness could be classified into three general categories: (p. 29)

   a. spiritual, demonic, and exorcised.

   b. paranoid, depressed, and schizophrenic.

   c. blood, phlegm, and bile.

   d. mania, melancholic, and phrenitis.

4. According to ancient Greek and Egyptian medicine, hysteria was a result of a(n) (p. 30)

   a. imbalance of the four humors.

   b. wandering womb.

   c. demonic possession.

   d. godly possession.

5. _____ has been called the "Hippocates of China." (p. 33)

   a. Ben-Teans Ng

   b. Huang Ti

   c. Chung Ching

   d. Tai Chi

6. During the middle ages mentally disturbed people were accused of being (p.34)

   a. witches and often killed.

   b. werewolves and incarcerated.

   c. willfully disruptive.

   d. demons and treated with great comfort.

7. Dorothea Dix is noted for her highly successful campaign to do something about the (p. 40)

   a. inhumane treatment accorded the mentally ill.

   b. problem of heroin abuse during the Civil War.

   c. view that women were biologically inferior.

   d. overcrowded conditions in large mental hospitals in rural areas.

8. In the early part of the 19th century, psychiatrists were known as (p. 40)

   a. lay people.

   b. saints.

   c. alienists.

   d. scientists.

9. The last half of the 20th century saw a change in the mental hospital environment because of which scientific development? (p. 42)

   a. effective use of psychoanalysis

   b. understanding the need to rehabilitate people with mental illnesses

   c. effective medication

   d. effective use of group therapy

10. Believing that mentally disturbed people were better off in the community, which could provide integrated and humane treatment, leaders in psychiatry during the latter decades of the 20th century began a movement of (p. 43)

   a. communitization.

   b. deinstitutionalization.

   c. networking.

   d. modernization.

11. Surprisingly, many breakthroughs in mental health treatment have been made as a result of psychologists and psychiatrists working with (p. 40)

    a. the military in relation to war.

    b. the severely retarded.

    c. animals.

    d. healthy adults.

12. Emil Kraeplin's most important contribution to mental health treatment was developing a system of (p. 46)

    a. therapeutic treatments for mental illness.

    b. medications for the treatment of mental illness.

    c. mental health asylums.

    d. classification for mental disorders.

13. Wilhelm Wundt is known for (p. 49)

    a. establishing the first experimental psychology lab.

    b. the first European mental health spa.

    c. the first mental hospital to treat patients humanely.

    d. a dream analysis clinic.

14. John Watson is known for his studies of the (p. 49-50)

    a. role of the environment in conditioning personality development and behavior.

    b. role of neurochemistry in abnormal behavior.

    c. dream analysis in predicting abnormal behavior.

    d. role of internal factors in predicting mental illness.

15. Behaviorism emerged out of (p. 49)

    a. experimental psychology.

b. the unconscious.

c. cathartic experiences.

d. Pavlov's experiments.

TRUE - FALSE

1. T / F Mental patients were placed in pleasant settings and exposed to activities, parties and music in Alexandria Egypt (p. 30)

2. T / F Contrariis contrarius was a treatment plan used by ancient Roman doctors to treat patients. (p. 31)

3. T / F During the Middle Ages, Europe was more enlightened in its treatment of the mentally ill than the Middle East. (p. 32)

4. T / F Scientific questioning is a key component of behaviorism. (p. 35)

5. T / F Freud based his research on exacting scientific methods. (p.48-50)

6. T / F Throughout history, mental asylums have treated patients humanely. (p. 41)

7. T / F Moral management was a success because antipsychotic drugs were used to help patients. (p 39)

8. T / F Dorothea Dix waged a campaign to oppose mental health care reform. (p. 39-40)

9. T / F Early Psychiatrists were called alienists because they believed mental health were caused by space aliens. (p. 40)

10. T / F Classical Conditioning is most concerned with the consequences of a behavior. (p. 49)

11. T / F Operant Conditioning focuses on the pairing of stimuli. (p. 50-51)

ESSAY QUESTIONS

1. Why was deinstitutionalization advocated and what have been the problems with the policy? (p. 42)

2. Explain the disagreement between the Charcot and the Nancy School. (p. 48-49)

WEB LINKS TO ITEMS OR CONCEPTS DISCUSSED IN CHAPTER 2

Nancy School

www.thenancyschool.com

www.wordreference.com/English/definition.asp

?en=tarantism

Abnormal Behavior

http://library.thinkquest.org/26618/en-

4.1.1=defining%20abnormal%20behavior.htm

http://www.usnews.com/usnews/health/articles/050502/2sick.b.htm

USE IT OR LOSE IT

Provide an answer to the thought question below, knowing that there is more than one way to respond. Possible answers are presented in the Answer Key.

Why do you think we continue to teach Freud's theories even though many of them have not stood the test of time?

CRISS-CROSS

Now that you know all there is to know about this chapter, here's your chance to put that knowledge to work.

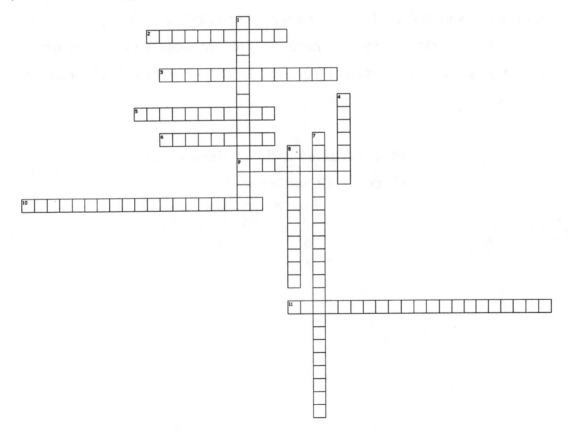

CRISS-CROSS CLUES

Across

2. A school of psychology that formerly restricted itself primarily to study of overt behavior

3. Method Freud used to study and treat patients

5. Delusion of being a wolf

6. Theories of animal magnetism(hypnosis) developed by Anton Mesmer

9. 13th-Century, Italian dancing mania

10. Form of learning in which a response is reinforced

11. Basic form of learning using a neutral stimulus with an unconditioned stimulus repeatedly to eventually elicit a conditioned response

Down

1. Method for probing the unconscious by having patients talk freely about themselves

4. Institutions meant solely for the care of the mentally ill

7. Movement to close mental hospitals and treat patients in the community

8. A major portion of the mind containing a hidden mass of instincts, impulses, and memories

Puzzle created with Puzzlemaker at DiscoverySchool.com

ANSWERS TO TEST QUESTIONS - CHAPTER TWO

WHO'S WHO IN THE HISTORY OF ABNORMAL PSYCHOLOGY

THE ANCIENT WORLD

Plato (429-347 B.C.)
Galen (130-200 A.D.)
Hippocrates *(460-377 B.C.)*
Aristotle *(384-322 B.C.)*
Martin Luther *(1483-1546)*
Teresa of Avila *(1515-1582)*
Avicenna *(980-1037)*
Paracelsus *(1490-1541)*

THE 16th THROUGH THE 18th CENTURIES

Reginald Scott *(1538-1599)*
William Tuke *(1732-1822)*
Johann Weyer *(1515-1588)*
Robert Burton *(1576-1640)*
Philippe Pinel *(1745-1826)*
Dorothea Dix *(1802-1887)*
Benjamin Rush *(1745-1813)*
Clifford Beers *(1876-1943)*

THE 19th AND EARLY 20th CENTURIES

Emil Kraepelin *(1856-1926)*
Franz Anton Mesmer *(1734-1815)*
Sigmund Freud *(1856-1938)*
Wilhelm Wundt *(1832-1920)*
Lightner Witmer *(1867-1956)*
J. McKeen Cattell *(1860-1944)*
William Healy *(1869-1963)*
Ivan Pavlov *(1849-1936)*
John B. Watson *(1878-1958)*
B. F. Skinner *(1904-1990)*
E. L. Thorndike (1874-1949)

SHORT ANSWERS
(Your answer should contain the following points.)

1. Hippocrates:
    a. did not believe gods and demons possessed the mentally ill
    b. thought mental illness had natural causes

c. thought the brain was the central organ of intellectual activity and that brain pathology caused mental illness

d. and believed that heredity, predisposition, and head injuries would cause sensory and motor disorders

2. Mass madness was so common during the 14th and 15th centuries because of the following factors:
   a. social oppression, famine, and epidemics like the Black Death
   b. depression, fear, and wild mysticism
   c. unable to control their environment

3. Early asylums:
   a. were storage places for the insane
   b. were filthy and cruel
   c. put patients on exhibition for the public
   d. forced people to beg on the streets
   e. shackled patients to walls, unable to lie down
   f. provided inadequate food, clothing, and other comforts

4. Moral management of the mentally ill had been abandoned by the end of the 19th century because of :
   a. ethnic prejudice
   b. failure of the movement's leaders to train replacements
   c. overextension of hospital facilities
   d. rise of the mental hygiene movement, which focused on physical well-being
   e. advances in biomedical science

5. The important events that lead to the biomedical breakthrough in discovering a cure for general paresis were:
   a. 1825—French physician Bayle differentiated general paresis as a specific type of mental disorder.
   b. 1897—Viennese psychiatrist Richard von Krafft-Eging inoculated paretic patients with matter from syphilitic sores.
   c. 1906—von Wasserman developed a blood test for syphilis.
   d. 1917—von Wagner-Tauregg, chief of psychiatric clinic at the University of Vienna, introduced malarial fever treatment.
   e. 1978—First controlled studies of malarial treatment by Bahr and Brutsch were very successful.

THE DOCTOR IS IN

1. The patient is melancholic because their bile is out of balance. He recommended that they live a regular, tranquil life, including sobriety, abstinence from all excesses, a vegetable diet, celibacy, and exercise short of fatigue and bleeding. He might have removed the patient from their family as well.

2. *Diagnosis*: shattered senses of neurasthenics.   *Cause*:using up of precious nerve force excesses in living lifestyle problems

3. *Cause*: thoughts/experiences in the unconscious. *Treatment:* hypnosis, emotional release through catharsis, free association, and dream analysis.

PRACTICE TESTS

Q#	TEST 1	TEST 2	TEST 3
1	B	D	C
2	C	A	A
3	D	B	D
4	C	B	C
5	D	A	D
6	C	A	B
7	D	B	D
8	A	A	A
9	D	B	D
10	B	A	B

COMPREHENSIVE PRACTICE TEST

Q#	MULTIPLE CHOICE	T/F
1	A	T
2	A	T
3	D	T
4	B	F
5	C	F
6	A	F
7	A	F
8	C	F
9	C	T
10	B	F
11	A	F
12	D	
13	A	
14	A	
15	A	

ESSAY QUESTIONS
(Your answer should contain the following points.)

1. Motives for deinstitutionalization: –more humane treatment –more cost effective –eliminate the possibility of people becoming "chronically sick" in institutions –new medication would allow people to lead productive lives outside the hospital Problems with deinstitutionalization –"abandonment" of chronic patients to harsh existence of living on the streets –no planned community efforts to fill the gaps in community services

2. Nancy School—Bernheim and Liebeault hypothesis that hypnotism and hysteria were related and due to suggestion. Basis for hypothesis—symptoms of hysteria could be produced by hypnosis and eliminated by hypnosis. Charcot believed hysteria caused by degenerative brain changes. Debate between physiological cause and psychological cause. Nancy School triumphed—first recognition of a psychologically caused mental disorder

USE IT OR LOSE IT

Although many questions have been raised about Freud's theories we still discuss his theories because he introduced the idea of the unconscious and its role in motivating behavior. In its time this was a revolutionary concept.

CRISS-CROSS ANSWERS

Across
2. behaviorism
3. psychoanalysis
5. lycanthropy
6. mesmerism
9. tarantism
10. operant conditioning
11. classical conditioning

Down
1. free association
4. asylums
7. deinstitutionalization
8. unconscious

Chapter 3: Causal Factors and Viewpoints In Abnormal Psychology

BEFORE YOU READ

This chapter will compare a range of possible explanations for abnormal behavior. Biological and genetic factors will be discussed alone and in relation to their interaction with environment experiences. Psychosocial viewpoints including Freud's psychodynamic approach, behavioral, and cognitive-behavioral models will be explored. The impact of social interactions will be considered, since humans are social beings who are profoundly affected by the cultures in which they live, as well as by their early environmental experiences. Given the complexity of the human experience, it is probable that most abnormal behaviors are the result of complex, interactive factors, rather than a single cause.

- **CAUSES AND RISK FACTORS FOR ABNORMAL BEHAVIOR**
  Necessary, Sufficient, and Contributory Causes

  Feedback and Circularity in Abnormal Behavior

  Diathesis-Stress Models

- **VIEWPOINTS FOR UNDERSTANDING ABNORMAL BEHAVIOR**

- **THE BIOLOGICAL VIEWPOINTS AND BIOLOGICAL CAUSAL FACTORS**
  Neurotransmitter and Hormonal Imbalances

  Genetic Vulnerabilities

  Temperament and Other Constitutional Liabilities

  Brain Dysfunction and Neural Plasticity

  The Impact of the Biological Viewpoint

- **THE PSYCHOSOCIAL VIEWPOINTS**
  The Psychodynamic Perspectives

  The Behavioral Perspective

The Cognitive-Behavioral Perspective

What the Adoption of a Perspective Does and Does Not Do

• **PSYCHOSOCIAL CAUSAL FACTORS**

Early Deprivation or Trauma

Inadequate Parenting Styles

Marital Discord and Divorce

Maladaptive Peer Relationships

• **THE SOCIOCULTURAL VIEWPOINT**

Uncovering Sociocultural Factors Through Cross-Cultural Studies

• **SOCIOCULTURAL CAUSAL FACTORS**

The Sociocultural Environment

Pathogenic Societal Influences

Impact of the Sociocultural Viewpoint

• **UNRESOLVED ISSUES**

Theoretical Viewpoints and the Causes of Abnormal Behavior

OBJECTIVES

After reading this chapter, you should be able to:

1. Discuss the different conceptual approaches to understanding the causes of abnormal behavior. These approaches will include: (a) necessary, sufficient, and contributory causes; (b) feedback and circularity models; and (c) the diathesis-stress model.

2. Summarize the biological theories of abnormal behavior, including neurotransmitter/hormonal imbalances, genetic and constitutional influences, and physical damage to brain structures.

3. Outline the major psychosocial theoretical approaches to abnormal

behavior, including the psychodynamic, behavioral, and cognitive-behavioral perspectives.

4. Discuss the substantive contributions of the psychosocial factors of deviant cognitions (schema and self-schema), early deprivation or trauma (e.g., parental deprivation, institutionalization, abuse, etc.), inadequate parenting and pathogenic family structures, and problems with peer relationships.

5. Describe the sociocultural perspective and its contributions to understanding abnormal behavior.

6. Explain why simplistic explanations rarely account for the complexity of abnormal behaviors.

AS YOU READ

Answers can be found in the Answer Key at the end of the chapter.

KEY WORDS

Each of the words below is important in understanding the concepts presented in this Chapter. Write the definition next to each of the words. The page numbers are provided in case you need to refer to the book.

Term	Page	Definition
Adoption method	69	
Association studies	71	
Attachment theory	79	
Attributions	85	
Behavior genetics	69	
Biopsychosocial viewpoint	63	
Castration anxiety	78	
Chromosomes	66	
Classical conditioning	81	
Cognitive-behavioral	84	

conditioning)		
Interpersonal perspective	79	
Intrapsychic conflicts	76	
Libido	76	
Linkage analysis	71	
Necessary cause	58	
Neurotransmitters	64	
Object-relations theory	78	
Observational learning	83	
Oedipus complex	78	
Phenotype	68	
Pituitary gland	66	
Pleasure principle	76	
Primary process thinking	76	
Protective factors	60	
Psychosexual stages of development	76	
Reality principle	76	
Reinforcement	82	
Resilience	61	
Schema	84	
Secondary process thinking	76	
Self-schema	84	
Spontaneous recovery	81	
Sufficient cause	59	
Superego	76	
Synapse	64	
Temperament	71	
Twin method	69	

Who's Who?
Match each of the following people with her/his accomplishment or theory.

Theory
A. believed that people are inherently social beings motivated primarily by the desire to belong to and participate in a group.
B. focused on dispositions that people adopt in their interactions.
C. vigorously rejected Freud's demeaning female psychology.
D. broadened Freud's psychosexual stages into more socially-oriented concepts.
E. maintained that the term "personality" was best defined in terms of an individual's characteristic way of relating to others.

Psychologist
_____ Karen Horney
_____ Harry Stack Sullivan
_____ Erik Erikson
_____ Erich Fromm
_____ Alfred Adler

What's What?
Match each of the following terms with its definition.

___E___ Discrimination
___C___ Generalization
___B___ Intermittent
___D___ Reinforcement
___A___ Avoidance conditioning

A. A person, previously bitten, avoids dogs.
B. An occasional win at gambling keeps the behavior going.
C. A person, beaten as a child by an authority figure, has an involuntary fear of anyone in authority.
D. A child performs a response that produced candy in the past.
E. A child learns that although red and green strawberries look somewhat similar, only the red ones taste good.

Match each of the following parenting styles with its description of the result of using this type of parenting.

Parenting Style
___C___ Authoritative
___D___ Authoritarian
___A___ Permissive-indulgent
___B___ Neglecting-uninvolved

Descriptions

A. impulsive and aggressive; spoiled, selfish, inconsiderate, and demanding; exploit people for their own purposes
B. disruptions in attachment in childhood; moodiness, low self-esteem, and conduct problems later in childhood; problems with peer relations and academic performance
C. energetic and friendly, competent in dealing with others and the environment
D. conflicted, irritable, moody; poor social and cognitive skills

SHORT ANSWERS
Provide brief answers to the following questions.

1. List the five methods used in behavior genetics to study the heritability of mental disorders and give description of each. (p. 69)

2. Define and give an example of each of the following defense mechanisms: (p.76 - 78)

   a. acting out

   b. denial of reality

   c. displacement

   d. fixation

   e. projection

   f. rationalization

THE DOCTOR IS IN...PSYCHIATRIC HELP—5¢
Read the following scenarios and diagnose the client. Remember to look carefully at the criteria for the disorder before you make a decision as to the diagnosis. Make a list of other information you might need to help you understand the causal factors.

1. Roger comes to your office because he has recently been laid off from his job as a store manager. He is concerned because he has started to drink heavily as a result of this and finds himself feeling incredibly sad and depressed. His wife is supportive but he is afraid she will get tired of dealing with his moods and leave. Although she says she won't, he is becoming preoccupied with the idea of her leaving him. He tells you that his father abused alcohol and that his mother ended up leaving when she couldn't take it any more. His father always drank, according to Roger, would get really down, and, on at least one occasion, talked about suicide. Roger doesn't want to become like his father but finds himself acting in similar ways. He is thinking that maybe he should just tell his wife to leave him, then move to another state, and start all over.

Look at Roger's situation from psychodynamic, behavioral, and cognitive-behavioral perspectives. What in Roger's story would you emphasize from each of these perspectives and how would you treat him? (p. 74 - 84)

AFTER YOU READ

PRACTICE TESTS
Take the following three multiple-choice tests to see how much you have comprehended from the chapter. Each represents roughly one-third of the chapter. As you study the chapter, use these to check your progress.

PRACTICE TEST NUMBER 1

1. Disorders could be classified and diagnosed better if their causes could be better understood instead of relying on (p.58)
   a. clusters of symptoms.
   b. clusters of test results.
   c. interview techniques.
   d. unconscious motivations.

2. The etiology of abnormal behavior means the (p. 64)
   a. method of treatment.
   b. treatment outcome.
   c. causal pattern.
   d. all of the above.

3. The response of an individual to demands that he or she perceives as taxing or exceeding his or her personal resources is referred to as (p.60)

a. stress.
b. fixated.
c. socialized.
d. diathesis.

4. The diathesis is a relatively _____ necessary or contributory cause. (p. 60)
   a. proximal
   b. distal
   c. unimportant
   d. a and c

5. Jimmy's parents use drugs and his father is often abusive toward his mother. In spite of this, Jimmy is doing well in school and has made the football team. Jimmy's success is a form of (p. 61)
   a. good genes.
   b. good luck.
   c. resilience.
   d. diathesis.

6. Jimmy had an uncle who took him under his wing and helped him get through some rough times. This uncle provided the warmth and support that Jimmy lacked at home. Jimmy's uncle provided a (p. 61)
   a. protective factor.
   b. relief to Jimmy's parents.
   c. proximal cause.
   d. distal cause.

7. When Sharon went to school, she was taught the theory and practice of the psychoanalytical viewpoint. The methods she used in her practice reflected this viewpoint and she believed totally in this perspective. At a conference, she was introduced to the cognitive-behavioral viewpoint and became intrigued by it. She went on to study this perspective and incorporate it into her practice. Sharon's new insights constituted a (p.63)
   a. breakthrough.
   b. paradigm shift.
   c. break from tradition.
   d. cognitive shift.

8. Malfunction of the negative feedback system in the hypothalamic-pituitary-adrenal-cortical axis has been implicated in such psychopathologies as (p. 66)
   a. post-traumatic stress disorder.
   b. depression.

c. OCD.

d. a and b

9. The fact that a number of disorders, such as depression, schizophrenia, and alcoholism, show heredity as an important predisposing causal factor is consistent with which perspective? (p. 63)

a. biological

b. behavioral

c. cognitive

d. psychoanalytical

10. The observed structural and functional characteristics that result from an interaction of the person's total genetic endowment and the environment are referred to as a person's (p. 64)

a. phenotype.

b. genotype.

c. self.

d. linotype.

PRACTICE TEST NUMBER 2

1. The flexibility of the brain to make changes in organization and/or function in response to prenatal or postnatal experiences is called (p.72)

a. neural flexibility

b. syntaptic pruning

c. synaptogenesis

d. neural plasticity

2. At what age can we identify approximately five dimensions of temperament development that may affect personality? (p. 71)

a. one to two years

b. two to three months

c. six months to one year

d. four to five years

3. The _____ acknowledges that genetic activity influences neural activity, which, in turn, influences behavior, which, in turn, influences the environment, and that these influences are bidirectional. (p. 73)

a. brain activity approach

b. neural regulatory approach

c. developmental systems approach

d. none of the above

4. Because biological treatments seem to have more immediate results

than other available therapies, these have been seen as a possible (p.73)
a. cure-all.
b. band-aid approach.
c. short cut.
d. answer to all of the problems with therapy.

5. When we adopt a perspective, it will influence (p.74 - 84)
a. our perceptions of maladaptive behavior.
b. the types of evidence we look for.
c. the way in which we interpret data.
d. all of the above

6. The process of working new experiences into existing cognitive frameworks, even if the new information has to be reinterpreted or distorted to make it fit, is known as (p.85)
a. integration.
b. accommodation.
c. assimilation.
d. incorporation.

8. Amato and Keith (1991a, 1991b) found that the negative effects of divorce seemed to be decreasing, particularly since 1970, because divorce was decreasing in (p. 95)
a. stigmatization.
b. number.
c. amount parents blamed each other.
d. availability.

9. Jill, who is 20 years old, is popular with many people and is comfortable in all settings. Jill has a good deal of (p.96)
a. luck.
b. intuition.
c. social competence.
d. social ineptitude.

10. Jennifer, who is five years old and in kindergarten, is clueless when it comes to reading her peers' emotions, especially fear and sadness. This behavior can predict aggressive behavior toward peers in the (p. 96)
a. third grade.
b. first grade.
c. ninth grade.
d. the behavior really can't predict anything.

PRACTICE TEST NUMBER 3

1. Studies done by sociocultural researchers made it clear that there is a relationship between mental disorders and (p. 103)
    a. individual schema.
    b. cultural schema.
    c. sociocultural conditions.
    d. none of the above.

2. In our society, the lower the SES, the higher the incidence of (p. 101)
    a. therapy.
    b. intervention of some sort.
    c. mental disorder.
    d. a and b

3. Many more women than men suffer from various emotional disorders. This may be in part due to sexual discrimination. The primary types of discrimination are (p. 102.)
    a. work and wage.
    b. access and treatment.
    c. educational and career.
    d. all of the above

4. Estimates are that approximately _____ of the homeless are affected by mental illness. (p.103)
    a. one-half
    b. one-quarter
    c. 75%
    d. one-third

5. Since Kleinman and Good consider cultural factors so important to understanding depressive disorders, they have urged the psychiatric community to do what? (p.103)
    a. incorporate it into all therapeutic treatment
    b. incorporate it into all educational programs
    c. incorporate another axis in the DSM
    d. create a new paradigm

6. Dr. Smith combines many different approaches/techniques when assessing and working with clients. What is Dr. Smith's approach? (p. 104)
    a. confusing
    b. eclectic
    c. purist
    d. practical

7. A factor that increases the probability of developing a disorder without being either necessary or sufficient is a _____ cause. (p..59)
   a. distal
   b. proximal
   c. reinforcing
   d. contributory

8. When the ego resorts to irrational protective measures of dealing with anxiety, it is called a(n) (p. 76)
   a. compatability response
   b. stress reducer
   c. anxiety reduction method
   d. ego defense mechanism

9. The ability to discriminate may be brought about by (p 82)
   a. classical conditioning.
   b. shaping.
   c. responding differently to similar stimuli, based on which ones are reinforced.
   d. avoidance conditioning.

10. Which of the following was not proposed as a strong factor in popularity among juveniles? (p 91)
   a. parents' income
   b. intelligence
   c. being seen as friendly and outgoing
   d. physical attractiveness

COMPREHENSIVE PRACTICE TEST
The following tests are designed to give you an idea of how well you understood the entire chapter. There are three different types of tests: multiple choice, true-false, and essay.

MULTIPLE-CHOICE
1. A predisposition toward developing a disorder is termed (p. 60)
   a. stress.
   b. fixated.
   c. socialized.
   d. diathesis.

2. The death of a parent would be considered a _____ stressor for a child's grief reaction. (p. 60)
   a. proximal
   b. distal
   c. unimportant

d. b and c

3. A rapidly growing field of psychology that focuses on determining what is abnormal at any point in development by comparing and contrasting it with normal and expected changes that occur in the course of development is called (p. 62)
   a. cognitive-behavioral psychology.
   b. psychodevelopmental psychology.
   c. developmental psychopathology.
   d. cognitive-developmental psychology.

4. The belief that _____ in the brain can result in abnormal behavior is one of the basic tenets of the biological perspective today. (p 64.)
   a. diseases
   b. disorders of the central nervous system
   c. neurotransmitter imbalances
   d. none of the above

5. The _____ is referred to as the master gland of the body. (p. 66)
   a. adrenal gland
   b. hypothalamus
   c. endocrine gland
   d. pituitary gland

6. A person's total genetic endowment is referred to as her or his (p. 68)
   a. phenotype.
   b. genotype.
   c. self.
   d. linotype.

7. The _____ perspective views human nature as basically "good." (p. 75)
   a. existential
   b. behavioral
   c. psychoanalytical
   d. humanistic

8. The _____ perspective places more emphasis on the irrational tendencies and the difficulties inherent in self-fulfillment—particularly in a modern, bureaucratic and dehumanizing mass society. (p. 75)
   a. existential
   b. behavioral
   c. cognitive

d. humanistic

9. Evidence suggests that disordered _____ make a significant
   contribution to child and adolescent psychopathology, especially to
   problems such as depression, conduct disorder, delinquency, and
   attention deficit disorder. (p.92)
   a. mothers
   b. brothers
   c. grandparents
   d. fathers

10. Your book mentions that, at present, the only unified perspective is
    called the (p. 105)
    a. unification viewpoint.
    b. cognitive viewpoint.
    c. cognitive-behavioral viewpoint.
    d. biopsychosocial viewpoint.

11. The specialized structure on the postsynaptic neuron at which the
    neurotransmitter exerts its effect is the (p.65)
    a. synaptic cleft.
    b. synaptic vesicle.
    c. receptor site.
    d. enzyme.

12. After being released into the synaptic cleft, the neurotransmitter
    substance may be reabsorbed into the presynaptic axon button, a
    process called (p 65.)
    a. re-uptake.
    b. deactivation.
    c. recapture.
    d. active transport.

13. In genetic studies the subject, or carrier, of the trait or disorder in
    question who serves as the starting point is known as the (p.69)
    a. proband.
    b. zygote.
    c. risk person.
    d. initiation point.

14. According to Freud's psychoanalytic perspective, the source of all
    instinctual drives is the (p.76)
    a. ego.
    b. id.
    c. libido.
    d. superego.

15. Margaret Mahler focused on the process by which children come to understand that they are different from other objects. This process involves a developmental phase called (p.78)
    a. assimilation-accommodation.
    b. introjection-identification.
    c. introversion-extroversion.
    d. separation-individuation.

16. Instead of Freud's concept of fixation, Erikson proposed that parental deprivation might interfere with the development of (p 89.)
    a. high self-esteem.
    b. tolerance for stimulation.
    c. self-control.
    d. basic trust.

17. The form of learning in which an individual learns to achieve a desired goal is (p. 82)
    a. classical conditioning.
    b. operant conditioning.
    c. modeling.
    d. avoidance conditioning.

18. The behaviorist tradition has been criticized for (p.83)
    a. its precision and objectivity.
    b. its research orientation.
    c. its failure to demonstrate effectiveness.
    d. its over concern with symptoms.

19. The tendency to explain one's success as due to luck—as compared to hard work—is best categorized as an example of a specific (p. 85)
    a. attributional style.
    b. contributory effect.
    c. proximal schema.
    d. internal representation.

20. A basic goal of psychosocial therapies is (p 85.)
    a. accommodation.
    b. social skills training.
    c. reduction of anxiety.
    d. assimilation.

21. Bowlby found that when young children were separated from their parents during prolonged periods of hospitalization, their reaction upon reunion was (p 91.)

    a. strong dependence.
    b. detachment.
    c. joy.
    d. despair.

22. A(n) _____ parental style is likely to produce a
    child who is impulsive and aggressive, spoiled, selfish,
    inconsiderate, and demanding, and who will exploit people for
    his/her own purposes. (p.93)
    a. authoritative
    b. authoritarian
    c. permissive-indulgent
    d. neglecting-uninvolved

23. Epidemiological studies that have linked psychopathology with social
    class are (p 95)
    a. based on controlled experimentation.
    b. correlational in nature.
    c. establishing a clear-cut cause-effect relationship.
    d. good examples of analogue studies.

True - False

1. T / F The behavioral sciences have no difficulty distinguishing between what is cause and effect. (p.60)

2. T / F Protective factors are not necessarily positive experiences. (p. 61)

3. T / F Some forms of psychopathology have been linked to hormonal imbalances. (p. 64)

4. T / F Genes affect behavior directly. (p. 64)

5, T / F The temperament of an infant has profound effects on many developmental processes. (p. 72)

6. T / F Assimilation is the basic goal of psychosocial therapies. (p. 85)

7. T / F Children deprived of needed resources normally supplied by parents or parental surrogates may be left with irreversible psychological scars. (p. 89)

8. T / F Candy is a loner and Brian is a bully. Each of them will probably have healthy mental health outcomes. (p 96.)

9. T / F When social roles are conflicting, unclear, or difficult to achieve, unhealthy personality development may occur. (p 101)

10. T / F Prejudice against minority groups may play a role in explaining why these groups sometimes show increased prevalence of certain mental disorders.   (p. 102)

11. T / F The sociocultural viewpoint has been readily embraced by the therapeutic community and incorporated into treatment. (p. 97)

ESSAY QUESTIONS

1.   List the misconceptions and stereotypes that exist about studies of genetic influences on behavior, traits and psychopathology, and give examples of each. (p.70)

WEB LINKS TO ITEMS OR CONCEPTS DISCUSSED IN CHAPTER 3

Fetal Alcohol Syndrome

> www.nofas.org/

> www.acbr.com/fas/s

Sigmund Freud

> plaza.interport.net/nypsan/freudarc.html

> www.psychoanalysis.org

USE IT OR LOSE IT

Provide an answer to the thought question below, knowing that there is more than one way to respond. Possible answers are presented in the Answer Key.

> Discuss how drugs and medications can effect the actions of neurotransmitters at the synapse.

CRISS-CROSS

Now that you know all there is to know about this chapter, here's your chance to put that knowledge to work.

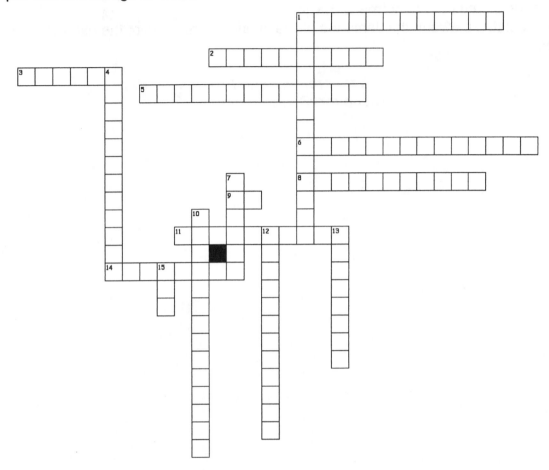

CRISS-CROSS CLUES

Across

1. fitting new experiences into one s existing cognitive framework
2. gradual lessening of a conditioned response, when the UCS is omitted
3. one's frame of reference through the complexities of modern living
5. delivery of a reward or pleasant stimulus; aids in conditioning
6. distinguishing between similar stimuli and responding differently to these
8. one's reactivity and characteristic ways of self-regulation
9. the source of instinctual drives
11. the ability to adapt successfully
14. the outgrowth of internalizing the taboos and moral values of society

Down

1. changing existing cognitive framework to incorporate new discrepant information
4. the process of assigning causes to things that happen

7. life instincts and death instincts
10. when one stimulus (or set of stimuli) can be evoked by another, similar stimuli
12. an internal process in which the infant or child incorporates symbolically
13. causal pattern of abnormal behavior
15. mediates between the demands of the id and the realities of the external world

Puzzle created with Puzzlemaker at DiscoverySchool.com

ANSWERS TO TEST QUESTIONS - CHAPTER THREE

WHO'S WHO
C. Karen Horney
E. Harry Stack Sullivan
D. Erik Erikson
B. Erich Fromm
A. Alfred Adler

E. Discrimination
C. Generalization
B. Intermittent
D. Reinforcement
A. Avoidance conditioning

C. Authoritative
D. Authoritarian
A. Permissive-indulgent
B. Neglecting-uninvolved

SHORT ANSWERS
(Your answer should contain the following points.)

1. The five methods used in behavior genetics to study the heritability of mental disorders are:
    a. pedigree or family-history method—observation of samples of relatives of each proband case to see whether the incidence increases in proportion to the degree of hereditary relationship.
    b. twin method—the study of monozygotic and dizygotic twins to look at concordance rates for mental disorders.
    c. adoption method—the study of adopted offspring of parents with a mental disorder and those who parents did not have a disorder to see if a disorder develops.
    d. linkage analysis—studies that capitalize on currently known locations of chromosomes of genes for physical characteristics or biological processes to see if the same could apply for mental disorders.
    e. association studies—studies of large groups of people with and without a disorder, followed by a comparison of the frequencies of certain genetic markers that are known to be located on particular chromosomes in the people with and without the disorder.

2. a. acting out
    b. denial of reality
    c. displacement
    d. fixation
    e. projection
    f. rationalization

THE DOCTOR IS IN

Psychodynamic: Emphasize the unconscious motives for Roger's behaviors—hurtful memories from his childhood about his mother and father. You might also say that his drinking is a result of the breakdown of his ego—an ego-defense mechanism
Treatment: Use free association and dream analysis to become acquainted with the conscious and the unconscious, also might want to include interpersonal therapy.
Behavioral: Look at Roger's behavior and the stimuli, and reinforcing conditions that control it. For instance, his drinking is getting him attention from his wife and because he is drinking so much it reinforces that he can't get a job. His drinking also reinforces his sadness and depression (alcohol is a depressant).
Treatment: Create a situation where alcohol is not a reinforcement but is substituted for something else that is positive, e.g. Roger and his wife walking together or looking through employment opportunities together. Attendance of AA meetings to continue to strengthen the behavior of not drinking.
Cognitive-Behavioral: Look at Roger's basic information-processing mechanisms, his internal reinforcements, and how these are distorted. Explore his attributional style and the meaning he gives to his wife's behavior about leaving him and his thoughts of leaving her.
Treatment: Change thought patterns through logical reanalysis and by having Roger experiment with different behaviors/actions that would then be looked at in therapy.

PRACTICE TESTS

Q#	TEST 1	TEST 2	TEST 3
1	A	D	C
2	C	B	C
3	A	C	B
4	B	A	D
5	C	D	C
6	A	C	D
7	B	B	B

8	D	A	D
9	A	C	C
10	A	A	A

COMPREHENSIVE PRACTICE TEST

Q#	MULTIPLE CHOICE	T/F
1	D	F
2	A	T
3	C	T
4	C	F
5	D	T
6	B	F
7	D	T
8	A	F
9	D	T
10	D	T
11	C	T
12	A	
13	A	
14	B	
15	D	
16	D	
17	B	
18	D	
19	A	
20	A	
21	D	
22	C	
23	B	

ESSAY QUESTIONS
(Your answer should contain the following points.)

Myth: Strong genetic effects mean that environmental influences must be unimportant. Example: Height—genetically determined but nutrition can play a role.

Myth: Genes provide a limit to potential. Example: Children born to socially disadvantaged parent and adopted by and reared by socially advantaged parents.

Myth: Genetic strategies are of no value for studying environmental influences. <u>Example:</u> Monozygotic twins with less than 100% concordance rates for mental illness and personality.

<u>Myth:</u> Nature and nurture are separate. <u>Example</u>: Babies born with PKU only develop the disease if exposed to diets with phenylalanine.

<u>Myth:</u> Genetic effects diminish with age. <u>Example:</u> Dizygotic twins show greater differences over time than monozygotic twins.

<u>Myth:</u> Disorders that run in families must be genetic and those that do not run in families must not be genetic. <u>Example:</u> Autism doesn't run in families but shows a very powerful genetic effect.

USE IT OR LOSE IT

Employers may use the MMPI to assist in determining whether prospective employees exhibit stable patterns of thought and emotion. They may also want to compare the responses to new hires with those of people they know to be successful in their field.

CRISS-CROSS ANSWERS

Across
1. assimilation
2. extinction
3. schema
5. reinforcement
6. discrimination
8. temperament
9. id
11. resilience
14. superego

Down
1. accommodation
4. attributions
7. libido
10. generalization
12. introjection
13. etiology
15. ego

Chapter 4: Clinical Assessment

BEFORE YOU READ

The ability to accurately assess and diagnose psychological problems is a key aspect of mental health care. Chapter 4 is devoted to a discussion of the goals, methods, and issues involved in clinical assessment. These include the identification, description, and diagnosis of an individual's presenting symptoms. Clinical assessment depends on data from observation and interviews, as well as tests of physical, psychological, neuropsychological, and neurological function. This chapter describes what the different types of tests are, how these are constructed, how valid they are considered to be, and the types of information they provide. Psychosocial and environmental pressures such as stress are also considered in the process. The use of the DSM system of classification commonly used in the United States is also discussed in detail. Finally, the practical and ethical implications of labeling people with a diagnosis are discussed.

- **THE BASIC ELEMENTS IN ASSESSMENT**
    - The Relationship Between Diagnosis and Assessment
    - Taking a Social History
    - The Influence of Professional Orientation
    - Trust and Rapport Between the Clinician and the Client
- **ASSESSMENT OF THE PHYSICAL ORGANISM**
    - The General Physical Examination
    - The Neurological Examination
    - The Neuropsychological Examination
- **PSYCHOSOCIAL ASSESSMENT**
    - Assessment Interviews
    - The Clinical Observation of Behavior
    - Psychological Tests Advantages and Limitations of Objective

Personality Tests

A Psychological Case Study: Esteban

- **• THE INTEGRATION OF ASSESSMENT DATA**

Ethical Issues in Assessment

- **• CLASSIFYING ABNORMAL BEHAVIOR**

Reliability and Validity

Differing Models of Classification

Formal Diagnostic Classification of Mental Disorders

OBJECTIVES

After reading this chapter, you should be able to:

1. Describe the basic elements of clinical assessment, including:
   a) its nature and purpose, b) the relationship between diagnosis and assessment, c) the types of information sought, and d) the different types of data of interest.

2. Describe the influence of professional orientation on the assessment process.

3. Explain what is meant by rapport between the clinician and client, and outline the components of a relationship that leads to good rapport.

4. Summarize the various approaches to assessment of physical problems, including the general, physical, neurological, and neuropsychological examples.

5. List types of psychosocial assessments.

6. Discriminate between structured and unstructured interviews for the assessment of psychosocial functioning, and evaluate the relative merits of each.

7. Discuss various approaches to the clinical observation of behavior and identify the advantages of each.

8. Explain the importance of rating scales in clinical observations.

9. Describe the major intelligence tests.

10. Discuss the advantages and disadvantages of projective personality tests.

11. Discuss the advantages and disadvantages of objective personality tests.

12. Summarize the process of integrating assessment data into a model for use in planning or changing treatment.

13. Explain the ethical issues involved in assessment.

14. Explain the purpose of classification systems for abnormal behavior.

15. Discuss reliability and validity as they relate to a classification system.

16. Describe the differing models of classification.

17. Explain the DSM classification of mental disorders.

AS YOU READ

Answers can be found in the Answer Key at the end of the chapter.

KEY WORDS

Each of the words below is important in understanding the concepts presented in this chapter. Write the definition next to each of the words.

Term	Page	Definition
Actuarial procedures	127	
Acute	137	
Comorbidity	133	
Computerized axial tomography (CAT scan)	111	
Dysrhythmia	111	
electroencephalogram (EEG)	111	

Episodic	137	
Functional MRI (fMRI)	112	
Magnetic resonance imaging ((MRI)	112	
Mild	137	
Minnesota Multiphasic Personality Inventory (MMPI)	122	
Moderate	137	
Neuropsychological assessment	113	
Objective tests	122	
Positron emission tomography (PET Scan)	112	
Projective tests	119	
Rating scales	116	
Recurrent	137	
Reliability	132	
Role playing	116	
Rorschach Test	119	
Self-monitoring	110	
Sentence completion test	122	
Severe	137	
Signs	134	
Symptoms	108	
Thematic Apperception Test (TAT)	110	

Validity	117	

MATCHING

Who's Who and What's What?

Match the following psychological tests with the appropriate description of each test's purpose.

Psychological Test

_____ Rorschach Test

_____ Thematic Apperception Test

_____ Minnesota Multiphasic Personality Inventory (MMPI)

_____ WAIS-R

_____ WISC-R

_____ Brief Psychiatric Rating Scale (BPRS)

_____ Sentence Completion Test

Purpose

A. Rating scale based on standardized interview

B. Intelligence scale for children

C. Intelligence scale for adults

D. Projective test using inkblots

E. Projective test using pictures

F. Structured personality test

G. Test that pinpoints topics that should be explored

SHORT ANSWERS

Provide brief answers to the following questions.

1. Discuss

   a) the benefits of using computers in psychological testing and

b) why some clinicians are reluctant to use them? (p.118)

2. Compare the functions, advantages, and disadvantages of the CAT, MRI, fMRI, and PET scans. (p. 112-113.)

3. Explain the purpose of classifying abnormal behavior. (p.131)

4. Discuss the problem of labeling. (p. 137)

THE DOCTOR IS IN...PSYCHIATRIC HELP—5¢

Read the following scenarios and diagnose the client. Remember to look carefully at the criteria for the disorder before you make a decision as to the diagnosis. Make a list of other information you might need to help you understand the causal factors.

1. You are a famous neuropsychologist, and a new patient has been referred to you. This patient's history leads you to believe that some sort of brain injury has occurred. You believe that a preselected battery of standard tests is the most beneficial. What test battery would you use? What are its component parts, and what are its limitations? (p. 113 - 119.)

2. Tim, a 21-year-old man, has just been admitted to the hospital. He was found wandering the streets, talking to himself. It looks as if he has been homeless for some time. You are called in to do a clinical observation. What would you include in your observation of Tim? (p. 113-119)

3. You are seeing a new patient who has been referred to you by his primary-care doctor. Ben, a 29-year-old truck driver, went to his doctor thinking he was having a heart attack. When he drove across bridges, his heart would pound, his hands got sweaty, he would feel short of breath, and begin to hyperventilate. Several months ago, Ben was involved in an accident that left three people dead and several injured. Though it wasn't his fault (there had been heavy fog), he felt that as an experienced truck driver, he should have been able to prevent the accident. The symptoms began shortly after the accident and have lasted for six months. His primary doctor reports that Ben is not having any heart problems and is generally in good health.

As Ben's psychologist, what type of interview would you conduct? What diagnosis would you give him on Axis I, II, and III? Why? (p. 130-136)

AFTER YOU READ

PRACTICE TESTS

Take the following three multiple-choice tests to see how much you have comprehended from the chapter. Each represents roughly one-third of the chapter. As you study the chapter, use these to check your progress.

PRACTICE TEST NUMBER 1

1. Formal diagnosis is necessary after assessment for (p. 108)

    a. insurance claims.

    b. planning treatment.

    c. deciding on which treatment facilities would be best for the client.

    d. all of the above.

2. When taking a social history, the clinician notes key dimensions that help her/him to understand the individual's problem. The key dimensions are (p.109)

    a. excesses, deficits, and appropriateness.

    b. excesses, desires, and dreams.

    c. behaviors, subconscious wishes, and fantasies.

    d. thought association and results of CAT scans.

3. The orientation of a clinician can affect   (p.110)

    a. The way she interviews a patient.

    b. Her interpretation of data.

    c. Her treatment recommendations.

    d. all of the above

4. A significant divergence of normal brain patterns recorded on an EEG, which may be a result of some abnormality, is referred to as (p. 111)

    a. dysthmia.

    b. dysrhythmia.

    c. a brain tumor.

    d. none of the above.

5. Mrs. Smith, 73, is experiencing some significant difficulty with cognitive activities and has lost some coordination. She is referred to a specialist

who will test her cognitive, perceptual, and motor performance. This
specialist is a (p.113)

a. neuropsychologist.

b. cognitive behaviorist.

c. psychoanalyst.

d. biologist.

6. Mrs. Smith is administered a battery of tests to assess the psychological
components of her brain injury. The test she probably was given was a (p.
113.)

a. TAT.

b. MRI.

c. Brief Psychiatric Rating Scale.

d. Halstead-Reitan.

7. You have scheduled an assessment interview for a new client. You have
chosen a standardized interview format that you hope will yield a clear
picture of your client's situation. This will be a(n) _____ interview.
(p. 115)

a. structured

b. unstructured

c. insightful

d. constructed

8. You have scheduled an assessment interview for another new client. There
are several questions you want the client to answer, but you want to be
free to explore responses in more depth. This format is considered a(n)
_____ interview. (p.110.)

a. structured

b. unstructured

c. insightful

d. constructed

9. Tim has been admitted to the hospital, and you, a renowned doctor, are about to administer several clinical observations using a rating scale. It is called the (p. 117)

    a. TAT.

    b. WISC-R.

    c. BPRS.

    d. MMPI-2.

10. You are going to conduct research on depression. You use what instrument to select your research subjects? (p.121)

    a. TAT

    b. HRSD

    c. BPRS

    d. MMPI-2

PRACTICE TEST NUMBER 2

1. Which of the following is an example of an intelligence test? (p. 117-119)

    a. WISC-III

    b. WAIS-III

    c. Standard-Binet Intelligence Scale

    d. all of the above

2. When Dr. Taylor asked the client to respond to an inkblot picture he was probably administering the _____ test. (p. 110)

    a. Thematic Apperception

    b. Rorschach

    c. Sentence-Completion

    d. Stanford-Binet

3. When Dr. Zimmer asked the client to make up a story based on the picture she was probably administering the _____ test. (p. 121)
    a. Thematic Apperception
    b. Rorschach
    c. Sentence completion
    d. Stanford-Binet

4. Dr. Jones gives her client the beginning of sentences and asks that she complete each one. This is known as the _____ test. (p.122)
    a. Thematic Perception
    b. Rorschach
    c. Sentence completion
    d. Stanford-Binet

5. Tests which are controlled and objective are called a(n) _____ personality test. (p. 119)
    a. subjective
    b. deductive
    c. objective
    d. carefully constructive

6. The MMPI consists of _____ clinical scales, each designed to measure tendencies to respond in psychologically deviant ways. (p. 122)
    a. 10
    b. 15
    c. 8
    d. The MMPI doesn't have clinical scales, because it is a projective test.

7. As a psychiatrist in a large mental hospital, you and several of your colleagues

often work together to evaluate assessment data. You are part of a (p. 130)

a. collective-bargaining unit.

b. ward-management team.

c. administrative team.

d. interdisciplinary team.

8. The degree to which a measuring device produces the same results each time it is used to measure the same thing is referred to as (p. 115)

a. reliability.

b. validity.

c. usability.

d. consistency.

9. The extent to which a measuring instrument actually measures what it is supposed to measure is referred to as (p. 132)

a. reliability.

b. validity.

c. usability.

d. measurability.

10. Good reliability in diagnostic classification does not in itself guarantee (p. 134)

a. usefulness.

b. validity.

c. concreteness.

d. all of the above.

PRACTICE TEST NUMBER 3

1. The psychiatric classification system widely used in Europe is the (p.133)

    a. ICD-10.

    b. DSM.

    c. UCS.

    d. TAT.

2. The psychiatric classification system used in the United States is the (p.133)

    a. ICD-10.

    b. DSM.

    c. UCS.

    d. TAT.

3. Although purporting to be a categorical model of classification, the authors of
    the book say the DSM is, in fact, a (p. 134)

    a. prototypal model.

    b. dimensional model.

    c. category within itself.

    d. b and c.

4. A diagnostic interview that follows no preexisting plan is called a(n) (p. 138)

    a. structured interview.

    b. unstructured interview.

    c. spontaneous interview.

    d. organized interview.

5. A diagnostic interview that follows a sort of master plan is called a(n) (p. 138.)

    a. structured interview.

    b. unstructured interview.

    c. spontaneous interview.

    d. organized interview.

6. A neurological diagnostic aid that reveals how an organ is functioning by

measuring metabolic processes is the (p. 112)

a. PET scan.

b. CAT scan.

c. EEG.

d. angiogram.

7. Which of the following is the most highly regarded six-hour neuropsychological test? (p. 114)

a. Halstead-Reitan

b. Luria-Nebraska

c. Stanford-Binet

d. Wechsler Adult Intelligence Scale

8. According to the text, the rating scale specifically targeted for depression that has almost become the standard for selecting clinically depressed research subjects is the (p. 117)

a. Beck Depression Inventory.

b. Schedule for Rating Depressive Temperament.

c. Leeds Depression Rating Scale.

d. Hamilton Rating Scale for Depression.

9. Responsible examiners (p. 119)

a. never release client information

b. never administer tests unless they are adequately trained

c. avoid basing conclusions on a single test

d. lie to clients so they won't worry about a test's results

10. The two general categories of psychological tests are (p.117)

a. projective and objective

b. objective and multiphasic

c. projective and inventory

d. structured and personality

COMPREHENSIVE PRACTICE TEST

The following tests are designed to give you an idea of how well you understood the entire chapter. There are three different types of tests: multiple-choice, true-false, and essay.

MULTIPLE-CHOICE

1. The initial clinical assessment is used to (p. 108)

    a. identify the main dimensions of the problem.

    b. predict the likely course of events.

    c. establish a baseline.

    d. all of the above.

2. When assessing an individual, the clinician integrates information concerning the person's personality traits, behavior patterns, environmental demands, etc. into a consistent, meaningful picture often called a(n) (p. 109)

    a. Rorschach.

    b. TAT.

    c. dynamic formulation.

    d. hypothesis.

3. _____ testing provides a clinician with behavioral information on how organic brain damage affects a person's functions. (p. 113)

    a. TAT

    b. Rorschach

    c. MMPI

    d. Neuropsychological

4. A classification system's usefulness depends upon its (p. 132)

    a. reliability.

    b. validity.

    c. a and b

    d. none of the above

5. A _____ approach for classifying abnormal behavior assumes that human behavior can be divided into either healthy or disordered, and that within the disordered category, there are non-overlapping types with a high degree of homogeneity in both symptoms displayed and underlying organization of the disorder. (p. 133)

    a. dimensional

    b. prototyped

    c. behavioral

    d. categorical

6. A _____ approach for classifying abnormal behavior assumes that a person's typical behavior is the product of different strengths of behaviors along several definable dimensions. (p. 133)

    a. dimensional

    b. prototypal

    c. behavioral

    d. categorical

7. An approach to classifying abnormal behavior that compares an active behavior to an ideal is called (p. 133)

    a. dimensional

    b. prototypal

    c. behavioral

    d. categorical

8. A limitation of the DSM classification system is that (p. 134)

a. the differentiation of disorders is too wide.

b. it contains too few disorders.

c. real patients often don't fit into the precise lists of signs and symptoms.

d. a and b

9. The first three axes in the DSM system deal with (p. 134)

   a. psychosocial stresses.

   b. global assessment of functioning.

   c. assessing an individual's present clinical status.

   d. b and c

10. The fourth and fifth axes of the DSM-IV-TR deal with (p. 135)

    a. psychosocial stresses.

    b. global assessment of functioning.

    c. assessing an individual's present clinical status.

    d. b and c

11. Clinical interviews have been criticized as unreliable, and evidence of this unreliability includes the finding that different clinicians often arrive at different formal diagnoses. For this reason, recent versions of the DSM have emphasized an approach that (p. 115)

    a. employs a hierarchical structure.

    b. employs multidimensional assessments.

    c. requires confirmation by convergent information.

    d. employs "operational" assessment.

12. Two general categories of psychological tests used in clinical practice are (p.117)

    a. intelligence and personality.

    b. philosophy and religion.

    c. speech perception and reaction time.

d. tactual performance and auditory perception.

13. Personality tests are often grouped into two categories: (p. 117)

    a. behavioral and psychodynamic.

    b. conscious and unconscious.

    c. projective and objective.

    d. verbal and performance.

14. The aim of a projective test is to (p. 119)

    a. predict a patient's future behavior.

    b. compare a patient's responses to those of persons who are known to have mental disorders.

    c. assess the way a patient perceives ambiguous stimuli.

    d. assess the role of organic factors in a patient's thinking.

15. Behaviorists have criticized the MMPI for being too (p.123-124)

    a. action-oriented.

    b. "mentalistic."

    c. objective.

    d. superficial.

TRUE - FALSE

1. T / F In cases of severe disorders, decisions regarding treatment may be made about a client with his or her consent or consultation with family members. (p.109)

2. T / F Assessment of an individual may involve coordinated use of physical, psychological, and environmental assessment procedures. (p. 109)

3. T / F Confidentiality is not an important issue for clients, because they want as many people as possible to know about their problems. (p.110)

4. T / F Rating scales, when used in clinical observation and self-reports, encourages reliability, objectivity, and allows the rater to indicate the presence, absence, or prominence of a behavior. (p. 116)

5. T / F Two general categories of psychological tests used for clinical practice are general medical exams and intelligence tests. (p.117)

6. T / F An agreed-upon classification system allows clinicians to be confident of communicating clearly. (p. 131)

7. T / F The classification of mental disorders is intended to give direct insight into a person's problems. (p. 134)

8. T / F A classification system, once completed, is not changed. (p. 134)

9. T / F Validity presupposes reliability. (p. 132)

10. T / F The number of recognized mental disorders has remained constant from the first DSM-I to the DSM-IV. (p. 134)

11. T / F Acute mental disorders are relatively short in duration. (p. 138)

12. T / F Chronic mental disorders are relatively short in duration. (p. 138)

ESSAY QUESTIONS

1. What assessment techniques would be favored by the following clinicians? (p.

110)

    a. Biologically oriented clinician

    b. Psychoanalytically oriented clinician

    c. Behaviorally oriented clinician

    d. Cognitively oriented behaviorist

    e. Humanistically oriented clinician

    f. Interpersonally oriented clinician

2. What are the elements of psychological assessment? (p. 110)

WEB LINKS TO ITEMS OR CONCEPTS DISCUSSED IN CHAPTER 4

Clinical assessment

    www.ncaa.nhs.uk/

    www.sci.sdsu.edu/CAL/CAL.html

USE IT OR LOSE IT

Provide an answer to the thought question below, knowing that there is more than one way to respond. Possible answers are presented in the Answer Key.

Why do you suppose that some employers ask prospective employees to take the MMPI, and what they might be looking for?

CRISS-CROSS

Now that you know all there is to know about this chapter, here's your chance to put that knowledge to work.

CRISS-CROSS CLUES

Across

7. Procedure using psychological testing, observation, and interviews to develop a summary of a client s symptoms and problems

9. Disorder patterns that tend to come and go

10. Objective observations of a patient's physical or mental disorder by a diagnostician

11. Patient's subjective description of a physical or mental disorder

12. Long-standing or frequently recurring disorders

13. Structured tests used in psychological assessment

Down

1. Computerized method of storing and analyzing data about many subjects

2. Situations that emulate the conditions thought to lead to abnormality

3. Occurrence of two or more identified disorders in the same individual

4. Sudden onset of a disorder

5. Degree to which a measuring device produces same results each time it is used

6. Statistical technique used to reduce large array of intercorrelated measures to the minimum number needed to account for the overlap or association

8. A disorder that tends to abate and to recur

14. Extent to which a measuring instrument actually measures what it purports to measure

Puzzle created with Puzzlemaker at DiscoverySchool.com

ANSWERS TO TEST QUESTIONS - CHAPTER FOUR

Psychological Test
D. Rorschach Test
E. Thematic Apperception Test
F. Minnesota Multiphasic Personality Inventory (MMPI)
B. WAIS-III
C. WISC-III
A. Brief Psychiatric Rating Scale (BPRS)
G. Sentence Completion Test

SHORT ANSWERS
(Your answer should contain the following points.)

1. Benefits:
* effective assessment function by getting together and evaluating all the information gathered
* can perform with a wide range of assessment tasks by comparing information in the memory banks
* can supply probable diagnosis
* indicate likely behavior
* suggest appropriate treatment
* predict outcome
* print summary reports
* low cost

Reluctance:
* some clinicians are uncomfortable with computers
* some practitioners do not do extensive pretreatment assessments
* the computers are impersonal and mechanical
* computer-bases assessment a threat to clinicians and will replace human functionality

2.   a. CAT—Computerized Axial Tomography
Function: • uses X-rays across patients brain to produce images and locate abnormalities
Advantage: • don't need surgery to look at brain abnormalities
Disadvantage: • exposes patients to prolonged radiation
• images not as clear
b. MRI—Magnetic Resonance Imaging
Function: • measurement of variations in magnetic fields caused by varying amounts of water in various organs
• to look at the anatomical structure of any cross-section of an organ Advantage: • less complicated than a CAT scan
• very clear and able to give a look at all but the smallest brain abnormalities
• noninvasive

Disadvantage: • some patients claustrophobic in narrow cylinder

c. fMRI—function Magnetic Resonance Imaging

Function: • used to measure brain activity

• measures oxygenation (blood flow) of specific areas of brain tissue Advantages: • less expensive than PET scans

• can map on-going psychological activity, e.g., sensations, images, and thoughts

Disadvantage: • some minor problems with distraught psychiatric patients

d. PET—Postiron Emission Tomography

Function: • shows how an organ is functioning by measuring metabolic processes Advantages: • images of metabolic activity allow for better diagnosis

• can see problems that aren't just anatomical

Disadvantages: • low fidelity pictures

• better as a research technique than the clinical diagnostic procedure

3. Classifying abnormal behavior:

    a. provides clear communication

    b. attempts to delineate meaningful side variations of maladaptive behavior

    c. introduces order into discussion of the nature, causes, and treatment of abnormal behavior

    d. allows communication about particular clusters of abnormal behavior

    e. gathers statistics on how common are various disorders

    f. meets needs of medical insurance companies

4. Labeling can be a problem because:

    a. psychiatric diagnosis, as a label, applies to a category of socially disapproved, problematic behavior

    b. a label is too easily accepted as description of an individual, rather than a person's behavior

    c. individuals may accept the label and redefine themselves to play out that role

    d. labeling can effect a person's morale, self-esteem, and relationships with others

THE DOCTOR IS IN

1. Use: Holstead-Reitan battery

    Components: *Factual Performance Test*—measures motor speed

        Rhythm Test—measures attention and sustained concentration

        Speech Sound Perception Test—identification of spoken words, measures concentration, attention, and comprehension

        Finger Oscillation Test—speed of which person can depress a lever

        Holstead Category Test—measures person's ability to learn and remember material

Limitations: Takes about six hours to administer; cost of time, examination fatigue

2. Included in the observation:

a. objective description of Tim's appearance and behavior

b. personal hygiene, emotional responses, depression, anxiety, aggression, hallucination, or delusions

c. could also include staged role playing, event re-enactment, family interaction assignments— analogue situations

3. You would conduct either a structured interview (SCAN) or unstructured interview

• Axis I:

a. Post Traumatic Stress Disorder. Symptoms occurred after an accident and have lasted more than a month.

b. Panic or disorder (could also be phobia). Rapid heart beat, sweaty hands, shortness of breath in a specific situation.

• Axis II: None

• Axis III: None

PRACTICE TESTS

Q#	TEST 1	TEST 2	TEST 3
1	D	D	A
2	A	B	B
3	D	A	A
4	B	C	B
5	A	C	A
6	D	A	A
7	A	D	A
8	B	A	D
9	C	B	A
10	B	B	A

COMPREHENSIVE PRACTICE TEST

Q#	MULTIPLE CHOICE	T/F
1	D	T
2	C	T
3	D	F
4	C	T
5	D	F
6	A	T
7	B	F
8	C	F

9	C	T
10	D	F
11	D	T
12	A	F
13	C	
14	C	
15	B	

ESSAY QUESTIONS
(Your answer should contain the following points.)

1.   a. Biologically oriented clinician
   • biological assessment focusing on underlying organic malfunctioning
   b. Psychoanalytically oriented clinician
   • use of TAT or Rorschach Test
   • focuses on intrapsychic conflicts
   c. Behaviorally oriented clinician
   • looks at functional relationships between environmental events or reinforcements and abnormal behavior
   • uses behavioral absencations and self-monitoring techniques to identify maladaptive learned patterns
   d. Cognitively oriented behaviorist
   • would shift to dysfunctional thoughts rethinking maladaptive learned patterns
   e. Humanistically oriented clinician
   • interview techniques to uncover blocked or distorted personal growth
   f. Interpersonally oriented clinician
   • use of personal confrontations and behavioral observations to pinpoint difficulties in interpersonal relationships

2. The elements of psychological assessment are:
   a. identify presenting problem – situational / more persuasive and long-term / combination of the two
   b. recent deterioration in cognitive faculties
   c. how long the person has been dealing with the problem
   d. whether prior help has been sought
   e. self-defeating behavior and personality deterioration
   f. whether the problem is affecting the person's performance in social roles
   g. whether the symptoms fit DSM-IV-TR diagnostic patterns

USE IT OR LOSE IT

Employers may use the MMPI to assist in determining whether prospective employees exhibit stable patterns of thought and emotion. They may also want to compare the responses to new hires with those of people they know to be successful in their field.

CRISS-CROSS ANSWERS

Across
7. clinical assessment
9. recurrent
10. signs
11. symptoms
12. chronic
13. objective tests

Down
1. actuarial procedures
2. analogue situations
3. comorbidity
4. acute
5. reliability
6. factor analysis
8. episodic
14. validity

Chapter 5: Stress and Adjustment Disorders

BEFORE YOU READ

Chapter 5 begins with a detailed discussion of stress, a topic of increasing concern as modern life becomes more complicated and pressured. The text discusses potential sources of stress, the factors that predispose people to stress and the biological and psychological aspects of stress responses. The definitions and symptoms of Adjustment Disorder and Post Traumatic Stress Disorder are also explained and compared. Particular sources of stress such as unemployment, bereavement, divorce, rape, military combat, torture, POW experiences, and large scale disasters are explored. Finally, possible coping strategies and their applications and efficacy are described, with particular emphasis on prevention, treatment strategies, the use of medication, and crisis interventions. A better understanding of how stress impacts us, and how we can best cope with the stressful events in our lives is essential if we are to flourish in our complex world.

- **WHAT IS STRESS?**
  Categories of Stressors
  Factors Predisposing a Person to Stress
  Factors Predisposing a Person to Stress
  Coping with Stress

- **THE EFFECTS OF SEVERE STRESS**
  Biological Effects of Stress
  Psychological Effects of Long-Term Stress

- **ADJUSTMENT DISORDER: REACTIONS TO COMMON LIFE STRESSORS**

Stress from Unemployment

Stress from Bereavement

Stress from Divorce or Separation

- **POST-TRAUMATIC STRESS DISORDER; REACTIONS TO CATASTROPHIC EVENTS**

  Prevalence of PTSD in the General Population

  Distinguishing Between Acute Stress Disorder and Post-Traumatic Stress

  The Trauma of Rape

  The Trauma of Military Combat

  Severe Threats to Personal Safety and Security

  Causal Factors in Post-Traumatic Stress

  Long-term Effects of Post-Traumatic Stress

- **PREVENTION AND TREATMENT OF STRESS DISORDERS**

  Prevention of Stress disorders

  Treatment for Stress Disorders

  Challenges in Studying Crisis Victims

  What We Are Learning About Crisis Intervention

- **UNRESOLVED ISSUES**

  Psychotropic Medication in the Treatment of PTSD

OBJECTIVES

After reading this chapter, you should be able to:

1. Define the concepts of stressor, stress, and coping, describe the basic categories of stressors, and discuss factors that increase or decrease a person's vulnerability to stress.

2. Contrast the two major categories of coping responses and outline the numerous negative consequences of a failure to cope successfully.

3. Characterize the DSM-IV-TR diagnosis of adjustment disorder and describe three major stressors and the consequences that increase the risk of adjustment disorder.

4. List the diagnostic criteria for acute stress disorder and post-traumatic stress disorder (PTSD), and compare and contrast the two disorders.

5. Summarize what is known about the major features of reactions to catastrophic events.

6. Identify the factors that influence the effects of rape on the victim and describe the typical immediate and long-term consequences of rape.

7. Characterize the phenomenon of combat-related stress and of PTSD in connection with battlefield stress.

8. List and illustrate the long-term effects of being a prisoner of war or in a concentration camp, and note the methodological problems associated with biased sampling.

9. Outline the factors that appear to influence combat-related stress problems, and describe the long-term effects of PTSD.

10. Describe the psychological problems associated with being tortured, with being a refugee, and with being held hostage.

11. Summarize the approaches that have been used to treat or to prevent stress disorders and evaluate their effectiveness.

12. Discuss the issue of using psychotropic medications to treat PTSD.

AS YOU READ

Answers can be found in the Answer Key at the end of the chapter.

KEY WORDS

Each of the words below is important in understanding the concepts presented in this chapter. Write the definition next to each of the words.

Term	Page	Definiton
Acute stress disorder	144	
Adjustment disorder	144	
Coping strategies	144	
Crisis	147	
Crisis intervention	172	
Debriefing sessions	172	
Defense-oriented response	150	
Disaster syndrome	158	
Distress	144	
Eustress	144	
General adaptation syndrome	151	
Personality or psychological decompensation	151	
Post-traumatic stress disorder	144 -5	
Psychoneuroimmun- ology	153	
Stress	144	
Stress tolerance	148	
Stress-inoculation training	171	
Stressors	144	
Task-oriented response	150	

MATCHING

Who's Who and What's What

Match the following terms with their definitions.

Term

_____ Post-Traumatic Stress Disorder

_____ psychoneuroimmunology

_____ adjustment disorder

_____ crisis

_____ stress

_____ stressor

_____ eustress

_____ stress tolerance

_____ stress-inoculation training

Definition

A a maladaptive response within three months of a stressor

B one's ability to withstand stress

C. an adjustment demand

D. severe psychological and physical symptoms as a reaction to unexpected environmental crises

E. preventative strategy, prepares people to meet stressful situations

F. a by-product of poor or inadequate coping

G. new field of study which focuses on the effects of stress on the immune system

H. when a stressful situation exceeds one's adoptive capacities

I. positive stress

SHORT ANSWERS

Provide brief answers to the following questions.

1. Explain the Social Readjustment Rating Scale and what it predicts. (p. 147)

2. Name the three interactional levels in coping with stress and give examples of each. (p. 150)

3. Selye (1956, 1976b) found that the body's reaction to sustained and excessive stress typically occurs in three major phases. Name and briefly explain each. (p. 151)

4. Explain how the sympathetic nervous system (SNS) reacts when an organism is faced with danger—the fight-or-flight response. Also, explain why there may be a danger connected to this. (p.151-152)

5. Following a disaster, a victim's initial responses typically follow three stages. Name and briefly explain these. (p.158)

6. Name and explain five areas of life functioning that may be affected by a rape. (p. 161)

7. The trauma of military combat was called "shell shock" in World War II,

"operational fatigue," or "combat exhaustion" in the Korean and Vietnam wars, and, currently, "acute stress disorder." Discuss its causes and effects. (p. 157 - 9)

THE DOCTOR IS IN...PSYCHIATRIC HELP—5¢

Read the following scenarios and diagnose the client. Remember to look carefully at the criteria for the disorder before you make a decision as to the diagnosis. Make a list of other information you might need to help you understand the causal factors.

1. Becky came to your office because she was sexually assaulted six months ago and is having difficulty. She tells you that she feels anxious and depressed. The rapist was an acquaintance of hers and she is questioning her ability to judge people. She is also having difficulty developing trust. Her self-esteem is really low and she is having problems concentrating at school because she keeps having thoughts about the rape. Becky has been having nightmares and has started to drink a lot to help her sleep. Her friends have been supportive, but they seem to be getting tired of her mood swings and angry outbursts. Becky feels like she is going crazy.

How would you diagnose Becky and why? What treatment would you recommend for her? (pp. 160-162)

AFTER YOU READ

Answers can be found in the Answer Key at the end of the chapter.

PRACTICE TESTS

Take the following three multiple-choice tests to see how much you have comprehended from the chapter. Each represents roughly one-third of the chapter. As you study the chapter, use these to check your progress.

PRACTICE TEST NUMBER 1

1. A wide range of obstacles, such as prejudice and discrimination, loneliness, inadequate self-control, the death of a loved one, fall into the category of (p. 145)
   a. adjustments.
   b. acutes.
   c. frustrations.
   d. pressures.

2. The simultaneous occurrence of two or more incompatible needs or motives, such as career versus family needs, is described as (p. 145)
   a. pressure.
   b. conflict.
   c. frustration.
   d. adjustment.

3. Feeling the need to achieve goals or behave in particular ways—internal or external—is known as (p.145)
   a. pressure.
   b. frustration.
   c. conflict.
   d. post-traumatic.

4. The term, "_____," is used to refer to times when a stressful situation approaches or exceeds the adaptive capacities of a person or group. (p. 147)
   a. crisis

b. traumatic

c. frustrating

d. acute

5. A crisis or trauma may occur as a result of (p.147)

    a. a disaster, such as a flood.

    b. a nasty divorce.

    c. an injury or disease.

    d. all of the above

6. The faster the changes, the greater the (p. 147)

    a. frustration.

    b. stress.

    c. excitement.

    d. LCU.

7. A person's _____ of the stressor has an impact—one person's stressor is another person's thrill. (p. 148)

    a. perception

    b. use

    c. level

    d. accumulation

8. The term, "_____," refers to a person's ability to withstand stress without becoming seriously impaired. (p.148)

    a. frustration

    b. intervention

    c. stress tolerance

    d. vulnerability

9. _____ can moderate the effects of stress on a person, and can

even reduce illness and early death. (p. 149)

a. Lack of support

b. Positive social and family relationships

c. Bureaucracy

d. Understanding national politics

10. _____ can make a stressor more potent and weaken a person's capacity to cope with it. (p.149)

a. Lack of support

b. Positive social and family relationships

c. Bureaucracy

d. Understanding national politics

PRACTICE TEST NUMBER 2

1. When confronting stress, a challenge is (p. 150)

a. to meet the requirements of the stressor.

b. to protect oneself from psychological damage and disorganization.

c. to remain calm and in control.

d. a and b

2. Severe stress may result in alterations that can impair the body's ability to fight off (p. 151)

a. family relatives.

b. invading bacteria and viruses.

c. coping resources.

d. biological adaptation.

3. In using its resources to meet one severe stressor, an organism may _____ tolerance for other stressors. (p. 151)

    a. suffer a lowering of

    b. experience greater

    c. be better prepared for

    d. not develop a

4. Five years after the nuclear accident at Three Mile Island, people exposed to the incident showed (p. 152)

    a. a high tolerance for radioactivity.

    b. a high level of radioactivity.

    c. symptoms of high stress.

    d. a dislike of islands.

5. One extremely stressful situation is loss of (p. 155)

    a. direction.

    b. gainful employment.

    c. the car keys.

    d. all of the above

6. The sudden unexpected death of a loved one accounts for about _____ of all PTSD cases seen in a community. (p. 156)

    a. one-third

    b. 1.732 percent

    c. three-quarters

    d. 10 percent

7. A normal grieving process typically lasts up to _____ and may involve negative health effects, such as high blood pressure, changes in eating habits, and even thoughts of suicide. (p. 155)

    a. a week or two

    b. a month

    c. about a year

d. decades

8. In the U.S., Post-Traumatic Stress Disorder (PTSD) appears to occur in about _____ adults at some time in their lives, but the reported rates are lower in national populations with fewer natural disasters and a lower crime rate. (p. 157)

    a. 1 in 12

    b. 1 in 100

    c. 1 in 1,000

    d. 1 in 1,000,000

9. There is a _____ ratio of female to male prevalence of PTSD, due largely to the occurrence of assaultive violence against women. (p. 157)

    a. 1:1

    b. 2:1

    c. 1:2

    d. 10:1

10. The symptoms of PTSD may vary greatly, depending on the (p. 157.)

    a. nature and severity of the terrifying experience.

    b. degree of surprise.

    c. personality make-up of the person.

    d. all of the above

PRACTICE TEST NUMBER 3

1. Regarding PTSD causal factors, (p. 169)

    a. personality seems to play a role.

    b. the nature of the event itself appears to account for most of the stress-response variance.

c. there appears to be a greater likelihood of post-traumatic disorder among women than men.

d. all of the above

2. An extensive survey of college health behavior reported that _____ percent of female students acknowledged having been forced to have sexual intercourse. (p. 161)

a. 2

b. 5

c. 10

d. 20

3. _____ is the most frequent cause of PTSD in women. (p.161)

a. Childbirth

b. Rape

c. Being in a traffic accident

d. a and c

4. In stranger rape, initially the victim is likely to have a strong fear of (p. 161)

a. the consequences of the rape.

b. physical harm or death.

c. betrayal.

d. guilt.

5. In acquaintance rape, the reaction may be (p. 161)

a. physical harm or death.

b. betrayal.

c. guilt.

d. b and c

6. Survivors of POW camps commonly showed (p. 165-166.)

    a. impaired resistance to physical illness.

    b. low frustration tolerance.

    c. frequent dependence on alcohol and drugs.

    d. all of the above

7. Many adults who emigrate—especially those forced to leave their homes—experience a high degree of stress and psychological adjustment problems. However, even greater degrees of stress can occur with (p. 167)

    a. those left behind.

    b. their children.

    c. their spouses.

    d. their new neighbors.

8. Torture induces psychological effects independent of other stressors, but the impact of torture could be lessened if victims were able to (p. 167)

    a. escape.

    b. predict and ready themselves for the pain they were about to experience.

    c. meditate and place themselves into a higher plane.

    d. none of the above

9. A process of stress-inoculation training prepares people to tolerate an anticipated threat by (p. 171)

    a. providing information about the situation and ways people can deal with such dangers.

    b. providing self-statements that promote effective adaptation are rehearsed.

c. having the person practice making such self-statements while being exposed to stressors.

d. all of the above

10. A study found that brief therapy treatment _____ the traumatic event significantly reduced PTSD symptoms. (p. 158-159)

a. occurring before

b. immediately following

c. anytime within the first year or two after

d. none of the above

COMPREHENSIVE PRACTICE TEST

The following tests are designed to give you an idea of how well you understood the entire chapter. There are three different types of tests: multiple-choice, true-false, and essay.

MULTIPLE-CHOICE

1. The term, "stress," has typically been used to refer to the _____ placed on an organism, and the organism's internal biological and psychological responses to such demands. (p.144)

a. conflicts

b. adjustive demands

c. pressures

d. crisis

2. The symptoms of stress _____ when a person is more closely involved in an immediately traumatic situation. (p.147)

a. go away

b. intensify

    c. remain constant

    d. cause acne

3. The longer a stressor operates, the _____ its effects. (p. 146-147)

    a. more acute

    b. less frustrating

    c. more severe

    d. less severe

4. Encountering a number of stressors at the same time will make these _____ than when occurring separately. (p.147)

    a. less acute

    b. more exciting

    c. more severe

    d. less severe

5. Stress operating through the hypothalamic-pituitary-adrenal system can result in a _____, making persons vulnerable to diseases to which they would normally be immune. (p. 153)

    a. raising of blood pressure

    b. lowering of blood levels

    c. higher perspiration output

    d. suppression of the immune system

6. What seems to push a normal reaction into the category of post-traumatic stress disorder is (p. 155)

    a. higher perspiration output.

    b. suppression of the immune system.

    c. the inability to function as usual.

    d. rising blood pressure.

7. Acute stress disorder occurs (p.158)

    a. at least four weeks after the traumatic event and lasts longer than four weeks.

    b. within four weeks and lasts from two days to four weeks.

    c. early and is long-lasting and late-arising.

    d. none of the above

8. Post-traumatic stress disorder differs from acute stress disorder in that it (p.158)

    a. lasts longer than four weeks.

    b. occurs within four weeks of the traumatic event and lasts from two days to four weeks.

    c. may be long-lasting or late-arising.

    d. a and c

9. _____ following a traumatic experience is considered important in preventing conditioned fear from establishing itself and becoming resistant to change. (p. 169)

    a. Obtaining medical attention

    b. Applying a tourniquet

    c. Prompt psychotherapy

    d. Getting back into a regular routine

10. After suffering a rape (female or male), a victim is very likely to (p. 163.)

    a. suffer anxiousness.

    b. experience disturbed concentration and intrusive thoughts.

    c. behave atypically, such as aggressively, or through substance abuse.

    d. all of the above

11. Most physically wounded soldiers have shown _____ symptoms than non-physically wounded soldiers (except in cases of permanent mutilation). (p. 164)

    a. more anxiety

    b. less anxiety or less combat exhaustion

    c. extreme anxiety or combat exhaustion

    d. more mental exhaustion

12. A study of a large sample of former POWs found that half reported symptoms of PTSD in the year following their releases, and _____ met PTSD criteria 40 to 50 years after their wartime experiences. (p. 166)

    a. none

    b. a few

    c. nearly a third

    d. only six

13. Among returning WW II POWs, within the first six years, (p.166)

    a. nine times as many died from tuberculosis as would have been expected in civilian life.

    b. four times as many died from gastrointestinal disorders, over twice as many from cancer, heart disease, and suicide as the norm.

    c. three times as many died from accidents.

    d. all of the above

14. A causal factor in combat stress problems is (p 169)

    a. temperament—a soldier's emotional and physical stamina.

    b. psychosocial—personal freedom frustrations, stresses from combat, personality.

    c. sociocultural—esprit de corps, acceptability of war goals, quality of leadership.

d. all of the above

15. Psychological symptoms experienced after having been tortured include (p. 167-8)

a. pain, nervousness, insomnia, tremors, weakness, fainting, sweating, and diarrhea.

b. night terrors and nightmares, depression, suspiciousness, social withdrawal and alienation, irritability, and aggressiveness.

c. concentration problems, disorientation, confusion, memory deficits, aggressiveness, impulsivity, and suicide attempts.

d. all of the above

TRUE - FALSE

1. T / F All situations, positive and negative, that require adjustment can be stressful. (p. 144)

2. T / F Stresses can be damaging if they are too severe for our coping resources—or if we believe as if they are. (p. 148)

3. T / F Severe and sustained stress on any level has very little effect on an organism's overall adaptive capacity. (p. 151)

4. T / F People who are recently divorced or separated are markedly overrepresented among people with psychological problems. (p.156)

5. T / F Even though PTSD can have a large impact on a person, young people, in particular, don't feel the need to avoid social situations or excitable stimuli. (p.158)

6. T / F Training and preparation can insulate persons from PTSD. This is why police officers never suffer from it. (p.169)

7. T / F PTSD can result in the traumatic event being persistently re-experienced by the person, or, conversely, deliberate avoidance of any stimuli associated with the trauma, such as cars, if the event were a car crash. (p. 158)

8. T / F Everyone has a breaking point, and at sufficiently high levels of stress, the average person can be expected to develop some psychological difficulties following a traumatic event. (p.169)

9. T / F Being held hostage can produce disabling psychological symptoms in victims for months following the incident. (p.166)

ESSAY QUESTIONS

1. Explain the three responses of personality decompensation. (p. 154)

2. Coping with rape: Describe the feelings and problems victims experience at different points during the trauma of a rape. (p.160-162)

3. Identify and briefly explain the approaches to treating the symptoms of PTSD. (p. 153-157)

WEB LINKS TO ITEMS OR CONCEPTS DISCUSSED IN CHAPTER 5

Crisis intervention:

www.nasponline.org/NEAT/crisis_0911.html

www.crisisinterventionnetwork.com/

Adjustment Disorder

www.mentalhealth.com/dis/p20-aj01.html

www.mftsource.com/Treatment.Adjust.htm

Stress Inoculation

mentalhelp.net/psyhelp/chap5/chap5n.htm

www.prevention.psu.edu/SIT2.htm

Psychoneuroimmunology

www.lifecoachusa.com/aaapni

USE IT OR LOSE IT

Provide an answer to the thought question below, knowing that there is more than one way to respond. Possible answers are presented in the Answer Key.

Explain why stressing about an exam in this class could contribute to your developing a cold?

CRISS-CROSS

Now that you know all there is to know about this chapter, here's your opportunity to put that knowledge to work.

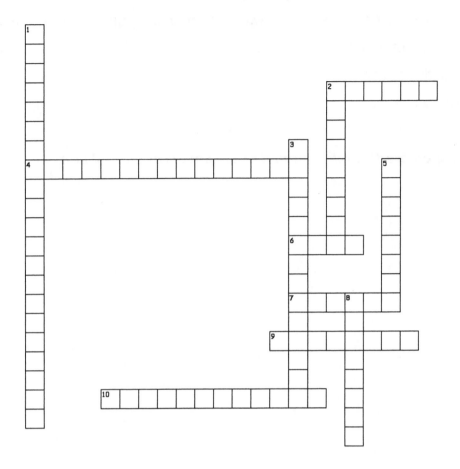

CRISS-CROSS CLUES

Across

2. time when a stressful situation approaches or exceeds the adaptive capacities of a person or group

4. an ability to withstand stress

6. disorder resulting from a major, severe stressor; may be short-term or long-lasting

7. a by-product of poor or inadequate coping

9. known as an adjustment demand

10. obstacles causing stress

Down

1. PTSD that occurs within four weeks of event; lasts more than two days, but not more than four weeks

2. simultaneous occurrences of two or more incompatible needs or motives

3. lowering of adaptive functioning

5. negative stress

8. positive stress

Puzzle created with Puzzlemaker at DiscoverySchool.com

ANSWERS TO TEST QUESTIONS - CHAPTER FIVE

Who's Who and What's What?
D. Post-Traumatic Stress Disorder
G. psychoneuroimmunology
A. adjustment disorder
H. crisis
F. stress
C. stressor
I. eustress
B. stress tolerance
E. stress-inoculation training

SHORT ANSWERS
(Your answer should contain the following points.)

1. The Social Readjustment Rating Scale is an objective method for measuring the cumulative stress to which a person has been exposed over a period of time in terms of "life-change units (LCU). More stressful events had more LCUs assigned. Death of a spouse rates 100 LCUs; minor violation of the law is 11. An experiment found that persons with 300 or more in recent months were at significant risk for getting a major illness.

2. The three interactional levels in coping with stress are a) biological ; there are immunological defenses and damage-repair mechanisms b) psychological and interpersonal; there are learned coping patterns, self-defenses, and support from family and friends c) sociocultural; group resources, such as labor unions, religious organizations, and law-enforcement agencies.

3. Selye found that the body's reaction to sustained and excessive stress typically occurs in three major phases.
a. Alarm reaction, in which the body's defensive forces are activated.
b. Stage of resistance, in which biological adaptation is at the maximum level.
c. Exhaustion, in which bodily resources are depleted and the organism loses its ability to resist.

4. In the fight or flight response:
a. The heart rate and blood flow are increased to large muscles.
b. Pupils are dilated so that more light enters the yet.
c. The skin constricts to limit blood loss in the event of injury.
d. Blood sugar is increased to provide more energy.
e. Possible problem: If the threat vanishes (usually the case), the body remains activated for physical combat, and, although it seeks to return to the previous restful state, there is a degree of wear and tear on the system, and "…each exposure leaves an indelible scar…"

5. Following a disaster, a victim's initial responses typically follow three stages.
a. Shock—stunned, dazed, and apathetic.
b. Suggestible stage—tends to be passive, suggestible, and willing to take directions.
c. Recovery stage—may be tense and apprehensive, general anxiety. PTSD may develop at this point.

6. Five areas of life functioning that may be affected by a rape:
a. Physical disturbances, including hyperaroulas or anxiousness.
b. Emotional problems, such as anxiety, depression, low self-esteem.
c. Cognitive dysfunction, including disturbed concentration and intrusive thoughts.
d. Atypical behavioral acts, such as aggression, antisocial actions, and substance abuse.
e. Interference in social relationships, including sexual problems, intimacy problems, and further victimization in a sexual relationship.

7. The causes and effects of the trauma of military combat are:
Causes - Ever-present threat of death or mutilation.
        Experiencing or participating in horrific events during combat.
Effects - The first symptoms are increasing irritability and sensitivity
        Sleep disturbances, and often-recurrent nightmares
        The feeling of overwhelming anxiety.

THE DOCTOR IS IN

Post-traumatic stress disorder: Symptoms have lasted longer than one month. She feels anxious and depressed, is having difficulty concentrating and intrusive thoughts regarding the rape. She is having mood swings and is starting to drink to keep the nightmares away. Treatment: Seek specialized rape crisis counseling services for short-term counseling. Services might include advocacy for Becky if she goes to court, possibly direct-exposure therapy if symptoms persist. Give her number to the telephone hotline and possibly use psychotropic medications.

PRACTICE TESTS

Q#	TEST 1	TEST 2	TEST 3
1	C	D	D
2	B	B	D
3	A	A	B
4	A	C	A
5	D	B	D
6	B	A	A
7	A	C	B
8	C	A	B
9	B	B	D

10	A	D	B

COMPREHENSIVE PRACTICE TEST

Q#	MULTIPLE CHOICE	T/F
1	B	T
2	B	T
3	C	F
4	C	T
5	D	F
6	C	F
7	B	T
8	D	T
9	C	T
10	D	
11	B	
12	C	
13	D	
14	D	
15	D	

ESSAY QUESTIONS

1. The three responses of personality decompensation are:

a. Alarm and mobilization
• Emotional arousal, increased tension, vigilance, heightened sensitivity; first signs of maladjustment may appear.

b. Resistance
• Utilizing task-oriented coping measures, ego-defense mechanisms. Indications of strain may exist. May revert to previously developed defenses.

c. Exhaustion
• Adaptive resources are depleted; coping patterns begin to fail. May employ exaggerated and inappropriate defensive measures. Delusions and hallucinations may occur. Severe exhaustion may lead to uncontrolled violence, apathy, stupor, and perhaps even death.

2. The feelings and problems rape victims experience at different points during their traumas:

a. Anticipatory phase: Before the rape, defense mechanisms, such as denial: "This can't be happening."

b. Impact phase:
• Recognition that she is actually going to be raped
• Fear for her life, may lead to inability to act
• Continues until rape is over

c. Post-traumatic recoil phase:
• Begins immediately after rape

• May include crying and sobbing, or control masked by a calm subdued facade
• Guilt, self-blame
d. Reconstitution phase:
• Victim starts to make plans for the future
• Self-protective activities, changing phone number, moving
• Frightening nightmares about the rape
• Phobias develop, including fear of being alone, fear of crowds

3. The approaches to treating the symptoms of PTSD:
a. Short-term therapy—brief, focuses on the immediate problem
b. Post-disaster debriefing sessions—"unwind" in a safe environment following a traumatic situation
c. Direct exposure to therapy for those whose PTSD symptoms persist—victim is reintroduced to stimuli that have come to be feared or associated with the traumatic event
d. Telephone hotlines—available in most major cities and many smaller ones to help people undergoing periods of severe stress
e. Psychotropic medications—antidepressants and other medication focused on specific symptoms

USE IT OR LOSE IT
Stress triggers the fight-or-flight response which cause changes in hormonal and neurotransmitters which inhibit immunological responses. Since the body has limited energy sources, responses which enable an individual to escape danger are given precedence over immune responses. Consequently, experiencing a stressor may make the body more susceptible to infections and illnesses.

CRISS-CROSS ANSWERS
Across
2. crisis
4. stress tolerance
6. PTSD
7. stress
9. stressor
10. frustrations

Down
1. acute distress disorder
2. conflicts
3. decompensation
5. distress
8. eustress

Chapter 6: Panic, Anxiety, and Their Disorders

BEFORE YOU READ

Chances are that simply reading this paragraph will make you worry about learning all of this new material, and to some degree, that worry is likely to increase the chances that you will study. However, when worry becomes anxiety it can actually interfere with performance. For the more than 23 million Americans a year coping with an anxiety disorder, worry, fear and anxiety can feel as though they are taking over their lives. Chapter 6, provides you with an overview and understanding of panic, anxiety disorders. You will learn there are many different types of anxiety disorders, from phobias (specific and social) to panic disorders, which can be so severe that people think they are having a heart attack. You will also be introduced to generalized anxiety and obsessive-compulsive disorders, their prevalence rates, causes, and the types of treatment to help people manage their anxiety.

- **THE FEAR AND ANXIETY RESPONSE PATTERNS**

- **OVERVIEW OF THE ANXIETY DISORDERS**

- **SPECIFIC PHOBIAS**
  - Blood-Injection-Injury Phobia Age of Onset and Gender
  - Differences in Specific Phobias
  - Psychosocial Causal Factors
  - Genetic and Temperamental Causal Factors
  - Treating Specific Phobias

- **SOCIAL PHOBIAS**
  - Interaction of Psychosocial and Biological Causal Factors
  - Treating Social Phobias

- **PANIC DISORDER WITH AND WITHOUT AGORAPHOBIA**

    Distinguishing Between Panic and Anxiety

    Agoraphobia Prevalence

    Gender, and Age of Onset of Panic Disorder with and without Agoraphobia

    Comorbidity with Other Disorders

    The Timing of a First Panic Attack

    Biological Causal Factors

    Behavioral and Cognitive Causal Factors

    Treating Panic Disorder and Agoraphobia

- **GENERALIZED ANXIETY DISORDER**

    General Characteristics Prevalence and Age of Onset

    Comorbidity with Other Disorders

    Psychosocial Causal Factors

    Biological Causal Factors

    Treating Generalized Anxiety Disorder

- **OBSESSIVE-COMPULSIVE DISORDER**

    Prevalence and Age of Onset Characteristics of OCD

    Psychosocial Causal Factors

    Biological Causal Factors

    Treating Obsessive-Compulsive Disorder

- **GENERAL SOCIOCULTURAL CAUSAL FACTORS FOR ALL ANXIETY DISORDERS**

    Cultural Differences in Sources of Worry

    Taijin Kyofusho

OBJECTIVES

After reading this chapter, you should be able to:

1. Compare and evaluate the merits of Freud's use of the concept of

anxiety in the etiology of the neuroses versus the descriptive approach used in DSM since 1980.

2. Distinguish between fear and anxiety.

3. Describe the major features of phobias

4. Identify and differentiate different subtypes of phobia

5. Explicate the major etiological hypotheses, and discuss the most effective treatment approaches.

6. List the diagnostic criteria for panic disorder, and compare and contrast panic attacks and other types of anxiety and explain its association with agoraphobia.

7. Summarize prevalence, age of onset, and comorbidity.

8. Describe recent findings on biological, behavioral, and cognitive influence for anxiety proneness.

9. Summarize the evidence that anxiety sensitivity constitutes a diathesis for development of panic attacks.

10. Describe how safety behaviors and cognitive biases help to maintain panic.

11. Compare and contrast the major treatment approaches for panic disorder and agoraphobia.

12. Summarize the central features of generalized anxiety disorder, and distinguish among psychoanalytic, conditioning, and cognitive theories of etiology.

13. Identify the central nervous system processes and structures associated with generalized anxiety disorder, and evaluate treatments for the disorder.

14. Describe the defining features of obsessive-compulsive disorder, summarize theories of etiology along with supporting evidence (or the lack thereof), and outline the treatment of OCD.

15. Provide several examples of sociocultural effects on anxiety disorders.

AS YOU READ

Answers can be found in the Answer Key at the end of the chapter.

KEY WORDS

Each of the words below is important in understanding the concepts presented in this Chapter. Write the definition next to each of the words.

Term	Page	Definition
Agoraphobia	194	
Amygdala	188	
Anxiety	180	
Anxiety disorders	180	
Anxiety sensitivity	201	
Blood-injection-injury phobia	184	
Compulsions	211	
Fear	181	
Generalized anxiety disorders	180	
Interoceptive fears	200	
Neuroses	180	
Neurotic behavior	180	
Obsessions	211	
Obsessive-compulsive disorder	182	
Panic	181	
Panic disorder	182	
Panic provocation agent	201	
Phobia	183	
Social phobia	183	
Specific phobia	183	

MATCHING

Who's Who and What's What?

Match the following terms with the appropriate description.

_____ Neuroticism

_____ Neurotic behavior

_____ Inflation effect

_____ Vicarious conditioning

_____ Nocturnal panic

_____ Introceptive avoidance

_____ Anxious apprehension

_____ CRH

_____ Bed nucleus of the stria terminali

_____ TKS

_____ Aaron Beck

_____ O. H. Mowrer

Definition

A. the transmission of a phobia from one person or animal to another by observing a person or animal behaving fearfully

B. credited with devising a two-process theory of avoidance learning in OCD

C. panic attack that occurs during sleep

D. persistent and disproportionate fear of some specific object or situation that presents little or no actual danger

E. avoidance of activities that create arousal sensations

F. exaggerated use of avoidance behaviors or defense mechanisms

G. basic personality trait—a proneness to experience negative mood states

H. cognitive psychologist who coined the phrase, "automatic thoughts," which are associated with panic triggers

I. when a person is exposed to a more intense traumatic experience (not paired with the conditioned stimulus) after a first traumatic experience, thus becoming more fearful of the conditioned stimulus

J. future-oriented mood state in which a person attempts to be constantly ready to deal with negative upcoming events

K. anxiety disorder found in Japan related to Western social phobia

L. extension of the amygdala believed to be important brain area mediating generalized anxiety

M. anxiety producing hormone recently implicated as playing a role in GAD

SHORT ANSWERS

Provide brief answers to the following questions.

1. List the five subtypes of specific phobia and give examples of each. (p.183)

2. Discuss methods used to treat social phobias. (p. 189-190)

3. You are a psychoanalyst and a client comes to see you with GAD. How would explain the causal factors for this disorder? (pp. 205)

4. Describe the different types of obsessive thoughts and compulsions. (p. 211)

THE DOCTOR IS IN...PSYCHIATRIC HELP—5¢

Read the following scenarios and diagnose the client. Remember to look carefully at the criteria for the disorder before you make a decision as to the diagnosis. Make a list of other information you might need to help you understand the causal factors.

1. Teresa comes to your office. She has been referred to you by her primary care doctor who could find nothing wrong with her. She tells you she feels as if she is losing control and going crazy. She says that for the last two months, she has been unexpectedly having shortness of breath, heart palpitations, dizziness, and sweating. These experiences seem to come out of the blue and make her so afraid that she is afraid to leave her house.

> How would you diagnose her and what would your treatment plan be? (pp.181- 203)

2. Ned visits your office at the urging of his family. Ned tells you he has been feeling anxious about the future and says that he needs to be ready to deal with any negative thing that might come up—like his car breaking down or getting lost when trying to get to a new area. Both of these would affect his work, thus, his financial well-being, and, ultimately, his family. He tells you he can't seem to control the constant state of apprehension and always feels tense and over aroused. He hasn't been sleeping well and has had difficulty concentrating at work. His family says he is constantly irritable and he has felt a lot of muscle tension, especially in his neck and shoulders.

> How would you diagnose Ned and what would be the most effective treatment for him? (pp. 181- 203)

3. In the past few months, Jean has been washing her hands 50 to 75 times a day. Her hands are now cracked and bleeding and she is unable to work. In addition to hand washing she has to constantly check her stove and door locks and she must do this in a particular way or she has to start all over again. She has come to see you because she is about to lose her marriage as a result of her behavior. Jean knows her behaviors are senseless and excessive but she can't control them.

How would you diagnosis Jean and what treatment plan would you create? (pp. 211- 215)

AFTER YOU READ

PRACTICE TESTS

Take the following three multiple-choice tests to see how much you have comprehended from the chapter. Each represents roughly one-third of the chapter. As you study the chapter, use these to check your progress.

PRACTICE TEST NUMBER 1

1. Who believed that neuroses were the result of intrapsychic conflict?(p. 180)
   a. Pavlov
   b. Ellis
   c. Freud
   d. Beck

2. The components of fear and panic are (p. 181)
   a. cognitive/subjective.
   b. physiological.
   c. behavioral.

d. all of the above

3. Anxiety, unlike fear, is a complex blend of emotions and cognitions that
   is oriented to the(p. 181)
   a. object of fear.
   b. past experience.
   c. future.
   d. all of the above

4. Many human and animal experiments have established that the basic
   fear and anxiety response patterns are highly (p. 182)
   a. predictable.
   b. conditionable.
   c. inevitable.
   d. a and c

5. A reduction in phobic behavior tends to occur when a person
   _____ the feared situation (p. 181)
   a. faces
   b. clarifies
   c. avoids
   d. understands

6.) _____is a phobia which, unlike most phobias, begins with an
   initial acceleration of blood pressure and heartrate, then a rapid
   decrease in both heartrate and blood pressure (p. 185)
   a. Blood-injection-injury
   b. Agoraphobia
   c. Arachnophobia
   d. Social phobia

7. Which viewpoint explains phobias as a defense against anxiety? (p. 185)

    a. behavioral

    b. cognitive

    c. psychodynamic

    d. humanistic

8. By watching her older sister react in a fearful way to spiders, Keri also learned to be afraid of spiders. This is called (p. 186)

    a. aping conditioning.

    b. mimicking conditioning.

    c. vicarious conditioning.

    d. none of the above.

9. John had dogs all of his life and was quite comfortable being around dogs. When John was bitten by a dog, he did not develop a phobia. Why? (p.187)

    a. He didn't care.

    b. It didn't hurt.

    c. The dog didn't mean it.

    d. His experiences had immunized him.

10. Steve, who has an unreasonable fear of elevators, watches as his therapist goes up and down an elevator in a calm and nonchalant way. Later, he walks into the elevator with his therapist and goes up one floor. This is an example of (p.188)

    a. participant modeling.

    b. specific phobia modeling.

    c. reality modeling.

    d. none of the above

PRACTICE TEST NUMBER 2

1. Social phobias usually begin in (p. 185)

    a. early childhood.

    b. mid-life.

    c. adolescence or early adulthood.

    d. old age.

2. Phobias tend to develop in response to stimuli that (p.185)

    a. could actually be dangerous.

    b. are typically modern inventions.

    c. are depressing.

    d. are not actually dangerous.

3. Like other phobias, social phobias are often (p. 186)

    a. evolving.

    b. learned.

    c. easily ignored.

    d. none of the above

4. Unlike specific phobias, social phobia can sometimes be treated with (p. 193)

    a. cognitive therapy.

    b. behavioral therapy.

    c. medication.

    d. none of the above

5. What distinguishes panic attacks from other types of anxiety? (p. 194)

    a. brevity

    b. intensity

    c. physiological symptoms

d. a and b

6. Panic attacks are about twice as prevalent in women as in men. This is thought to be a result of _____ factors. (p. 197)
   a. behavioral
   b. gender
   c. sociocultural
   d. unconscious

7. In family and twin studies, panic disorders have a _____ heritable component. (p. 198)
   a. high
   b. low
   c. moderate
   d. predictable

8. The _____ is the central area involved in what has been called a "fear network" with connections to lower (locus coeruleus) and higher (prefrontal cortex) areas of the brain. (p. 199)
   a. hippocampus
   b. amygdala
   c. limbic system
   d. all of the above

9. Beck and Emery (1985) and Clark (1986, 1988, 1997) proposed a model of panic that says clients are hypersensitive to their bodily sensations and prone to giving them the worst possible interpretations. What is this theory called? (p. 200)
   a. fear of fear theory
   b. comprehensive learning theory
   c. cognitive theory

d. biological readiness theory

10. Ken often has an upset stomach. He is very anxious about this condition. Although Ken does not have any panic attacks, his preexisting high level of _____ makes him more prone to developing a panic disorder. (p. 201)

a. awareness

b. cognition

c. a and b

d. anxiety sensitivity

PRACTICE TEST NUMBER 3

1. It is estimated that GAD is experienced by approximately _____ percent of the population in any one-year period and _____ percent at some point in their lives. (p. 207)

a. 10; 70

b. 2; 4

c. 8; 11

d. 3; 5

2. For people with GAD, worry (p. 207-8)

a. has both positive and negative consequences.

b. has minor and major consequences.

c. has no known affect at this time.

d. is irrelevant.

3. A(n) _____ is a overt repetitive behavior or more covert mental act. (p. 211)

a. compulsion

b. obsession

c. behavior

d. GAD

4. Cognitive factors that contribute to OCD behavior are (p. 216)

a. attention drawn to disturbing material relevant to obsession.

b. difficulty blocking out negative irrelevant input.

c. low confidence in memory skills.

d. all of the above

5. Biological causal factors are _____ implicated in the causes of OCD. (p.216)

a. strongly

b. mildly

c. superficially

d. somewhat

6. According to biological psychiatrists, which of the following drugs appears to block panic attacks in agoraphobics without affecting their anticipatory anxiety? (p. 203.)

a. minor tranquilizer

b. tricyclic antidepressant

c. barbiturate

d. monoamine oxidase inhibitor

7. Which of the following is not typically a part of cognitive-behavior therapy for panic disorder? (p. 201)

a. exposure to feared situations and/or feared bodily sensations

b. deep muscle relaxation and breathing retraining

c. identification and modification of logical errors and automatic thoughts

d. carbon dioxide inhalation and/or lactate infusion

8. The benzodiazepines are minor tranquilizers which probably exert their effects through stimulating the action of (p. 210)

    a. acetylcholine.

    b. GABA.

    c. serotonin.

    d. norepinephrine.

9. An impulse the person cannot seem to control is called a(n) (p.211)

    a. compulsion.

    b. delusion.

    c. hallucination.

    d. focal phobia.

10. The only disorder which shows virtually no difference in prevalence between men and women is (p. 212)

    a. OCD.

    b. social phobia.

    c. specific phobia.

    d. GAD.

COMPREHENSIVE PRACTICE TEST

The following tests are designed to give you an idea of how well you understood the entire chapter. There are three different types of tests: multiple-choice, true-false, and essay.

MULTIPLE-CHOICE

1. The term, "neurosis," was dropped from the DSM–III in the year (p. 180)

    a. 1969.

   b. 1980.

   c. 1975.

   d. 1990.

2. The most common way of distinguishing between fear and anxiety is that fear involves a(n) (p. 181)

   a. increase in heart rate.

   b. unpleasant interstate of something dreadful going to happen.

   c. inability to specify a clear danger.

   d. obvious source of danger.

3. Paula has been feeling extremely anxious and experiencing physical responses, such as a racing heart and dizziness. In all likelihood she will first consult her (p. 195.)

   a. primary care doctor.

   b. therapist.

   c. psychiatrist.

   d. dentist.

4. At the age of 21 months, Karen was a very timid and shy child. She hid behind her mother and rarely ventured over to play with other children in her play group. Based on the study done by Kagan and his colleagues, what can you predict about the risk of Karen developing multiple specific phobias by the age of seven or eight? It is (p.188)

   a. about the same as other children in her play group.

   b. less then uninhibited children in general.

   c. higher because of temperamental factors.

   d. higher because her play group has more boys than girls.

5. The most common specific social phobia is fear of (p. 190)

a. public speaking.

b. crowds.

c. urinating in public restrooms.

d. public affection.

6. From an evolutionary perspective, social phobia are a by-product of (p. 192)

    a. dominance hierarchies.

    b. learning.

    c. observing.

    d. modeling.

7. Billy, who is 25 months old, is behaviorally inhibited. What can you predict, based on the Hayward et. al. and Kagan's research, will be the likelihood of Billy developing a social phobia by the age of 13? He (p. 192)

    a. has increased risk.

    b. has no increased risk.

    c. will develop a social phobia.

    d. none of the above

8. An early hypothesis about the origins of agoraphobia was that it was a (p.200)

    a. fear of fear.

    b. fear of going shopping.

    c. fear of commitment.

    d. none of the above

9. Unlike other anxiety disorders that often have an acute onset, people with GAD report (p. 207)

    a. being anxious most of their lives.

b. a slow and insidious onset.

c. sudden onset.

d. a and b

10. Something that may account for why people with GAD feel constantly tense and vigilant for possible threats is their relative lack of (p. 208)

    a. interest in their surroundings.

    b. understanding.

    c. safety signals.

    d. something to be really worried about.

11. GAD seems to share a common genetic diathesis with (p. 210)

    a. personality disorders.

    b. PTSD.

    c. major depressive disorder.

    d. eating disorders.

12. A(n) _____ is a persistent and recurrent intrusive thought, image or impulse that is experienced as disturbing and inappropriate. (p. 211)

    a. compulsion

    b. obsession

    c. behavior

    d. GAD

13. OCD is characterized by?

    (p. 215)

    a. anxiety.

    b. compulsions..

    c. the fear of being responsible for something horrible happening.

d. all of the above

14. OCD may be characterized by excessively high levels of (p. 218)

    a. GABA.

    b. fluoxetine.

    c. serotonin.

    d. none of the above

TRUE - FALSE

1. T / F Fear or panic is a basic emotion that involves activation of the "flight or fight" response. (p.222)

2. T / F Anxiety involves a positive mood, worry about the future and the ability to predict the future threat. (p.180)

3 T / F It has been proven that classical conditioning does not produce fears and phobias. (p. 183)

4. T / F Life experiences influence a person's likelihood of developing a phobia. (p.187)

5. T / F The best treatment for specific phobia is cognitive therapy. (p. 188)

6. T / F The treatment of choice for specific phobias is exposure therapy. (p. 188)

7. T / F The term *social anxiety disorder* is increasingly preferred by researchers and clinicians, instead of social phobias. (p. 190)

8. T / F Social phobics have a deep sense of control over events in their lives. (p. 184)

9. T / F Agoraphobia can occur in the absence of full-blown panic attacks. (p. 197)

10. T / F Seven to 30 percent of adults who have experienced panic attacks will go on to develop panic disorder. (p. 200)

11. T / F The learning theory model is better able to explain why panic attacks often occur without any preceding negative automatic thoughts or during sleep at night better than the cognitive model. (p.211)

12. T / F People with panic disorder automatically pay attention to pleasant information in their environment. (p. 197)

13. T / F Most people with GAD manage to function in spite of their high levels of worry and anxiety. (p.207)

14. T / F People with GAD have a history of experiencing many important events in their lives which they feel are predictable and controllable. (p. 207)

15 T / F The neurotransmitter GABA is now strongly implicated in generalized anxiety. (p.199)

16. T / F OCD is different from other anxiety disorders in that there is a large gender difference in adults. (p.212)

17 T / F   When OCD clients were asked to suppress intrusive thoughts, they reported twice as many intrusive thoughts on those days as opposed to the days they were given no instructions. (p. 216)

ESSAY QUESTIONS

1. Discuss the criteria for diagnosing generalized anxiety disorder (GAD). (pp. 205-206)

2. Give examples of cultural differences in sources of worry. (p.221)

WEB LINKS TO ITEMS OR CONCEPTS DISCUSSED IN CHAPTER 6

Anxiety, panic

      www.anxietynetwork.com

      www.apa.org/pubinfo/panic.html

USE IT OR LOSE IT

Provide an answer to the thought question below, knowing that there is more than one way to respond. Possible answers are presented in the Answer Key.

Why do you think that people who have panic attacks frequently believe that they are having a heart attack?

CRISS-CROSS

Now that you know all there is to know about this chapter, here's your opportunity to put that knowledge to work.

CRISS-CROSS CLUES

Across

4. disturbing persistent, recurrent, intrusive thoughts, images, or impulses

5. the experienced emotion when the source of danger is not obvious

6. may involve fears of things (animals, water, heights, tunnels, spiders)

8. the exaggerated use of avoidance behaviors or defense mechanisms

9. a blend of emotions that is more oriented to the future and much more diffuse than fear

Down

1. clearly excessive ritualistic overt repetitive behaviors

2. involves fears of situations in which a person is exposed to the scrutiny of others

3. the experienced emotion when the source of danger is obvious

7. a collection of nuclei critical involved in the emotion of fear

Puzzle created with Puzzlemaker at DiscoverySchool.com

ANSWERS TO TEST QUESTIONS - CHAPTER 6

Who's Who and What's What
D. Phobia
G. Neuroticism
F. Neurotic behavior
I. Inflation effect
A. Vicarious conditioning
C. Nocturnal panic
E. Introceptive avoidance
J. Anxious apprehension
M. CRH
L. Bed nucleus of the stria terminali
K. TKS
H. Aaron Beck
B. O. H. Mowrer

SHORT ANSWERS
(Your answer should contain the following points.)

1. The five subtypes of specific phobias including examples of each:
a. Animal—snakes, spiders
b. Natural environment—heights or water
c. Blood-injection-injury—sight of blood or injury
d. Situational—airplanes or elevators
e. Atypical—choking or vomiting

2. Methods used to treat social phobias:
a. Behavior therapy—prolonged exposure to social situations in graduated manner
b. Cognitive behavior therapy—identify underlying negative automatic thoughts; help change negative automatic thoughts through logical reanalysis—the challenging of the automatic thought
c. Medication—can also be treated with beta-blockers, antidepressants, and anti-anxiety drugs.

3. a) unconscious conflict between the ego and id impulses that are not being dealt with because the person's defense mechanisms have broken down or become overwhelmed
b) perhaps defense mechanisms never developed
c) inoperative defense mechanisms leave the person anxious nearly all of the time

4. Examples of obsessions and compulsions:
a. Obsessive thoughts: contamination fears, fears of harming self or others, lack

of symmetry, pathological doubt, need for symmetry, sexual obsessions and religious or aggressive obsessions

b. Compulsions: five primary types – cleaning, checking, repeating, ordering/arranging, counting and primary obsessional slowness

THE DOCTOR IS IN

1. Teresa :

Diagnosis: Panic disorder with agoraphobia

Treatment: A variety of treatment methods could be used.

• Medication: not as good but could prescribe benzodiazepines or antidepressants

• Cognitive-Behavior Therapy (see Developments in Practice)

You would:

• teach Teresa about nature of anxiety and panic, and how to self-monitor her experiences

• teach her how to control her breathing

• help her identify her automatic thoughts during panic attacks

• teach her how to decatastrophize e.g., expose her to feared situations and feared bodily sensations (interceptive fears)

2. Ned:

Diagnosis: Generalized Anxiety Disorder

Treatment: • Medications—possibly busipirone or some antidepressants
                    • Cognitive-behavior therapy—training in applied muscle relaxation techniques and cognitive restructuring techniques aimed at reducing distorted cognitions, information processing biases and catastrophizing about minor events. GAD is still one of the most difficult anxiety disorders to treat.

Benefits:

• superstitious avoidance of catastrophe

• actual avoidance of catastrophe

• avoidance of deeper emotional topics

• coping and preparation

• motivating device

3. Jean :

Diagnosis: Obsessive-compulsive disorder

Treatment: Behavioral treatment involving a combination of exposure and compulsive response prevention is perhaps the most effective. SSRIs are a possibility, but there is a high relapse rate when the drugs are stopped. In severe intractable OCD, which has not responded to therapy or drugs, neurosurgical techniques may be considered.

PRACTICE TESTS

Q#	TEST 1	TEST 2	TEST 3
1	C	C	D
2	D	A	A

3	C	B	A
4	B	C	D
5	A	D	A
6	A	C	B
7	C	C	D
8	C	B	B
9	D	C	A
10	A	D	A

COMPREHENSIVE PRACTICE TEST

Q#	MULTIPLE CHOICE	T/F
1	B	T
2	D	F
3	A	F
4	C	T
5	A	F
6	A	T
7	A	T
8	A	F
9	D	T
10	C	F
11	C	T
12	B	F
13	D	T
14	C	F
15		T
16		F
17		T

ESSAY QUESTIONS
(Your answer should contain the following points.)

1. Generalized anxiety disorder (GAD) is characterized by:
a. chronic excessive worry about a number of events or activities—formerly used to be called free-floating anxiety
b. worry must occur more days than not for at least six months and be difficult to control
• cannot be associated with another concurrent Axis I disorder
• subjective experience of worry must be accompanied by at least three of the following symptoms
• restlessness, being keyed up
• sense of being easily fatigued
• difficulty concentrating or mind going blank

• irritability
• muscle tension
• sleep disturbance

2. Examples of cultural differences in sources of worry:
a. Yoruba culture of Nigeria—three primary clusters of symptoms associated with generalized anxiety:
• worry focusing on creating and maintaining a large family and fertility
• dreams may indicate the person is bewitched
• bodily complaints—water in my brain, "ants creeping in my brain," etc.
b. China—Koro, fear of penis shrinking or nipples retracting
c. Japan—Taijin Kyofusho—concern about doing something that will embarrass or offend others

USE IT OR LOSE IT

The symptoms of panic attacks can include rapid breathing, and heart beats, chest pain, and sweating, which can also accompany heart attacks. Since these symptoms can occur quite suddenly people may panic and believe that they are ill, and even dying.

CRISS-CROSS ANSWERS
Across
4. Obsessions
5. Panic
6. Specific phobia
8. Neuroses
9. Anxiety

Down
1. Compulsions
2. Social phobia
3. Fear
7. Amygdala

Chapter 7: Mood Disorders and Suicide

BEFORE YOU READ

As you know, both happiness and sadness are normal parts of life. However, these normal variations in emotion are not the same as the changes in mood and functioning seen in mood disorders. For example, depressed individuals typically experience extraordinary sadness and dejection, while those who experience a manic episode show a markedly elevated euphoric mood. However, even within these categories there are significant differences in the severity and duration of the disorder. This chapter will explore the biological and psychosocial causes of mood disorders and the ways in which they can be differentiated. The types of treatments available for mood disorders will be explained, as well as their application and efficacy. Cultural differences in the experience and treatment of mood disorders will also be addressed. Lastly, people who suffer from mood disorders are at risk for suicide. The final portion of this chapter discusses the risk factors for suicide, and what can be done to intervene or prevent suicidal attempts.

- **WHAT ARE MOOD DISORDERS?**
    The Prevalence of Mood Disorders

- **UNIPOLAR MOOD DISORDERS**
    Depressions That Are Not Mood Disorders
    Dysthymia
    Major Depressive Disorder

- **CAUSAL FACTORS IN UNIPOLAR MOOD DISORDERS**
    Biological Causal Factors
    Psychosocial Causal Factors

- **BIPOLAR DISORDERS**

Cyclothymia Biopolar Disorders

• CAUSAL FACTORS IN BIPOLAR DISORDER

Biological Causal Factors

Psychosocial Causal Factors

• SOCIALCULTURAL FACTORS AFFECTING UNIPOLAR AND BIPOLAR DISORDERS

Cross-Cultural Differences in Depressive Symptoms

Relieving Losses

Cross-Cultural Differences in Prevalence

Demographic Differences in the United States

• TREATMENTS AND OUTCOMES

Pharmacotherapy

Alternative /Biological Treatments

Psychotherapy

• SUICIDE

The Clinical Picture and the Causal Pattern

OBJECTIVES

After reading this chapter, you should be able to:

1. Define the characteristics of mood disorders

2. Explain the prevalence of mood disorders

3. Describe unipolar mood disorders

4. Differentiate depressions that are not mood disorders from those that are

5. Identify the mild to moderate depressive disorders

6. Describe criteria for diagnosing major depressive disorder and its subtypes

7. Discuss biological and psychosocial causal factors in unipolar and bipolar mood disorders

8. Describe various types of bipolar disorders

9. Explain how various sociocultural factors affect unipolar and bipolar disorders

10. Assess treatments and outcomes of mood disorders

11. Explain prevalence rates of suicide among people with mood disorders

12. Describe who is likely to attempt suicide versus who is likely to complete suicide

13. Describe the various motives for why someone takes his or her own life

14. Explain the sociocultural and biological variables that affect suicide

KEY WORDS

Each of the words below is important in understanding the concepts presented in this chapter. Write the definition next to each of the words. The page numbers are provided in case you need to refer to the book.

Term	Page	Defintion
Attributions	243	
Bipolar I disorder	254	
Bipolar disorder with a seasonal pattern	255	
Bipolar II disorder	255	
Chronic major depressive disorder	234	
Cyclothymia	253	

Depression	226	
Depressongenic schemas	244	
Diathesis - stress model	242	
Dysfunctional beliefs	244	
Dysthymias	234	
Hypomanic episode	253	
Learned helplessness	246	
Major depressive disorder	229	
Major depressive episode with atypical features	233	
Major depressive episode with melancholic features	232	
Mania	226	
Manic episode	227	
Mixed episode	226	
Mood disorders	226	
Mood-congruent delusions	233	
Negative automatic thoughts	244	
Pessimistic	242	

Rapid cycling	256	
Recurrence	234	
Relapse	234	
Seasonal affective disorder	234	
Severe major depressive episode with psychotic features	233	
Specifiers	232	
Suicide	227-228	
Unipolar disorder	226	

AS YOU READ

Answers can be found in the Answer Key at the end of the chapter.

MATCHING

Who's Who and What's What

Match each of the following people with her/his accomplishment or theory.

Psychologist

_____ Martin Seligman

_____ Emile Durkheim

_____ Aaron Beck

_____ Sigmund Freud

_____ Emil Kraepelin

_____ Abramson et al., 1989

Accomplishment or Theory

A. depressogenic schemas/negative automatic thoughts

B. "Mourning and Melancholia"

C. learned helplessness theory

D. hopelessness theory

E. introduced the term, *manic-depressive insanity"*

F. French sociologist who studied the sociocultural factors in suicide

SHORT ANSWERS

Provide brief answers to the following questions.

1. A friend of yours recently lost a grandparent. You have just finished studying mood disorders in your Abnormal Psychology class. What could you tell him about the normal response phases to the loss? (p.228)

2. In the Brown and Harris 1978 study, what factors were associated with the women who experienced stressful life events but did not become depressed? (p.242)

3. Discuss the ways interpersonal problems can play a causal role in depression and how depression affects others. (pp. 247-248)

THE DOCTOR IS IN...PSYCHIATRIC HELP—5¢

Read the following scenarios and diagnose the client. Remember to look carefully at the criteria for the disorder before you make a decision as to the diagnosis. Make a list of other information you might need to help you understand the causal factors.

1. Helen comes into your office asking for help. She is a 29-year-old woman, married with no children. She reports that she has been feeling sad for a long time—almost three years now. Although she does have periods of feeling normal, these don't last. Recently her husband has been making comments about how little she has been eating. Helen says that she has no energy and can't seem to sleep through the night. She is starting to think of herself as a worthless person for not being able to just snap out of it. How would you diagnose Helen? (p.229-232)

2. As a leading expert on adolescent suicide, you have been asked to give a talk on known risk factors. What would you include in your speech? (pp. 270)

3. Winter is coming, and Miles is feeling incredibly sad. He moved to Minnesota three years ago to take a new job. He likes his job and finds it very rewarding. When he finally comes to see you, he reports that it takes a lot of effort for him to get out of bed. He tells you that the last two years were about the same. He tells you that he feels much better, even normal, when spring comes around. (p. 234)

4. Ed was brought to the hospital by the police. His wife called them when he became aggressive. She had refused to give him a credit card. He had been awake for almost three days straight, working on a very big plan to buy a city and become the mayor. He had been spending money that they didn't have, and his wife was worried. When he was admitted to the hospital, he talked non-stop about needing a phone, because the deal was about to go through. He kept telling the hospital staff he was going to become famous and be able to save the city from ruin. (p

After talking to his wife, you discover that not too long ago, Ed had been very depressed. Before he became so "crazy," as she put it, she thought that maybe he was getting better. How would you diagnose Ed? Why? (p. 254-255)

AFTER YOU READ

PRACTICE TESTS

Take the following three multiple-choice tests to see how much you have comprehended from the chapter. Each represents roughly one-third of the chapter. As you study the chapter, use these to check your progress.

PRACTICE TEST NUMBER 1

1. The most common form of mood episode is (p. 227)
   a. a fugue.
   b. a manic episode .
   c. a dissociative disorder.
   d. a major depressive episode.

2. Mania is characterized by (p. 226)
   a. sadness and dejection.
   b. shame and confusion.
   c. excitement and euphoria.
   d. frustration and anxiety.

3. Depression is characterized by (p. 226)
   a. sadness and dejection.

b. shame and confusion.

c. excitement and euphoria.

d. frustration and anxiety.

4. Mood disorders are differentiated by (p. 227)

a. severity.

b. frequency.

c. duration.

d. a and c

5. A person who has been diagnosed with dysthymia may experience normal mood periods that last (p. 230)

a. a few days or weeks, up to a maximum of two months.

b. six months or more.

c. several days but no more than one month.

d. none of the above

6. Sue meets the criteria for major depressive disorder. However, her therapist also notes some patterns of symptoms that she feels are important for understanding the disorder and treating Sue effectively. These additional patterns are called (p. 232)

a. equalizers.

b. identifiers.

c. noteworthy.

d. specifiers.

7. Which of the following is true? (p.255-257)

a. Genetics plays a greater role in a person's developing bipolar depression than it does in that person developing unipolar depression.

b. Genetics plays a greater role in a person's developing unipolar depression than it does in that person developing bipolar depression.

c. Genetics have no impact on bipolar disorder.

d. Genetics have no impact on unipolar disorder.

8. Twin studies have provided evidence that there may be a

_____ genetic component to unipolar depression. (p. 235)

    a. significant

    b. minimal

    c. moderate

    d. overwhelming

9. In the 1960s and 70s, research focused on the following neurotransmitters and their effect on depression: (p. 236)

    a. norepinephrine, dopamine and serotonin.

    b. serotonin and epinephrine.

    c. coritsol, norephinephrine and DST.

    d. none of the above

10. Originally, diathesis-stress models assumed that diatheses were biological. Recently, depression researchers have begun to propose diatheses that are (p. 242)

    a. cognitive.

    b. social.

    c. subconscious.

    d. a and b

PRACTICE TEST NUMBER 2

1. Two personality variables that may be a diathesis for depression are (p. 277)

    a. extroversion and introversion.

    b. neuroticism and low positive affectivity.

    c. vulnerability and anger.

    d. none of the above

2. The cognitive diatheses that have been studied for depression focus on _____ patterns of thinking. (p. 247)

    a. positive

    b. inconsistent

    c. negative

    d. a and b

3. Research has found that a person may have a vulnerability to depression if he/she experiences an early childhood loss of a parent and (p. 243)

    a. poor parental care.

    b. support of siblings.

    c. involvement with an extended family.

    d. all of the above

4. The psychodynamic approach to depression emphasizes the (p. 231)

    a. importance of dreams.

    b. importance of the id.

    c. importance of early loss (real or imagined).

    d. creation of defense mechanisms.

5. According to the behavioral theories of depression, people become

depressed when their responses no longer produce positive reinforcement or when (p.243)

   a. they learn depression is good.

   b. their rate of negative reinforcement increases.

   c. they generalize.

   d. none of the above

6. A psychological theory on why there are sex differences in unipolar depression proposes that women are more prone to experience (p. 248)

   a. a lack of control over negative life events.

   b. discrimination in the workplace.

   c. poverty.

   d. all of the above

7. The mild-to-moderate range of bipolar disorder is known as (p. 253)

   a. dysthymia.

   b. cyclothymia.

   c. hypermania.

   d. unipolar.

8. Who introduced the term, "manic-depressive," insanity to describe a series of attacks of elation and depression? (p. 254)

   a. Freud

   b. Hippocrates

   c. Kraepelin

   d. Charcot

9. People who commit suicide (p. 274)

   a. rarely tell others their intent.

   b. only talk about suicide in vague terms.

c. typically talk clearly about suicide or death in the weeks or months prior to the attempt.

d. usually tell mental health professionals but not friends about their intentions.

10. Suicide is committed most often during the _____ phase of a depressive episode. (p. 268)

    a. early onset

    b. peak of depression

    c. late onset

    d. recovery

PRACTICE TEST NUMBER 3

1. A disorder that involves mood swings between subclinical levels of depression and mania is (p. 226)

    a. bipolar disorder.

    b. manic depression.

    c. dysthymic disorder.

    d. cyclothymic disorder.

2. Bipolar mood disorder is distinguished from major depression by (p. 254)

    a. at least one episode of mania.

    b. disturbance of circadian rhythms.

    c. evidence of earlier cyclothymia.

    d. evidence of earlier dysthymia.

3. The original learned helplessness theory refers to the depressed patient's perception that (p. 246.)

    a. accustomed reinforcement is no longer forthcoming.

b. they have no control over aversive events.

c. reinforcement is inadequate.

d. the world is a negative place.

4. Since about 1990, the type of antidepressants increasingly prescribed because of fewer side effects are (p. 264)

    a. tricyclics.

    b. selective serotonin re-uptake inhibitors (SSRIs).

    c. imipramine.

    d. ECT.

5. _____ is a brief form of treatment for unipolar depression that is highly structured and attempts to teach people to evaluate their beliefs and negative automatic thoughts. (p.265)

    a. CBT

    b. ECT

    c. IPT

    d. none of the above

6. The treatment for unipolar depression which focuses on current relationships issues, is called (p. 267)

    a. CBT.

    b. ECT.

    c. IPT.

    d. none of the above

7. Two main thrusts of suicide prevention efforts are the treatment of the person's mental disorders and (p.)

    a. cognitive therapy.

    b. family therapy.

c. crisis intervention.

d. psychotherapy.

8. A disorder that involves mood swings between subclinical levels of depression and mania is (p. 226)

a. bipolar disorder.

b. manic depression.

c. dysthymic disorder.

d. cyclothymic disorder.

9. Creativity is associated with

a. unipolar but not bipolar disorder.

b. mood disorders in general and espeicially bipolar disorder.

c. cyclothymic but not bipolar disorder.

d. bipolar but not unipolar disorder.

10. All of the following are symptoms of the manic phase of bipolar mood disorder, **except** (p. 262)

a. a notable increase in activity.

b. euphoria.

c. high levels of verbal output.

d. deflated self-esteem.

COMPREHENSIVE PRACTICE TEST

The following tests are designed to give you an idea of how well you understood the entire chapter. There are three different types of tests, multiple-choice, true-false, and essay.

MULTIPLE-CHOICE

1. Simultaneous symptoms of mania and depression are referred to as (p. 226)

    a. a trouble syndrome.

    b. an overwhelming episode.

    c. a mixed episode.

    d. a unipolar episode.

2. Which of the following is true? (p 259)

    a. Low social support and stressful events independently predict depressive recurrences in bipolar events.

    b. Low social support but not stressful events predict depressive recurrences in bipolar events.

    c. Stressful events but not low social support predict recurrences in bipolar events.

    d. Low social support but not stressful events predict recurrences in bipolar events.

3. Which of the following mood disorders is most common and has actually increased in recent years? (p. 227)

    a. cyclothymia

    b. major depression

    c. dysthymia

    d. adjustment disorder with depressed mood

4. Mild depression may be seen as "normal and adaptive" if (p. 228)

    a. it is brief and mild.

    b. it involves looking at issues that would normally be avoided.

    c.it keeps us from using energy to obtain futile goals.

    d. all of the above

5. A diagnosis of major depressive disorder *cannot* be made if the person has experienced (p. 227)

    a. hypersomnia.

    b. psychomotor agitation.

    c. hypomania.

    d. diminished ability to concentrate.

6. Depression occurs during which of the following life cycle stages? (p. 228-229)

    a. infancy.

    b. adolescence.

    c. middle adulthood.

    d. all of the above

7. Depression in infants is known as (p. 232.)

    a. baby blues.

    b. anaclitic depression.

    c. infant unipolar disorder.

    d. none of the above

8. When major depression and dysthymia coexist in an individual, it is referred to as (p. 232)

    a. double trouble.

    b. double depression.

    c. two depressive disorders.

    d. comorbid depressive subtypes.

9. Because depressive episodes are time-limited, these are usually specified as (p. 234)

    a. starting and stopping.

b. first and second.

c. single and recurrent.

d. a. and b.

10. A neurophysiological finding that damage to the _____ but not the _____ anterior cortex often results in depression. (p. 238)

   a. right; left

   b. left; right

   c. frontal; middle

   d. middle; frontal

11. Circadian rhythms, which may play a causal role in depression, are controlled by strong and weak (p. 240)

   a. links.

   b. beats.

   c. oscillators.

   d. kentilators.

12. They typical treatment for seasonal affective disorder focuses on (p. 240)

   a. behavioral therapy.

   b. psychotherapy.

   c. R.E.T.

   d. light therapy.

13. Gary has fallen further and further behind in his rent. His roommates are threatening to kick him out. This stressful life event is known as a(n) (p. 240)

   a. independent life event.

   b. dependent life event.

c. secondary life event.

d. primary life event.

14. Women who are at a genetic risk for depression will experience more (p. 241)

a. good days than bad.

b. exhaustion.

c. stressful life events.

d. none of the above

15. In the brains of depressed patients, abnormalities have been detected in the (p. 258)

a. anterior cingulate cortex.

b. hippocampus.

c. amygdala.

d. all of the above

TRUE – FALSE

1. T / F Major depression is more common in men (21% lifetime prevalence rate) than women (13% lifetime prevalence rate). (p. 227)

2. T / F It is normal to feel depressed as a result of a recent loss or stress. (p. 227)

3. T / F Postpartum blues and postpartum depression are different names for the same disorder. (p. 229)

4. T / F People with dysthymia and major depression have periods of normal moods.   (p. 230)

5. T / F People with double depression rarely have relapses (p. 233)

6. T / F Seasonal affective disorders are an example of recurrent depressive episodes. (p. 234)

7. T / F Bipolar, but not unipolar depression runs in families. (p. 235)

8. T / F Hormones play a significant role in causing depression in women. (p. 248)

9. T / F Bipolar is distinguished from major depression by at least one episode of mania or a mixed episode. (p. 254)

10. T / F A recent survey documented that most people with depression don't receive treatment or receive inappropriate care. (p. 262)

11. T / F Tricyclics have been the antidepressants most commonly prescribed since about 1990. (p. 262)

12. T / F Discontinuing antidepressants when symptoms have remitted may cause relapse. (p. 264)

13. T / F Women are about three times as likely to attempt suicide as are men, but three times more men than women die by suicide each year. (p.269)

14. T / F Marital therapy has not been shown to be as effective as cognitive therapy for people who have unipolar depression and marital discord. (p. 268)

15. T / F Children are at increased risk for suicide if they have lost a parent or have been abused. (p. 269)

16. T / F Genetic factors, as well as alterations in serotonin functioning can contribute to causal factors for suicide. (p. 271)

17. T / F Suicidal ambivalence means the person wants to die. (p. 273)

18. T / F Those who threaten suicide seldom attempt suicide. (p. 274)

ESSAY QUESTIONS

1. Describe Aaron Beck's cognitive theory of depression. (p. 244)

2. Discuss the controversy regarding a person's right to die. (p.276)

3. Discuss the causal factors in bipolar disorder. (p. 257-259)

4. Explain the sociocultural factors affecting unipolar and bipolar disorders. (p. 260-262)

WEB LINKS TO ITEMS OR CONCEPTS DISCUSSED IN CHAPTER 7
Bipolar disorder
> www.pendulum.org/

> bipolar.about.com/mbody.htm www.frii.com/~parrot/bip.html

Unipolar disorder

www.mooddisordersinfo.com/html/ unipolar_or_bipolar.html

USE IT OR LOSE IT

Provide an answer to the thought question below, knowing that there is more than one way to respond. Possible answers are presented in the Answer Key.

Why do you think rates of depression and anxiety are increasing in Western

Societies despite increasing prosperity, and material comfort?

CRISS-CROSS

Now that you know all there is to know about this chapter, here's your opportunity

to put that knowledge to work.

CRISS-CROSS CLUES

Across
5. a markedly elevated, euphoric, and expansive mood
9. ending one's own life
10. different patterns of symptoms or features
11. major mood disorder and exhibiting two symptoms of schizophrenia
13. being persistently depressed for at least two years

Down
1. experiencing only depressive episodes
2. cyclical mood changes less severe than in bipolar disorder
3. elevated or euphoric episode
4. depression recurs at some point after remission
6. severe alterations in mood for a long period of time
7. answers humans give to Why?(as in why does everything happen to me?)
8. same as recurrence, except in a fairly short time
12. experiencing depressive and manic episodes

Puzzle created with Puzzlemaker at DiscoverySchool.com

ANSWERS TO TEST QUESTIONS – CHAPTER 7

MATCHING

C. Martin Seligman

F. Emile Durkheim

A. Aaron Beck

B. Sigmund Freud

E. Emil Kraepelin

D. Abramson et al., 1989

SHORT ANSWERS

(Your answer should contain the following points.)

1. Normal response phases to the loss of a grandparent:

a. Numbing and disbelief; a few hours to a week

b. Yearning and searching; weeks or months

c. Disorganization and despair

d. Some level of reorganization

2. The women who experienced stressful life events but did not become depressed had in common:

a. Having an intimate relationship with spouse or lover

b. Having no more than three children

c. Having a part-time or full-time job

d. Having a serious religious commitment

3. Interpersonal problems can play a causal role in depression and how depression affects others by:

a. Lack of social support: more vulnerable to depression

b. Lack of social skills: Speak more slowly or monotonously, maintain less eye contact, difficulty solving interpersonal problems

c. Behavior elicits negative feelings in others

d. Negative feelings make people less willing to interact with depressed person

e. Depression can lead to marital discord and marital discord, can lead to depression

f. Depression in one family member extends to infants, children, and adolescents

4. When working with someone who is contemplating suicide, suicide prevention centers:

a. Maintain supportive and directive contact with person for short period of time

b. Help the person realize acute distress is impairing his or her ability to access the situation accurately

c. Help the person see that present distress and emotional turmoil will not be endless

THE DOCTOR IS IN

1. Helen

Diagnosis: Dysthymia—persistent depressed mood for at least two years with symptoms of poor appetite, sleep disturbances, low energy, low self-esteem and fleeting periods of feeling normal.

Additional information: Family history of mood disorders, relationship with husband, last time she had a physical check-up, outside interests and how often the periods of feeling normal appear and how long do these last.

2. Expert - you

a. Conduct disorders and substance abuse common among completers

b. Mood disorders common among non-fatal attempts

c. Those with two or more disorders are at higher risk for completion

d. Availability of fire arms in the home more common for completers

e. Adolescents more sensitive to lack of control and may have maladaptive family settings

f. Limited problem-solving abilities

g. Exposure to suicide in media

3. Miles - <u>Diagnosis:</u> Seasonal affective disorder—depressed for two winters in a row with symptoms disappearing in the spring.

<u>Additional information:</u> Did Miles have any depressive episodes at other times of the year? Did he experience anything similar where he use to live?

4. Ed - <u>Diagnosis:</u> Bipolar. Manic behavior—excessive ideas, violent when wife wouldn't give him a credit card. Mania lasted a week. Depression preceded the manic episode.

PRACTICE TESTS

Q#	TEST 1	TEST 2	TEST 3
1	D	B	D
2	C	C	A
3	A	A	B
4	D	C	B
5	A	B	A
6	D	D	C
7	A	B	C
8	C	C	D
9	A	B	B
10	D	D	D

COMPREHENSIVE PRACTICE TEST

Q#	MULTIPLE CHOICE	T/F
1	C	F
2	A	T
3	B	F
4	D	T
5	C	F
6	D	T
7	B	F
8	B	F
9	C	T
10	B	T
11	C	F
12	D	T
13	B	T
14	C	F
15	D	T

16		T
17		F
18		F

ESSAY QUESTIONS

(Your answer should contain the following points.)

1 Aaron Beck's cognitive theory of depression:

a. Depressogenic schemas or dysfunctional beliefs—rigid, extreme and counterproductive thoughts

b. Negative automatic thoughts—thoughts just below the surface and are unpleasant pessimistic predictions

c. Negative cognitive triad—what negative automatic thought focus on. These are negative thoughts about self, negative thoughts about one's experience and surrounding world, and negative thoughts about one's future

d. The above is maintained by negative cognitive biases, which are dichotomous reasoning, selective abstraction, and arbitrary inference

2. The controversy regarding a person's right to die:

a. Has always been an issue with some cultures/societies supporting a person's right to commit suicide, e.g. classical Greece, the Netherlands, Hemlock Society, and the Oregon Death with Dignity Act

b. A terminally ill person has a right to die with dignity—legislative pressure to pass laws to allow physician assisted suicide, e.g. Dr. Kervorkian

c. Some people fear that people who are terminally ill will be pressured into taking their own lives

d. Another issue is someone who isn't terminally ill who wants to take his/her own life and the use of prevention tactics, such as involuntary hospitalization

e. Civil right suits, if a person is restrained against his/her will, thus raising legal issues

3. Causal factors in bipolar disorder:

Biological

• Genetic component—80% of the variance in the tendency to develop bipolar depression

• Abnormalities in the hypothelamic, pituitary, thyroid axis

• Disturbance in biological rhythms

• Shifting patterns of brain activity

Biochemical

• Perhaps excesses of neurotransmitters norepinephrine, serotonin, and dopamine

Psychosocial

• Stressful life events

• Personality and cognitive variables interacting with stressful life events associated with relapse

• Extreme defense against or reaction to depression

4. Explain the sociocultural factors affecting unipolar and bipolar disorders.

a. Depression occurs in all cultures, but form and prevalence vary.

b. China and Japan: some time and vegetative manifestations. No Western concept of guilt, self-recrimination.

c. Australian aborigines: no guilt or self-recrimination and no suicide. Vent hostility on to others.

d. Kaluli of New Guinea: relieve losses prevents hopelessness.

e. U.S.: unipolar depression higher in lower socioeconomic groups; bipolar more common in higher socioeconomic classes.

USE IT OR LOSE IT

Rates of depression are thought to be on the rise because of changes in mobility, media exposure, personal expectations, and social structure which have resulted in people in Western Cultures expecting more out of life, while dealing with rapid change and diminished social support.

CRISS-CROSS ANSWERS

Across
5. hypomania
9. suicide
10. specifiers
11. schizoaffective disorders
13. dysthymic

Down
1. unipolar
2. cyclothymic
3. manic
4. reoccurrence
6. mood disorders
7. attributions
8. relapse
12. bipolar

Chapter 8: Somatoform and Dissociative Disorders

BEFORE YOU READ

The somatoform disorders are characterized by physical complaints or disabilities in the absence of any physical pathology. Because of the absence of physical pathology, they presumably reflect underlying psychological difficulties. In the dissociative disorders, the central problem is a failure of certain aspects of memory due to an active process of dissociation. For example, in dissociative amnesia, individuals cannot remember their names, do not know how old they are, or where they live. According to the text, both types of disorders appear to be ways of avoiding psychological stress while denying personal responsibility for doing so. There are suggestions, as well, that both may be associated with traumatic childhood experiences. Because the dissociative disorders are unfamiliar, they are among the most difficult to grasp of the disorders we discuss in this book.

- **SOMATOFORM DISORDERS**
  Hypochondriasis
  Somatization Disorder
  Pain Disorder
  Conversion Disorder
  Body Dysmorphic Disorder

- **DISSOCIATIVE DISORDERS**
  Depersonalization Disorder
  Dissociative Amnesia and Fugue
  Dissociative Identity Disorder (DID)
  General Sociocultural Causal Factors in Dissociative Disorders
  Treatment and Outcomes in Dissociative Disorders

• UNRESOLVED ISSUES:

DID and recovered memories of abuse

OBJECTIVES

After reading this chapter, you should be able to:

1. Describe the major manifestations of somatoform disorders.

2. List the primary presenting symptoms of somatization disorder and hypochondriasis and note the similarities and differences between these closely related disorders.

3. Explain what is meant by a pain disorder. Discuss the difficulties of determining that pain is of psychological, rather than physical, origin and of reliably assessing an entirely subjective phenomenon.

4. Characterize the symptoms of conversion disorder, trace the history of the concept of "conversion," and describe the likely cause and chain of events in the development of a conversion disorder.

5. Discuss the etiological contributions of biological, psychosocial, and sociocultural factors to the somatoform disorders.

6. Compare and contrast the treatments for the somatoform disorders. What is known regarding their effectiveness, as compared to no treatment at all?

7. Compare the major features of dissociative amnesia and fugue, dissociative identity disorder, and depersonalization disorder.

8. Discuss the causal factors that contribute to the dissociative disorders, and note the critical difficulty caused by the fallibility of memory in determining the

contribution of childhood abuse to these disorders.

9. Describe the most appropriate treatments for the dissociative disorders, as well as the limitations of biological and psychological treatments.

10. Describe the issues related to DID and recovered memories.

KEY WORDS

Each of the words below is important in understanding the concepts presented in this chapter. Write the definition next to each of the words.

Term	Page	Definition
Alter identities	299	
Body dysmorphic disorder	281	
Conversion disorder	286	
Depersonalization disorder	295	
Derealization	295	
Dissociation	280	
Dissociative amnesia	296	
Dissociative disorders	280	
Dissociative fugue	297	
Dissociative identity disorder	297	
Factitious disorder	290	
Factitious disorder by proxy	291	
Host identity	299	
Hypochondriasis	281	
Hysteria	287	

Malingering	290	
Pain disorder	285	
Primary gain	287	
Secondary gain	285	
Soma	280	
Somatoform disorders	280	

AS YOU READ

Answers can be found in the Answer Key at the end of the chapter.

MATCHING
Who's Who and What's What?
Match the following psychological disorders with their descriptions.

Description

A. severe pain but no medical pathology to explain it

B. anxious preoccupation with having a disease based on a misinterpretation of bodily signs or symptoms

C. patterns of symptoms affecting sensory or voluntary motor functions, even though medical examination reveals no physical basis for these

D. psychological problems are manifested in physical disorders that often mimic medical conditions, for which no medical evidence can be found

E. many different complaints of physical ailments in four symptom categories spread over several years

F. inability to recall previously sorted information that cannot be accounted for by ordinary forgetting; common initial reaction to severe stress

G. person manifests two or more distinct identities or personality states that alternate in some way in taking control of behavior

H. normal processes regulating awareness and multichannel capacities of the mind apparently become disorganized, leading to various anomalies

I. a person not only goes into an amnesic state, but also leaves home surroundings and becomes confused about his or her identity

J. an obsessive preoccupation with some perceived flaw in one's appearance

Disorder

_____ somatoform disorder

_____ hypochondriasis disorder

_____ somatization disorder

_____ pain disorder

_____ conversion disorder

_____ body dysmorphic disorder

_____ dissociative disorders

_____ depersonalization disorder

_____ dissociative fugue

_____ dissociative identity disorder

_____ dissociative amnesia

SHORT ANSWERS

Provide brief answers to the following questions.

1. Briefly explain the four criteria for somatization. (p.284)

2. List four categories of symptoms for conversion disorder. (pp.287)

3. How can people with malingering/factitious disorders be distinguished from those with somatoform disorders. (p. 290)

4. Name and describe four types of psychogenic amnesia. (p. 297)

5. Describe the characteristics of Dissociative Identity Disorder (pp. 299-300)

THE DOCTOR IS IN...PSYCHIATRIC HELP—5¢

Read the following scenarios and diagnose the client. Remember to look carefully at the criteria for the disorder before you make a decision as to the diagnosis. Make a list of other information you might need to help you understand the causal factors.

1. As the psychiatrist in a large hospital, you have been called in to evaluate a patient who had been admitted two days before. The patient, Cathy, had awakened in the morning and had been unable to see. She was blind. A complete medical and neurological exam were done, but found nothing that would account for the blindness. You were called in to see if there could be a psychological cause. After talking to her for a while, you find out that husband had died unexpectedly about three months ago, leaving her with financial problems. She was going to have to get a job and she was worried about her employability. You ask if she has a picture of her husband. She says, "Yes," and walks to the shelf skirting a chair that is in her way.

How would you diagnose Cathy and why. How would you treat her?

2. Frank comes to see you because he has been urged him to talk to somebody. He is wearing sunglasses, even though he is in your office, and it is dark outside. When you ask him about the glasses, he tells you that his eyelids are horrible and ugly. He doesn't want anyone to see them—ever. Frank tells you that he spends much of the day checking his eyelids and trying to make them look better. He is saving for another surgery, his third, because he just can't stand the way his eyes look. You ask if he dates, has friends or a job. Frank says that he doesn't date (Who would want to be with someone as ugly as he is?), so he has started to withdraw even from his few friends. He recently lost his job because he was unable to meet clients, looking the way he does.

How would you diagnose Frank and why? How would you treat him?

3. Jackie comes to see you because she has been feeling rather odd lately. She tells you that she is feeling "unreal"—like she is not a part of her body. Jackie says that she is beginning to see her life as a movie because she feels so isolated from herself. She explains that when this experience occurs, it is like looking at the world through someone else's eyes. These experiences are now happening two or three times per week and last for several hours.

What would be your diagnosis for Jackie and why? How would you treat her and what would you expect treatment outcomes to be?

AFTER YOU READ

Answers can be found in the Answer Key at the end of the chapter.

PRACTICE TESTS

Take the following three multiple-choice tests to see how much you have comprehended from the chapter. Each represents roughly one-third of the chapter. As you study the chapter, use these to check your progress.

PRACTICE TEST NUMBER 1

1. Dissociative disorders are some of the most dramatic phenomena to be observed in the entire domain of psychopathology, for example, (p. 299)

   a. people who cannot recall who they are or where they may have come from.

   b. people who have two or more distinct identities or personality states that alternatively take control of the individual's behavior.

   c. people who have intense pain for which no medical symptoms can be found.

   d. a and b.

2. People with _____ are preoccupied with fears of having a serious disease, based on misinterpretation of one or more bodily signs or symptoms, and are not reassured when medical examination can find no physical problem. (p. 281)

   a. depersonalization disorder

   b. dissociative fugue

  c. hypochondriasis

  d. halitosis

3. Somatization disorder very commonly occurs with (p. 284)

  a. major depression.

  b. panic disorder and phobic disorders.

  c. generalized anxiety disorder.

  d. all of the above

4. Evidence exists that somatization disorder (p. 284)

  a. runs in families.

  b. is racially based.

  c. seems concentrated in individual communities.

  d. occurs mostly near oceans.

5. Patients with somatization disorder tend to think of themselves as (p. 285)

  a. physically weak.

  b. unable to tolerate stress.

  c. unable to tolerate physical activity.

  d. all of the above

6. All of the following are part of a chain of events in the development of a conversion disorder, **except** (p. 287)

  a. a conscious plan to use illness as an escape.

  b. a desire to escape from an unpleasant situation.

  c. a fleeting wish to be sick in order to avoid the situation.

  d. the appearance of the symptoms of some physical ailment.

7. A typical example of symptoms of conversion disorder would be

(p. 286)

a. partial paralysis.

b. blindness or deafness.

c. pseudoseizures.

d. all of the above

8. Freud used the term, "conversion hysteria," because he believed the symptoms were an expression of (p.287)

a. widespread anger.

b. built-up hostility.

c. repressed sexual energy.

d. being a parent.

9. Conversion disorder occurs _____ often in women than in men. (pp. 288)

a. much less

b. two-10 times more

c. about as

d. a little less

10. Although it can develop at any age, conversion disorder most commonly occurs (p. 288)

a. between early adolescence and early adulthood.

b. during middle age.

c. during infancy or early childhood.

d. about eight weeks before death.

PRACTICE TEST NUMBER 2

1. The prevalence of conversion disorders has _____ in the past 30 years or so. (p. 287)
   a. risen
   b. remained about the same
   c. declined
   d. stagnated

2. People with _____ disorders are intentionally producing or grossly exaggerating psychological or physical symptoms for external reasons, such as avoiding work or military service. (p. 290)
   a. malingering and factitious
   b. conversion
   c. pain
   d. somatoform

3. A person with _____ disorder is obsessed with a perceived or imagined flaw or flaws in his or her appearance. It is so intense that it causes clinically significant distress and/or impairment in social or occupational functioning. (p. 290)
   a. conversion
   b. pain
   c. factitious
   d. body dysmorphic

4. People with body dysmorphic disorder (BDD) may think (p. 290)
   a. their skin has ugly blemishes.
   b. their breasts are too small.

      c. their face is too thin.

      d. all of the above

5. Dissociative disorders are thought to represent attempts to avoid stress by (p. 287)

      a. escaping from personal identities.

      b. projecting blame on others.

      c. separating from significant others.

      d. facing stressful situations.

6. It is likely that some people may have certain _____ that make them more susceptible to developing dissociative symptoms than others. (p. 295)

      a. ineffective genes

      b. mystical properties

      c. lack of self control

      d. personality traits

7. In _____, one's sense of one's own self and one's own reality is temporarily lost, usually occurring during or after periods of severe stress. (p. 295)

      a. psychogenic pain disorder

      b. retrograde measles

      c. depersonalization

      d. hypochondriasis

8. When episodes of depersonalization become persistent and recurrent and interfere with normal functioning, _____ may be diagnosed. (p. 295)

      a. psychogenic pain disorder

      b. depersonalization disorder

    c. dissociative amnesia

    d. hypochondriasis

9. Retrograde amnesia involves the failure to remember (p. 296)

    a. previously learned information

    b. new information

    c. emotional information

    d. only names and dates

10. _____ is a fairly common initial reaction to intolerably stressful circumstances. (pp. 297)

    a. Dissociative amnesia

    b. Brain pathology

    c. Hypochondriasis

    d. Retrograde measles

PRACTICE TEST NUMBER 3

1. In very rare cases, called _____, a person is not only amnesic for some or all aspects of his or her past, but also departs from home surroundings. (p. 297)

    a. retrograde measles

    b. dissociative fugue

    c. disappropriate stressful symnabulolism

    d. multiple personality disorder

2. Dissociative identity disorder (DID) was formerly known as (p. 298)

    a. Scarlett O'Hara fever.

    b. dissociative fugue.

    c. multiple personality disorder.

    d. depersonalization disorder.

3. The identity switches in DID typically occur (p. 300)

    a. very quickly (in a matter of seconds).

    b. over a period of several hours.

    c. during a full moon.

    d. just prior to taking a test.

4. DID's alter identities may differ in (p. 299)

    a. gender, age, and sexual orientation.

    b. handedness, handwriting, and prescription for eyeglasses.

    c. foreign languages spoken and general knowledge.

    d. all of the above

5. _____ may or may not be aware of each other, or may attempt to take over control from the host identity. (p. 302)

    a. Escapists

    b. Malingerers

    c. Alter identities

    d. Localized amnesiacs

6. DID was rare until around _____, but now thousands of cases have been reported. (p. 301)

    a. 1800

    b. World War I

    c. 1979

    d. September 11, 2001

7. DID has now been identified throughout the world. It has been

found (p. 306)

    a. in all racial groups.

    b. in all cultures.

    c. in countries ranging from Nigeria and Ethiopia, to Turkey, Australia, and the Caribbean.

    d. all of the above

8. A major cause of DID appears to be (p. 306)

    a. the rise of individual anger and inner rage.

    b. childhood sexual abuse.

    c. air and water pollution.

    d. broken families and the fast pace of modern society.

9. For _____ patients, most therapists set integration of the previously separate alters, together with their collective merging into the host personality, as the ultimate goal of treatment. (p. 307)

    a. conversion disorder

    b. BDD

    c. DID

    d. JPG

10. A controversy exists concerning DID, including (p. 305-309)

    a. how it develops.

    b. whether it is real or faked.

    c. whether memories of childhood abuse are real, and if the memories are real whether the abuse played a causal role.

    d. all of the above

COMPREHENSIVE PRACTICE TEST

The following tests are designed to give you an idea of how well you understood the entire chapter. There are three different types of tests: multiple-choice, true-false, and essay.

MULTIPLE-CHOICE

1. Body dysmorphic disorder (BDD) usually occurs in adolescence when many people start to become preoccupied with their appearance and appears to be (p. 293)

   a. more prevalent in men than women.

   b. approximately equal in men and women.

   c. more prevalent in women than men.

   d. unheard of in Canada.

2. Treatment approaches for BDD focus on (p. 294)

   a. getting patients to identify and change distorted perceptions of their body.

   b. exposure to anxiety-provoking situations (e.g., wearing something that highlights, rather than disguises, their defect).

   c. prevention of checking responses (e.g., mirror checking, reassurance seeking, and repeatedly examining their imaginary defect).

   d. all of the above

3. Dissociative disorders have been a major research area in the field of cognitive psychology for the past (p. 295)

   a. few months

   b. few years

   c. quarter-century

   d. 150 years

4. Which of the following disorders is thought to mainly be a way of avoiding anxiety and stress and of managing life problems that threaten to overwhelm the person's usual coping resources. (p. 295)

    a. dissociative

    b. generalized

    c. hypochondriasis

    d. low-esteem

5. In which of the following disorders might a person feel drastically changed or unreal? (p. 295)

    a. depersonalization disorder

    b. psychogenic pain disorder

    c. hypochondriasis

    d. cognitive psychology

6. The loss of memory following a catastrophic event is called (pp. 297)

    a. psychogenic pain disorder.

    b. dissociative amnesia.

    c. hypochondriasis.

    d. alter ego.

7. In DID, the primary or host identity is most frequently encountered, but alter identities may (p. 300)

    a. be more concerned with personal-identity issues.

    b. take control at different points in time.

    c. become moody and refuse to cooperate.

    d. become an alter ego.

8. People with DID often show (p. 300)

a. moodiness and erratic behavior.

b. headaches, hallucination, and substance abuse.

c. post-traumatic symptoms, and other amnesic and fugue symptoms.

d. all of the above.

9. In _____ amnesia, the individual forgets his/her entire life history. (p. 297)

a. localized

b. selective

c. generalized

d. continuous

10. Approximately _____ more females than males are diagnosed as having the DID, believed by some to be due to the greater proportion of abuse among females than males. (p. 300)

a. 25%

b. 75%

c. 3-9 times

d. The numbers for females and males are about the same.

11. One of the primary techniques used in most treatments of DID is (p. 307)

a. esteem exercise.

b. hypnosis.

c. projection.

d. withdrawing stress.

12. DID patients who recover memories of abuse (often in therapy) have sued _____ for inflicting abuse. (p. 308)

a. each other

b. their parents

c. schools and teachers

d. anyone who seems to have a lot of money

13. DID patients have also sued _____ for implanting memories or abuse they later came to believe had actually not occurred. (p.308)

a. their parents

b. schools and teachers

c. therapists and institutions

d. everyone who seems to have any money at all

14. Some parents, asserting they had been falsely accused, formed an international support organization called _____ and have sometimes sued therapists for damages, alleging the therapists induced false memories of parental abuse in their child. (p. 308)

a. The False Memory Syndrome Foundation

b. Parents Against False Memories

c. The International Order of Falsely Accused Parents

d. The International Support Organization

15. Alter personalities would be expected in cases of (p. 308)

a. psychogenic pain disorder.

b. conversion disorder.

c. hypochondriasis.

d. dissociative identity disorder.

TRUE – FALSE

1. T / F Somatoform disorders are characterized by physical symptoms without a physical explanation. (p. 280)

2. T / F Somatization disorder is not extremely difficult to treat because much systematic research has been conducted. (p. 285)

3. T / F Indications exist that people with hypochondriasis often had an excessive amount of illness in their families while growing up. (p. 282)

4. T / F Contemporary views of conversion disorder see it as serving the function of providing a plausible excuse, enabling the individual to escape or avoid an intolerably stressful situation without having to take responsibility for doing so. (p. 287)

5. T / F Conversion disorder was not very common in the past and and hardly ever occurred prior to World War II. (p. 287-288)

6. T / F Conversion disorder typically involves unstable men (p. 287).

7. T / F Most of us have concerns about our appearance; but people with body dysmorphic disorder are unrealistically preoccupied with their bodies. (p. 290)

8 T / F   We all dissociate to a degree, occasionally. (p. 295)

9. T / F Dissociative disorders appear mainly to provide a way to

avoid anxiety and stress and of managing life problems that threaten to overwhelm the person's usual coping resources. (p. 295)

10. T / F Some have proposed that both eating disorders and BDD are variants of a "body image disorder" (not an official category). People with both BDD and eating disorders are preoccupied with their appearance and overemphasize their importance for relationships. (p. 294)

ESSAY QUESTIONS

1. Discuss pain disorder. (p. 285)

2. Describe the criteria commonly used for distinguishing between conversion disorders and true organic disturbances. (p. 289)

3. Discuss four controversies regarding DID. (p. 303-308)

WEB LINKS TO ITEMS OR CONCEPTS DISCUSSED IN THIS CHAPTER

Somatoform and Dissociative Disorders

www.psyweb.com/Mdisord/somatd.html

www.nlm.nih.gov/medlineplus/ency/article/000954.htm

www.multiple-personality.com/

USE IT OR LOSE IT

Dissociative Identity Disorder is characterized by the expression of different behaviors, voices, and even handwriting by the same person at different times. How would you explain this disorder to someone unfamiliar with psychological issues?

CRISS-CROSS

Now that you know all there is to know about this chapter, here's your opportunity to put that knowledge to work.

<u>CRISS-CROSS CLUES</u>

Across

9. may include partial paralysis, blindness, pseudoseizures, but without any known medical condition

Down

1. seemingly medical conditions without evidence of physical pathology to account for these

2. the human mind's capacity to engage in complex activity independent of conscious awareness

3. not only amnesic but leaves home and may assume a new identity

4. intentionally over-exaggerating physical symptoms to avoid work

5. when one's sense of the reality of the outside world is temporarily lost

6. failure to recall when that failure cannot be accounted for by ordinary forgetting

7. presence of persistent and severe pain without a purely medical cause

8. new term for multiple personality disorder

Puzzle created with Puzzlemaker at
DiscoverySchool.com

ANSWERS TO TEST QUESTIONS – CHAPTER 8

MATCHING

D. somatoform disorder

B. hypochondriasis disorder

E. somatization disorder

A. pain disorder

C. conversion disorder

J. body dysmorphic disorder

H. dissociative disorders

K. depersonalization disorder

I. dissociative fugue

G. dissociative identity disorder

F. dissociative amnesia

SHORT ANSWERS

(Your answer should contain the following points.)

1. Four criteria must be met for somatization disorder to be present:

    a. Four pain symptoms. The patient must report a history of pain experienced in at least four different sites or functions.

    b. Two gastrointestinal symptoms. The patient must report a history of at least two symptoms, other than pain, pertaining to the gastrointestinal system.

    c. One sexual symptom. The patient must report at least one reproductive system symptom other than pain.

    d. One pseudoneurological symptom. The patient must report a history of at least one symptom, not limited to pain, suggestive of a neurological condition.

2. Conversion disorder's four categories of symptoms:

    a. Sensory—most often visual, auditory, or sensitivity to feeling

    b. Motor—paralysis of an arm or leg

    c. Seizures—resemble epileptic seizures

    d. Mixed presentation from 1-3

3. One way of telling the difference between people with malingering/factitious disorders and other somatoform disorders is by the response given when asked to describe the symptoms. Fakers are inclined to be defensive, evasive, and suspicious, but individuals with conversion disorders are very willing to discuss them, often in excruciating detail.

4. Four types of psychogenic amnesia are recognized:

    a. localized—a person remembers nothing that happened during a specific period

    b. selective—a person forgets some, but not all, of what happened during a given period

    c. generalized—a person forgets his or her entire life history

    d. continuous—a person remembers nothing from a certain point in the past until the present

5. In very rare cases, called dissociative fugue, a person is not only amnesic for some or all aspects of his or her past, but also departs from home surroundings. During the fugue these persons are unaware of memory loss for prior stages in their life, but their memory for what happens during the fugue state itself is intact, during which they may live a quite normal life. Days, weeks, or ever years later, such persons may suddenly come out of the fugue state and find themselves in strange places working in a new occupation and not knowing how they got there.

THE DOCTOR IS IN

1. Cathy:

Diagnosis: Conversion disorder, blind with no medical or neurological cause, recent large stressors in life, doesn't seem to be faking it, walks around a chair but is blind

Treatment: behavioral approaches, possibly hypnosis combined with other problem-solving therapies

2. Frank:

Diagnosis: Body dysmorphic disorder, preoccupation with eyelids to the point of interfering with his life; two surgeries and saving for a third

Treatment: antidepressants and cognitive-behavioral therapy that focuses on having Frank identify and change distorted perceptions about his body.

3. Jackie:

Diagnosis: Depersonalization disorder—Jackie feels separate from her body and like she is in a movie. She feels unreal and sees herself and her friends as automatons.

Treatment: no real controlled research has been done on treatment for depersonalization disorder. This disorder is thought to be resistant to treatment making outcome difficult to predict. Treatment has focused on other psychopathology that may be associated with the disorder. Hypnosis and teaching self-hypnosis techniques may be useful but again no controlled research has been done.

PRACTICE TESTS

Q#	TEST 1	TEST 2	TEST 3
1	D	C	B
2	C	A	C
3	D	D	A
4	A	D	D
5	D	A	C
6	A	D	C
7	D	C	D
8	C	B	B

9	B	A	C
10	A	A	D

COMPREHENSIVE PRACTICE TEST

Q#	MULTIPLE CHOICE	T/F
1	B	T
2	D	F
3	C	T
4	A	T
5	A	F
6	B	F
7	B	T
8	D	T
9	C	T
10	C	T
11	B	
12	B	
13	C	
14	A	
15	D	
16		
17		

ESSAY QUESTIONS
(Your answer should contain the following points.)

1. Pain disorder essay:
   a. Two types:
   • pain disorder associated with psychological factors. Psychological factors are judged to play a major role in the onset or maintenance of the pain.
   • pain disorder associated with psychological factors and a general medical condition. The pain experienced is considered to result from psychological factors and some medical condition that could cause pain.
   b. Pain may be acute (duration of less than six months) or chronic (duration of more than six months).
   c. Unknown in the general population; fairly common among patients at pain clinics.
   d. More frequently diagnosed in women.
   e. Frequently comorbid with anxiety and/or mood disorders.
   f. Can lead to a vicious cycle of patient not being able to work or exercise and resulting inactivity may lead to depression and loss of physical strength and endurance. The loss of strength and fatigue can, in turn, exacerbate the pain.
   g. Cognitive-behavior treatment techniques have been widely used. They generally include relaxation training, support and validation that the pain is real, scheduling of daily activities, cognitive restructuring, and reinforcement of "no-pain" behaviors.

2. Criteria commonly used for distinguishing between conversion
disorders and true organic disturbances:
a. Patient must receive a thorough medical and neurological
examination.
b. The frequent failure of dysfunction to conform clearly to the
symptoms of the particular disease or disorder simulated—no
wasting away or atrophy of a "paralyzed" limb.
c. The selective nature of the dysfunction—"paralyzed" muscles
can be used for some activities but not others.
d. Under hypnosis or narcosis, the symptoms can be removed,
shifted, or reinduced at the suggestion of the therapist.

3. Four controversies regarding DID:
1. Concern whether DID is a real disorder or whether it is faked, and even if it
is real, can it be faked?
2. How does DID develop? a) DID is caused by early childhood trauma and
b) the development of DID involves some kind of social enactment of multiple
different roles that have been inadvertently encouraged by careless clinicians.
3. Those who maintain DID is caused by childhood trauma cite mounting
evidence that the vast majority of individuals diagnosed with DID report
memories of an early history of abuse. But are these memories of early abuse
real or false?
4. If abuse has occurred in most individuals with DID, did the abuse play a
causal role, or was something else correlated with abuse actually the cause?
Controversy rages.
a. Believers usually take DID and the idea of abuse as its cause to be
established beyond doubt.
b. Disbelievers are sympathetic to people suffering from DID symptoms, but
have tended to doubt that it is usually caused by childhood abuse, and have
challenged the validity or accuracy of recovered memories of abuse.

USE IT OR LOSE IT

Dissociative issues are often thought to be the result of self-hypnosis as a means of
coping with early adversity, and in particular sexual abuse. In order to avoid anxiety
or distress such individuals involuntarily slip into altered states, for which they may
have little memory. Normal individuals may experience a minor version of this
when they realize that they have engaged in an automatic behavior such as driving,
while thinking about something completely different.

CRISS-CROSS ANSWERS

Across	Down
9. conversion disorder	1. somatoform disorders
	2. dissociation
	3. dissociative fugue

4. malingering
5. derealization
6. dissociative amnesia
7. pain disorder
8. dissociative identity disorder

Chapter 9: Eating Disorders and Obesity

BEFORE YOU READ

Why are the majority of Americans obsessed with losing weight, despite the fact that obesity rates are rising? Why would countless young women, including celebrities like Princess Diana, get caught in a cycle of binge eating and then purging to maintain a supposedly "ideal" body? Why are more and more young men willing to take harmful steroids to build up their bodies? Chapter 9 provides insight into the complex world of diet, weight, obesity, and eating disorders. The clinical aspects of eating disorders such as anorexia nervosa, bulimia nervosa, and binge eating disorder will be discussed. The causes of these disorders will be discussed including biological factors such as set-point, and the roles of serotonin, leptin and ghrelin, as well as the impact of societal and cultural factors. The implementation and efficacy of eating disorder interventions will also be reviewed. Finally, the emergence of obesity as a worldwide health problem will be considered, with an emphasis on the causes and possible means of responding to this growing issue.

- **CLINICAL ASPECTS OF EATING DISORDERS**
    Age of Onset and Gender Differences
    Anorexia Nervosa
    Bulimia Nervosa
    Medical Complications of Anorexia Nervosa and Bulimia Nervosa
    Other Forms of Eating Disorders
    Distinguishing Among Diagnoses
    Comorbidity of Eating Disorders with Other Forms of
    Psychopathology
    Prevalence of Eating Disorders
    Eating Disorders Across Cultures Course and Outcome

- **RISK AND CAUSAL FACTORS IN EATING DISORDERS**

Biological Factors

Sociocultural Factors

Individual Risk Factors

Family Environment

- **TREATMENT OF EATING DISORDERS**

  Treatment of Anorexia Nervosa

  Treatment of Bulimia Nervosa

  Treatment of Binge-Eating Disorder

- **OBESITY**

  Biological Factors; Psychological Factors

  Learning Perspective

  Sociocultural Factors

  Treatment of Obesity

  The Importance of Prevention

OBJECTIVES

After reading this chapter, you should be able to:

1. Discuss the clinical aspects of eating disorders, such as age of onset and gender differences.

2. Define anorexia nervosa and bulimia nervosa and their subtypes.

3. Describe the medical complications of the various eating disorders.

4. Identify other forms of eating disorders, such as EDNOS and BED.

5. Explain the comorbidity of eating disorders with other forms of psychopathologies.

6. Discuss prevalence rates of eating disorders in this culture and across cultures.

7. Describe the biological, sociocultural, individual, and family risk and causal factors associated with eating disorders.

8. Explain the various methods used for treating eating disorders and be

able to evaluate each.

9. Define obesity and identify risk and causal factors.

10. Discuss prevention and treatment methods for obesity.

AS YOU READ

Answers can be found in the Answer Key at the end of the chapter.

KEY WORDS

Each of the words below is important in understanding the concepts presented in this chapter. Write the definition next to each of the words.

Term	Page	Definition
Anorexia nervosa	313	
Anorexia nervosa—restricting type	314	
Anorexia nervosa—binge-eating/purge type	314	
Binge eating disorder	319	
Cognitive behavioral therapy	332	
Eating disorder	312	

Eating disorders not otherwise specified (EDNOS)	319	
Grehlin	335	
Leptin	335	
Meta-analysis	322	
Negative affect	329	
Obesity	333	
Perfectionism	329	
Purge	314	
Randomized controlled trials	331	
Serotonin	323	

MATCHING

Who's Who and What's What

Match the following terms with their definitions.

Definition

A. published the first medical account of anorexia nervosa in 1689

B. comes from the Greek words meaning "ox" and "hunger"

C. suffered from bulimia nervosa

D. instrumental in naming the eating disorder, anorexia nervosa, in 1873.

E. suffered from anorexia nervosa which ultimately lead to her death

F. low weight is maintained by tightly controlling how much food is eaten

G. proposed the term, "bulimia nervosa," in 1979

H. breakdown of eating restraint, resulting in periods of binge-eating and efforts to purge

Name/Term

_____ Princess Diana

_____ Karen Carpenter

_____ Richard Morton

_____ Charles Lasegue and Sir William Gull

_____ Anorexia nervosa—restricting type

_____ Anorexia nervosa—binge-eating purging type

_____ Bulima nervosa

_____ Russell, a British psychiatrist

SHORT ANSWERS

Provide brief answers to the following questions.

1. Describe the risk factors for eating disorders in males. (p. 318)

2. What are the DSM-IV-TR criteria for bulimia nervosa? (318)

3. Mary was diagnosed with an eating disorder—anorexia nervosa. She sought treatment for the disorder. Based on the research done by Lowe in 2001, what can you say about her recovery possibilities? (p. 314)

4. Explain how the study done by Anne Becker of the women in Fiji illustrates the impact the media has on thinness. (pp. 325)

THE DOCTOR IS IN...PSYCHIATRIC HELP—5¢

Read the following scenarios and diagnose the client. Remember to look carefully at the criteria for the disorder before you make a decision as to the diagnosis. Make a list of other information you might need to help you understand the causal factors.

1. Mary is 5'6" tall and weighs 96 pounds. She tells you that whenever she looks in the mirror, all she sees is a fat person. Mary has restricted her eating to just a few pieces of celery and carrots each day. There is a ritual to her eating pattern. Mary's hair is thin and her nails are brittle. She is still having regular menstrual periods.

How would you diagnose Mary and why?

2. Glenn, a 45-year-old male, comes to your office. His wife insisted that he come in to see you. Glenn is 5'8" tall and weight 350 pounds. Even though his health is in jeopardy, he finds himself binging on all kinds of food from cakes and cookies to pizzas, fried chicken and hamburgers. He feels disgusted with his behavior. You ask if he purges and he tells you that he does not. He says that sometimes he will exercise excessively after binging, but not every time.

How would you diagnose Glenn and why?

3. Diane, a 14-year-old girl, is referred to you because she has anorexia nervosa. Her parents are very concerned, but a bit shocked, when you suggest that you would like to see the whole family in therapy, not just Diane. What would you expect to see as family characteristics when you talk to Diane's family? How would you proceed with treatment?

AFTER YOU READ

Answers can be found in the Answer Key at the end of the chapter.

PRACTICE TESTS

Take the following three multiple-choice tests to see how much you have comprehended from the chapter. Each represents roughly one-third of the chapter. As you study the chapter, use these to check your progress.

PRACTICE TEST NUMBER 1

1. An eating disorder that is found almost exclusively in men is (p. 318)

 a. anorexia nervosa.

 b. bulimia nervosa.

 c. male pattern eating disorder.

 d. reverse anorexia.

2. In this type of anorexia nervosa, every effort is made to limit how much food is eaten and caloric intake is tightly controlled. (p. 314)

 a. binge-eating purging type

 b. binge-eating disorder type

 c. restricting type

 d. bulimia nervosa

3. This type of anorexia nervosa involves a breakdown of restraint that results in periods of binge eating. (p. 316)

 a. binge-eating purging type

 b. binge-eating disorder type

 c. restrictive type

 d. bulimia nervosa

4. Karen has the eating disorder, bulimia nervosa. During her average

binge, she could consume as much as _____ calories. (p. 316)

a. 2,000

b. 10,000

c. 4,800

d. 1,200

5. The DSM-IV distinguishes between two types of bulimia nervosa. These are (p. 316)

a. purging and nonpurging.

b. starving and nonstarving.

c. binging and nonbinging.

d. none of the above

6. The difference between a person with the purging type of bulimia nervosa and a person with the restricting type of anorexia nervosa is (p. 316)

a. the non-purging methods of weight maintenance.

b. the fear of gaining weight

c. their actual weight.

d. negative self-evaluation

7. An eating disorder diagnosis found in the Appendix of the DSM-IV which warrants further study is (p. 320)

a. BED.

b. EDNOS.

c. OCD.

d. TNT.

8. What percentage of people with eating disorders also harm themselves? (p. 321)

a. more than one-half

b. about three-quarters

c. less than one-third

d. over 90 %

9. A common disorder found in relatives of patients with eating disorders is
(p. 323)

a. schizophrenia.

b. mood disorders.

c. anxiety disorders.

d. none of the above

10. Which of the following neurotransmitters is linked with mood disorders
and impulsivity and modulates appetite and feeding behavior? (p. 323)

a. serotonin

b. dopamine

c. GABA

d. all of the above

PRACTICE TEST NUMBER 2

1. The majority of girls and women who have anorexia come from a
(p.325)

a. single-parent home.

b. middle-class background.

c. higher social class background.

d. a and b

2. The first model to exemplify the current sociocultural ideal of extreme

thinness was (p. 325)

    a. Marilyn.

    b. Brittany.

    c. Sandra.

    d. Twiggy.

3. Internalizing the _____ is considered a risk factor for eating disorders. (p. 326)

    a. over-weight ideal

    b. Sleeping Beauty ideal

    c. Monroe ideal

    d. thin-ideal

4. There seems to be a perceptual discrepancy between how young girls and women regard their own bodies and the media representation of the (p. 327)

    a. "ideal" female form.

    b. natural looking woman.

    c. older woman.

    d. none of the above

5. Which of the following factors has the most controversy surrounding whether or not it is a causal factor in developing an eating disorder? (p. 328)

    a. dieting.

    b. internalizing the "ideal" female form.

    c. perfectionism.

    d. all of the above have been proven to be causal factors.

6. A causal risk factor for body dissatisfaction is. (p. 329)

    a. negative affect

b. upbeat attitude

c. high self-esteem

d. social support

7. Which of the following is true about bulimics after they have received intense CBT treatment? (p.332)

    a. Most fully recover.

    b. Most revert to their bulimic behavior.

    c. Most stop binging and purging. but continue to severely restrict their diets.

    d. Most continue to be very concerned with weight and body image.

8. Most studies show a _____ link between child sexual abuse and eating disorders.

    a. weak but correlational.

    b. moderate and correlational.

    c. strong and correlational.

    d. moderate and causal.

9. Some young women turn to _____ web sites for validation of the anorexic lifestyle. (p. 331)

    a. pro-ana

    b. pro-choice

    c. pro-life

    d. pro-food

10. This type of treatment has proven effective in treating anorexia and bulimia by helping to modify distorted beliefs about weight, food and self. (p. 332)

    a. EDT

    b. CNT

c. behavioral

d. CBT

PRACTICE TEST NUMBER 3

1. The _____ component of CBT for bulimia focuses on normalizing eating patterns. (p. 332)

   a. behavioral

   b. cognitive

   c. cathartic

   d. all of the above

2. The _____ component of CBT for bulimia challenges the dysfunctional thought patterns that perpetuate a binge cycle. (p. 332)

   a. behavioral

   b. cognitive

   c. cathartic

   d. all of the above

3. When patients with bulimia stop trying so hard to restrain their eating, they seem to (p. 332)

   a. get worse by eating more.

   b. stay about the same.

   c. improve.

   d. get better, then get worse.

4. Significant depression is a comorbid condition for binge-eaters, affecting around _____ during their lifetime. (p. 332)

   a. 25%

   b. 37%

  c. 76%

  d. 60%

5. Obesity is defined based on a statistic called the (p. 333)

  a. CBT.

  b. BMI.

  c. GABA.

  d. MMPI.

6. From a diagnostic perspective, obesity is not a(n) (p. 334)

  a. problem if the person recognizes it.

  b. treatable problem like other eating disorders.

  c. eating disorder.

  d. health risk.

7. Adult obesity is related to the number and size of the _____ in the body. (p. 336)

  a. hormones

  b. T-cells

  c. adipose cells

  d. lymphocytes

8. A key influence on excessive eating and obesity is (p. 336)

  a. television.

  b. family behavior patterns.

  c. magazines.

  d. peers.

9. Which of the following people is most likely to be obese? (p. 334)

  a. A young woman with no children

b. An older woman with 3 children who has never smoked

c. A low-SES married, black, ex-smoker

d. A high-SES, divorced, man with 2 children

10. Which of the following has NOT been implicated as a possible contributor to obesity?

a. genetic mutation of cells

b. a society which discourages activity

c. family influences

d. more free time as society becomes wealthier

COMPREHENSIVE PRACTICE TEST

The following tests are designed to give you an idea of how well you understood the entire chapter. There are three different types of tests: multiple-choice, true-false, and essay.

MULTIPLE-CHOICE

1. At the heart of anorexia nervosa and bulimia nervosa is an intense and pathological fear of becoming (p. 312)

a. too thin.

b. overweight and fat.

c. under nourished.

d. all of the above

2. People with anorexia and bulimia will compromise their health to achieve (p. 312)

a. muscle

b. obesity

c. thinness

d. a career

3. Although people of all different ages have been known to develop eating disorders, the period of greatest risk is in (p. 318)
   a. teenage years.
   b. early adulthood.
   c. middle age.
   d. a and b

4. The clinical picture of the binge-eating/purging type of anorexia has much in common with (p. 312)
   a. EDNOS.
   b. BED.
   c. bulimia nervosa.
   d. none of the above

5. If a person meets the criteria for anorexia nervosa he/she can't be diagnosed with bulimia nervosa because (p. 313)
   a. the two are very similar.
   b. bulimics continue to menstruate.
   c. you can only have one diagnosis.
   d. none of the above

6. Eating disorders are no longer confined to industrialized Western countries but can be found in (p. 322)
   a. India.
   b. Africa.
   c. Asia.
   d. all of the above

7. The long-term mortality rate for bulimia nervosa is around (p. 323)
   a. 10%

b. 6%

c. 0.5%

d. 1%

8. People with anorexia and bulimia often show a long-standing pattern of excessive (p. 329)

    a. upbeat attitude.

    b. high self-esteem.

    c. social support.

    d. perfectionism.

9. Currently there is not enough empirical evidence to show that _____ is a risk factor for eating disorders. (p. 329)

    a. overly indulgent grandmother

    b. single parent family

    c. childhood sexual abuse

    d. being an only child

10. Which of the following groups responds well to family treatment? (p. 332)

    a. adolescents

    b. mid-twenties

    c. young adults

    d. none of the above

11. Because many patients with bulimia also suffer from mood disorders, they are often treated with (p. 332)

    a. psychotherapy.

    b. behavioral therapy.

    c. antidepressants.

    d. hospitalization.

12. Which treatment for patients with bulimia has shown the greatest
    promise? (p. 312)
    a. CBT
    b. Antidepressants
    c. ECT
    d. A and B

13. Obesity can result in (p. 334)
    a. diabetes.
    b. high blood pressure.
    c. musculoskeletal problems.
    d. all of the above.

14. The rates of obesity are rising too quickly to be only a result of
    genetics. This rise implies what has become a significant influence?
    (p. 340)
    a. old age
    b. increase in activity
    c. unhealthy lifestyles
    d. all of the above.

15. Being obese is defined as having a body mass index of _____ or
    above. (p. 333)
    a. 30
    b. 10
    c. 25
    d. 35

16. An extreme method for treating obesity involves (p. 338)
    a. antidepressants.

b. psychotherapy.

c. psychosurgery.

d. gastric bypass surgery.

TRUE – FALSE

1. T / F Eating disorders in the elderly are easily diagnosed because doctors are aware of the problem. (p. 319)

2. T / F Even if they are painfully thin or emaciated, patients with anorexia often deny having any problems. (p. 313)

3. T / F Thirty to fifty percent of patients transition from the restricting type to the binge-eating purging type of anorexia nervosa during the course of their disorder. (p. 314)

4. T / F Death is often a direct outcome of the eating disorder bulimia nervosa. (p. 323)

5. T / F Psychiatric conditions often coexist with eating disorders. (p. 321)

6. T / F Recent research suggests that the restrictive type of anorexia has a genetic base. (p. 323)

7. T / F Body dissatisfaction is an important risk factor for pathological eating.   (p. 328)

8. T / F Dieting is not regarded as a risk factor for the development of eating disorders in young women. (p. 328)

9. T / F About 17% of patients with severe eating disorders have to be committed to a hospital for treatment against their will.   (p. 330)

10. T / F The most immediate concern with patients with anorexia is to restore their weight to a level that is not life-threatening. (p. 330)

11. T / F Young men never develop eating disorders (p. 318)

ESSAY QUESTIONS

1. Discuss the medical complications of anorexia nervosa and bulimia nervosa.

Anorexia

Bulima

2. Describe Garner's set-point theory and its relation to eating disorders.

WEB LINKS TO ITEMS OR CONCEPTS FOUND IN CHAPTER 9

Clinical assessment

bioinformatics.weizmann.ac.il/cytokine/

health.yahoo.com/health/encyclopedia/000818/0.html

www.uth.tmc.edu/schools/med/surgery/organ_transplant/

www.ash-us.org/

www.jhypertension.com/

www.phassociation.org/

www.mco.edu/whl/

www.cdc.gov/nchs/fastats/hyprtens.htm

USE IT OR LOSE IT

Provide an answer to the thought question below, knowing that there is more than one way to respond. Possible answers are presented in the Answer Key.

What role do you think the media plays in triggering Eating Disorders in young women?

CRISS-CROSS

Now that you know all there is to know about this chapter, here's your opportunity to put that knowledge to work.

CRISS-CROSS CLUES

Across

7. a statistic used to define obesity

8. A neurotransmitter that has been implicated in modulating appetite and feeding behavior

Down

1. means lack of appetite induced by nervousness

2. frequent occurrence of episodes of out-of-control binge-eating, followed by recurrent inappropriate behavior that is intended to prevent weight gain.

3. having a BMI above 30

4. physiologically regulated weight the body tries to defend or maintain

5. a causal risk factor; focusing on one's limitations and short-comings

6. may cause people to be much more likely to subscribe to the thin ideal; may help maintain bulimic pathology

Puzzle created with Puzzlemaker at DiscoverySchool.com

ANSWERS TO TEST QUESTIONS - CHAPTER 9

WHO'S WHO AND WHAT'S WHAT—MATCHING

Name/Term

C. Princess Diana - suffered from bulimia nervosa

E. Karen Carpenter - suffered from anorexia nervosa which ultimately lead to her death

A. Richard Morton - published the first medical account of anorexia nervosa in 1689

D. Charles Lasegue and Sir William Gull - instrumental in naming the eating disorder, anorexia nervosa, in 1873

F. Anorexia nervosa—restricting type - low weight is maintained by tightly controlling how much food is eaten

H. Anorexia nervosa—binge-eating purging type - breakdown of eating restraint, resulting in periods of binge-eating and efforts to purge

B. Bulimia nervosa - comes from the Greek words meaning "ox" and "hunger"

G. Russell, a British psychiatrist - proposed the term, " bulimia nervosa," in 1979

SHORT ANSWERS

(Your answer should contain the following points.)

1. Describe risk factors for eating disorders in males.

    a. homosexuality

    b. pre-morbid obesity

    c. being teased as a child

    d. subgroups who need to "make weight" in order to work

2. What are the DSM-IV-TR criteria for bulimia nervosa?

    a. frequent occurrence of episodes of binge-eating

    b. lack of control over eating

c. recurrent inappropriate behavior that is intended to prevent weight gain

d. person's self-evaluation has to be excessively influenced by weight and body shape

3. Mary was diagnosed with an eating disorder, anorexia nervosa. She sought treatment for the disorder. Based on the research done by Lowe in 2001, what can you say about her recovery possibilities?

Very difficult to treat—Lowe's study looked at outcomes 21 years after patients sought treatment. He found that 16% of women with anorexia nervosa had died from starvation or suicide, 10% were still suffering from anorexia 21% partially recovered, and 51% were fully recovered. Mary has a little better than 50% chance of recovery.

4. Explain how the study done by Anne Becker of the women in Fiji illustrates the impact the media has on thinness. In early 1990s when Becker was first conducting her research, fat was associated with being strong, capable of work, and being kind and generous. Being thin was considered negative, thought to be sickly, incompetent, or having received poor treatment. There was no such thing as an eating disorder. In 1998, when Becker returned to Fiji, television has been introduced to Fiji, and the people were able to see such shows as *Beverly Hills 90210* and *Melrose Place.* The young women were expressing concerns about their weight and dislike of their bodies and dieting in earnest. This research provides anecdotal information about how the introduction of Western values about thinness might insinuate themselves into different cultures.

PRACTICE TESTS

Q#	TEST 1	TEST 2	TEST 3
1	D	C	A

2	C	D	B
3	A	D	C
4	C	A	D
5	A	D	B
6	C	A	C
7	A	D	C
8	C	A	B
9	B	A	C
10	A	D	D

COMPREHENSIVE PRACTICE TEST

Q#	MULTIPLE CHOICE	T/F
1	B	F
2	C	T
3	D	T
4	C	F
5	B	T
6	D	T
7	C	T
8	D	F
9	C	T
10	A	T
11	C	F
12	D	
13	D	
14	C	
15	A	
16	D	

ESSAY QUESTIONS
(Your answer should contain the following points.)

1. Discuss the medical complications of anorexia nervosa and bulimia nervosa.

Anorexia

a. hair thins; nails and hair become brittle

b. skin becomes dry and downy hair grows on face neck, arms, back and legs (langugo)

c. skin develops a yellowish tinge

d. hands and feet feel cold

e. low blood pressure

f. Vitamin B1 deficiency, which could lead to depression and cognitive changes

g. sudden death from heart arrhythmias

h. low levels of potassium can result in kidney damage and renal failure

Bulimia

a. purging can cause electrolyte imbalances and hypokalemia

b. risk for heart abnormalities

c. damage to heart muscle caused by ipecac used to induce vomiting

d. callouses on their hands from sticking their fingers down their throat

e. damage to teeth from acid in stomach when throwing up

f. mouth ulcers and dental cavities

g. small red dots around eyes, caused by the pressure of throwing up

h. swollen parotid glands, caused by repeatedly vomiting

2. Describe Garner's set-point theory and its relation to eating disorders.

Weight is physiologically regulated around a weight that the body tries to defend, a set-point. If a person tries to radically deviate from this weight, there are "physiological compensations" that take place in order to restore the weight. Hunger drive is an example of a compensation. The more weight a person loses, the greater the hunger levels. This is an attempt to encourage eating, gain weight and return to a state of equilibrium. People with anorexia think about food all the time and try very hard to suppress their hunger. Chronic dieting increases likelihood of person having periods of binging impulses—eating very high-caloric foods.

Use IT OR LOSE IT

Many researchers believe that constant exposure to media images of extremely thin models may cause some young women to develop eating disorders in the pursuit of unrealistic body weights.

CRISS-CROSS ANSWERS
Across
7. Body Mass Index
8. serotonin

Down
1. anorexia nervosa
2. bulimia nervosa
3. obesity
4. set-point theory
5. negative affect
6. perfectionism

Chapter 10: Health Problems and Behavior

BEFORE YOU READ

In the past, people tended to see the mind and body as separate entities. However, in the latter half of the 20th century this distinction began to break down as the lines distinguishing mental and physical illness started to blur, and we realized that thoughts can impact illness and vice versa. It is now clear that stress, and negative emotions including anger, anxiety, and depression can predispose people to illness, and impact the severity of their illness and the course of their recovery. Conversely, we know that positive emotions such as hope and optimism can promote health, diminish the impact of illness and even predict such things as recovery time following surgery. The implications of these relationships are explored in regard to cardiovascular disease. Clearly, a better understanding of how the brain and body work together to control illness, and of how psychological factors impact this relationship will help us to identify those at risk for illness, and to treat those experiencing poor health. The emerging field of positive psychology is also discussed.

- **PSYCHOLOGICAL FACTORS IN HEALTH AND DISEASE**
  Stress and the Stress Response
  Physiological Aspects of Stress
  Stress and the Immune System
  Psychoneuroimmunology
  Lifestyle Factors in Health and Illness
  Health Attitudes and Coping Resources

- **CARDIOVASCULAR DISEASE**
  Hypertension Coronary Heart Disease
  What Psychological Factors are Implicated in Cardiovascular Disease?

- **GENERAL CAUSAL FACTORS IN PHYSICAL ILLNESS AND DISEASE**

Genetic Factors

Psychosocial Factors

Sociocultural Factors

• TREATMENTS AND OUTCOMES

Biological Interventions

Psychosocial Interventions

Sociocultural Interventions

• UNRESOLVED ISSUES:

Does Clinical Practice Ignore the Doctor-Patient Relationship?

OBJECTIVES

After reading this chapter, you should be able to:

1. Explain how psychological problems can cause or affect medical problems, and how medical problems can cause or affect psychological problems.

2. Discuss how and why behavioral medicine extends our conception of disease beyond the traditional medical focus on physical breakdown of organs and organs systems.

3. Explain the role cortisol and other hormones play in stress reaction, and why extended contact can be problematic over the longer term.

4. Describe the function of the immune system, and the specialized roles of B-cells, T-cells and macrophages.

5. Explain the interactions between the nervous system, the immune system, and behavior

6. Explain what cytokines are, how they work.

7. Explain why negative emotional states can impair the function of the immune system and the cardiovascular system.

8. Discuss damaging habits and lifestyles—such as smoking—and how they enhance risk for physical disease.

9. Explain the relationships between chronic negative emotions—such as anger, hostility, anxiety, and depression—and physical illness.

10. Discuss positive psychology as an emerging field associated with health and well-being.

11. Explain why a patient's physical factors—such as genetic vulnerabilities and possible organ weaknesses—need to be considered during treatment regardless of strong evidence of psychological contributions to its development.

12. Explain cognitive-behavior therapy's promise in helping an individual's coping resources for managing stressful life circumstances.

13. Describe the Positive Psychology movement and how it relates to health.

AS YOU READ

Answers can be found in the Answer Key at the end of the chapter.

KEY WORDS

Each of the words below is important in understanding the concepts presented in this chapter. Write the definition next to each of the words.

Term	Page	Definition
antigens		
b-cell		
behavioral medicine		
biofeedback		
chronic fatigue syndrome		
cortisol		
cytokines		
essential		

hypertension		
health psychology		
HPS axis		
immunosupression		
observational study		
placebo effect		
positive psychology		
psychoneuroimmun ology		
t-cell		
type A behavior pattern		

MATCHING

Match the following terms with their appropriate definitions.

Terms

_____ psychoneuroimmunology

_____ health psychology

_____ behavioral medicine

_____ positive psychology

_____ biofeedback

_____ Type A behavior pattern

_____ Type B behavior pattern

Definition

A. a focus on human traits and resources that might have direct implications for our physical and mental well-being

B. broad interdisciplinary approach involving many disciplines

C. focus on altering physiological states

D. relaxed, more laid-back, and less time-pressured people

E. the study of the interactions between behavior, the nervous system, and the immune system

F. excessive competitive drive, extreme commitment to work, impatience or time urgency, and hostility

G. subspecialty which deals with psychology's contributions to diagnosis, treatment, and prevention of psychological components of physical problems

SHORT ANSWERS

Provide brief answers to the following questions.

1. Cortisol is a good hormone to have around in an emergency. But there is also a down side to cortisol. Explain. (pp. 325-26)

2. Optimism and its opposite, hopelessness, can have a significant impact on one's health. Explain. (pp. 330-33)

3. Explain the prevalence of hypertension in the African-American community in the United States. (p. 334)

4. What is the importance of asking yourself, "In the past month, have I felt so sad, discouraged, hopeless or had so many problems that I

wondered if anything was worthwhile?" (p. 337)

5. Why should depression and CHD be linked? (p. 337)

AFTER YOU READ

Answers can be found in the Answer Key at the end of the chapter.

PRACTICE TESTS

Take the following three multiple-choice tests to see how much you have comprehended from the chapter. Each represents roughly one-third of the chapter. As you study the chapter, use these to check your progress.

PRACTICE TEST NUMBER 1

1. The emphasis of _____B_____ is on the role that psychological factors play
   in the occurrence, maintenance and prevention of physical illness. (p. 344)
   a. health attitude
   b. behavioral medicine
   c. psychoneuroimmunology
   d. biofeedback

2. Antigens in the blood stream are searched out and destroyed by (p. 348)
   a. B-cells.
   b. T-cells.
   c. macrophages.
   d. all of the above.

3. Gastric ulcers (p. 346)
   a. are caused by purely psychological origins.
   b. are caused by the Helicobacter pylori bacterium.
   c. may have psychological or physical, as well as common lifestyle factors.

d. are one of the great mysteries of life.

4. A person who is depressed because of an underactive thyroid would be a victim of (p. 346)

a. Mental Disorder Due to a General Medical Condition.

b. Psychological Factor Affecting a General Medical Condition.

c. extreme bad luck.

d. negative affects.

5. Cortisol (p. 347)

a. is necessary in an emergency, as it prepares the body for a fight or flight response.

b. can damage brain cells, especially in the hippocampus, if not shut off.

c. may cause an allergic reaction if allowed to accumulate.

d. a and b.

6. Long-term stress (p. 351)

a. might compromise the body's ability to heal and fight infections.

b. is being linked to diminished immune reactivity.

c. proves to be a good thing, as the body becomes stronger by dealing with it.

d. a and b.

7. The immune system has been likened to a police force, in that (p. 348)

a. if it is too weak, it cannot function effectively, and the body succumbs to damage from invading viruses and bacteria.

b. if it is too strong and not selective, it can turn on its own normal cells.

c. it protects and serves.

d. a. and b.

8. Negative emotions _____ the power of the killer cell cytotoxicity to

eradicate an antigen (p. 350)

a. have no affect on

b. greatly increase

c. significantly diminish

d. neutralize

9. Under specific conditions, immunosuppression can be (p. 364)

a. easily turned on or off at will.

b. classically conditioned.

c. controlled with music.

d. neutralized.

10. Conditions demonstrated to be associated with diminished immune function

include (p. 351)

a. sleep deprivation.

b. space flight.

c. death of a spouse.

d. all of the above.

PRACTICE TEST NUMBER 2

1. Lifestyle factors—habits or behavior patterns presumable under our own

control—play _____ role in three of the leading causes of death

in this country: coronary heart disease, automobile accidents, and alcohol-

related deaths. (p. 354)

a. no significant

b. a major

c. a small, but growing

d. a cameo

2. Which of the following is NOT a clinical manifestation of coronary heart disease?   (p. 356)

    a. angio myopathy.

    b. myocardial infarction

    c. angina pectoris

    d. disturbance of the heart's electrical conduction

3. Now that optimism is known to affect health (p. 352)

    a. many surgeons will delay a major operation until they are convinced that a patient is reasonably optimistic about the outcome.

    b. in an everyday sense, it seems to serve as a buffer against disease.

    c. people with too little optimism experience a psychological sense of helplessness.

    d. all of the above.

4. Chronic anger and hostility (p. 353)

    a. can be risk factors for coronary heart disease and death.

    b. typically have little effect on a person's health.

    c. are characteristic of type B personality.

    d. promote health

5. Neuroticism, anxiety, and depression are known as _____ emotions. (p. 369)

    a. empowering

    b. negative

    c. hurtful

    d. powerful

6. Positive psychology has shown the health benefits of (p. 369)

    a. humor and laughter.

b. positive affectivity.

c. forgiving people.

d. all of the above.

7. Stress causes the normal heartbeat, regular pulse, and low blood pressure to (p. 346)

a. to increase temporarily

b. to decrease temporarily

c. to cycle rapidly

d. to remain stable

8. High blood pressure is insidious and dangerous, due to the fact that it (p. 355)

a. puts a strain on the heart and cardiovascular system

b. underactivates the heart and cardiovascular system

c. impedes breathing

d. none of the above

9. People who _____ have the lowest blood pressure. (p. 356)

a. express their anger

b. suppress their anger

c. use their anger constructively

d. both a and b.

10. Investigating patients who had had heart attacks, researchers found that clinically depressed patients were _____ more likely to die in the next six months than were their nondepressed counterparts. (p. 357)

a. no

b. two times

c. five times

d. forty-two times

PRACTICE TEST NUMBER 3

1. A study that followed 1,500 men and women with no prior history of heart disease found that people who had suffered major depression were _____more likely to have had a heart attack. (p. 358)

    a. one and one-half times

    b. two times

    c. four times

    d. not

2. People with low levels of emotional support (unmarried, small social network, lack of friends) are _____ likely to develop CHD, _____ likely to have another cardiac event, and _____ likely to die over the next five years. (p. 359)

    a. more, three times more, three times more

    b. less, not, not

    c. just as, twice as, more

    d. not, not, less

3. Mental stress is known to (p. 359)

    a. raise systolic blood pressure.

    b. cause an elevation in epinephrine.

    c. reduce the oxygen supply to the heart muscle.

    d. all of the above.

4. African Americans are at greater risk for high blood pressure because, as a group (p.356)

    a. they are less likely to exercise than other ethnic groups.

    b. their bodies process the enzyme Renin differently.

    c. heavy salt use is their dietary preference.

    d. all of the above.

5. Marital problems or divorce have been linked to _____.

    (p. 362)

    a. high death rates

    b. decreased immune functions

    c. depression

    d. all of the above

6. People who have a good social support system (p. 362)

    a. have lower blood pressure.

    b. have higher natural killer cell activity in the blood.

    c. hardly ever get sick.

    d. a and b.

7. An appropriate treatment for CHD might include (p. 365)

    a. lipid lowering medications.

    b. anxiolytic (anxiety reducing) medications.

    c. anticoagulants.

    d. all of the above.

8. In the first study of emotional disclosure in people with rheumatoid arthritis, it
    was found that those who had engaged in emotional disclosure had
    _____ physical dysfunction than people in the control condition.
    (p. 365)

    a. no difference in

    b. much more

    c. significantly less

    d. slightly less

9. The benefits of emotional disclosure include

(p. 365)

a. emotional catharsis or "blowing off steam."

b. having the opportunity to re-think and re-appraise their problems.

c. neither a or b.

d. a and b.

10. Biofeedback (p. 366)

a. has been a glowing success in the treatment of negative events.

b. generally has failed to live up to the enthusiasm it originally generated.

c. may prove to be effective in the control of musculoskeletal pain.

d. b and c.

COMPREHENSIVE PRACTICE TEST

The following tests are designed to give you an idea of how well you understood the entire chapter. There are three different types of tests: multiple-choice, true-false, and essay.

MULTIPLE-CHOICE

1. It is becoming apparent that (p. 346)

a. medical conditions are usually entirely physical in origin.

b. psychosomatic disorders neve involve real symptoms.

c. psychological problems can be directly related to medical problems.

d. a and b.

2. Studies examining the association between stress and immune functioning established an association between the occurrence of stressful circumstances and (p. 348)

a. immune activity

b. diminished immune reactivity

c. change in liver function

d. denial

3. If a patient hears voices which tell him to refuse dialysis for his kidney disease his DSM-IV diagnosis might be a/an (p. 346)

a. alien abduction.

b. uncooperative disorder.

c. Mental Disorder Due to a General Medical Condition.

d. Psychological Factor Affecting a General Medical Condition.

4. A stress response involves biological responses, including (p. 346)

a. the hypothalamus, which stimulates the sympathetic nervous system, which stimulates the adrenal glands to secrete adrenaline and noradrenaline.

b. an increase in heart rate and a preparation to metabolize glucose more rapidly.

c. the pituitary gland secretes adrenocorticotropic hormone, which activates the adrenal cortex into producing the stress hormone called cortisol.

d. all of the above.

5. While stress has not been found to cause specific physical diseases, it (p. 347)

a. is becoming a key underlying theme in our understanding of the development and course of virtually all organic illness.

b. may serve as a predisposing, precipitating, or reinforcing factor in the causal pattern.

c. may interfere with the body's normal defensive forces or immunological system.

d. all of the above.

6. In studies of groups of uninfected high-risk and early stage HIV-infected men, it was found that (p. 350)

   a. behavioral interventions, such as aerobic exercise, had positive psychological and immunocompetence effects.

   b. depressed mood was associated with enhanced HIV-1 activity.

   c. psychological depression compromised immune function.

   d. all of the above.

7. Psychoneuroimmunology, the study of the interactions between behavior, the nervous system, and the immune system (p. 351)

   a. has shown that the immune system is not responsive only to external challenges.

   b. the nervous system and the immune system communicate.

   c. the brain influences the immune system and the immune system influences the brain.

   d. all of the above.

8. Research has shown that depression (or negative affect) (p. 353)

   a. is related to compromised immune function.

   b. causes stress in itself

   c. is reliably associated with lowered numbers of white cells

   d. all of the above.

9. Negative emotions (p. 353)

   a. can be damaging to our health.

   b. are associated with measurable and undesirable changes in immune function.

   c. are associated with the development of coronary heart disease, in men and women and to delay recovery from surgery.

   d. all of the above.

10. In 1998, the number of sudden cardiac deaths in the United States in people
    ages 15 to 34 was (p. 332)
    a. 9.
    b. 77.
    c. 467.
    d. 3,000.

11. Which of the following emotions is most closely related to coronary artery
    deterioration and development of heart disease? (p.357)
    a. hostility
    b. competitiveness
    c. impatience
    d. impulsivity

12. In a two-year study of 34,000 male professionals with panic disorder,
    agoraphobia, and generalized anxiety, men with the highest levels of
    phobic anxiety were _____likely to have a fatal heart attack and
    _____ likely to suffer sudden cardiac death than were men with
    the lowest levels. (p. 359)
    a. not, less
    b. three times more, six times more
    c. 1.414 times more, 1.732 times more
    d. 1.414 times less, 1.732 times less

13. Genetic contributions to disease may involve (p. 361)
    a. an underlying physical vulnerability for acquiring a disease.
    b. the psychological make-up of the individual and his/her stress
    tolerance.
    c. an interaction between a and b.
    d. all of the above.

14. Optimism has been shown to (p. 352)

    a. have no affect on recovery from surgery

    b. to lengthen the amount of time required to recover from surgery

    c. to decrease the amount of time required to recover from surgery

    d. none of the above

15. Biofeedback combines relaxation with information about

    a. physiological responses

    b. Meditation

    c. Behavior therapy

    d. Emotional disclosure

TRUE – FALSE

1. T / F The ailments to which people are most vulnerable—whether physical, psychological, or both—are determined in no small part by who we are, where we live, and how we live. (p. 344)

2. T / F The "fight-or-flight response" involves primarily the sympathetic division of the autonomic nervous system. (p. 346)

3. T / F Stress appears to speed up the onset or increase the severity of a disorder, and to interfere with the body's immunological defenses and other homeostatic repair functions. (p. 344)

4. T / F The immune system and the nervous system are separate, closed systems that operate independently of each other. (p. 351)

5. T / F Depression has little or no effect on the immune system. (p. 351)

6. T / F Stress has been shown to slow down the healing of wounds by as much as 24-40%. (p. 351)

7. T / F It is easy for people to make lifestyle changes. (p. 352)

8. T / F Had it not been for the placebo effect, the medical profession, as we know it, might not have survived to the twentieth century, because until the early 1900s, medical practitioners had little else to offer disease sufferers. (p. 354)

9. T / F Heart attack patients who are depressed at the time of their heart attacks or shortly afterward show a greatly increased risk for future coronary events and cardiac deaths. (p. 357)

10. T / F Stress does not have to be extreme or severe in order to have potentially lethal consequences. (p. 359)

11. T / F Some physical disorders may be acquired, maintained, or both in much the same way as other behavior patterns. (p. 364)

ESSAY QUESTIONS

1. Chronic fatigue syndrome can leave a person physically exhausted for months or even years. Discuss this disorder.

2. Discuss the behavioral medicine approach to physical illness.

WEB LINKS TO ITEMS OR CONCEPTS FOUND IN CHAPTER 10

Clinical assessment

      bioinformatics.weizmann.ac.il/cytokine/

      health.yahoo.com/health/encyclopedia/000818/0.html

      www.uth.tmc.edu/schools/med/surgery/organ_transplant/

      www.ash-us.org/

      www.jhypertension.com/

      www.phassociation.org/

      www.mco.edu/whl/

      www.cdc.gov/nchs/fastats/hyprtens.htm

USE IT OR LOSE IT

Provide an answer to the thought question below, knowing that there is more than one way to respond. Possible answers are presented in the Answer Key.

If you were told that your child had Attention Deficit Hyperactivity Disorder would you feel comfortable giving them a stimulant such as Ritalin to help control his/her behavior?

CRISS-CROSS

Now that you know all there is to know about this chapter, here's your opportunity to put that knowledge to work.

CRISS-CROSS CLUES

Across

7. broad, interdisciplinary approach of physical disorders thought to have psychosocial factors as a partial cause

10. study of interactions among behavior, the nervous system, and the immune system

Down

1. chemical messengers in the blood that appear to be of crucial importance for health

2. hypertension for which there is no known cause

3. a patient who believes a treatment is going to be effective and is likely to improve, even if the treatment has no effect

4. a leukocyte that matures in the thymus

5. a field that deals with psychology's contributions to diagnosis, treatment, and prevention

6. a treatment based on altering physiological states

8. a compromising of the body's immune system to the possible detriment of one's health

9. foreign bodies (viruses, bacteria, and others) in one's body

Puzzle created with Puzzlemaker at DiscoverySchool.com

ANSWERS TO TEST QUESTIONS - CHAPTER 10

MATCHING

Terms

E. psychoneuroimmunology
G. health psychology
B. behavioral medicine
A. positive psychology
C. biofeedback
F. Type A behavior pattern
I. Type B behavior pattern

SHORT ANSWERS
(Your answer should contain the following points.)

1. Cortisol:
   a. prepares the body for the fight or flight response, inhibits the innate immune system…
   b. If the cortisol response is not shut off, it can damage brain cells.

2. a. Hopelessness can accelerate the progression of atherosclerosis, the underlying process leading to heart attacks and strokes.
   b. Optimism seems to serve as a buffer against disease.
   c. People with too little optimism experience a psychological sense of helplessness.

3. There is a probably a higher prevalence of hypertension in African Americans because of:
   a. the stresses of inner-city life, poverty, and explicit racial prejudice.
   b. diet. African-American women are more likely to be overweight
   c. high salt use in the diet, and blacks, as a group, excessively retain ingested sodium.
   d. lower likelihood to exercise as a group.

4. a. Depressed people may engage in more behaviors known to put people at risk—not eating well, exercising, or smoking, etc.
   b. Depression may be linked to CHD through biochemical mechanisms, such as elevated levels of cortisol and norepinephrine.

PRACTICE TESTS

#	TEST 1	TEST 2	TEST 3
1	B	B	C
2	D	A	A
3	C	D	D
4	A	A	D
5	D	B	D
6	D	D	D
7	D	A	D
8	C	A	C
9	B	C	D
10	D	C	D

COMPREHENSIVE PRACTICE TEST

Q#	MULTIPLE CHOICE	T/F
1	C	T
2	B	T
3	D	T
4	D	F
5	D	F
6	D	T
7	D	F
8	D	T
9	D	T
10	D	T
11	A	T
12	B	
13	D	
14	C	
15	A	

ESSAY QUESTIONS
(Your answer should contain the following points.)

1. Chronic fatigue syndrome:
   a. Often begins with sudden flu-like illness or similar
   b. Debilitating fatigue that cannot be explained medically

c. Fluctuating disability, may be bedridden for months
d. Unremitting fever, chills, soaking sweats, acute light sensitivity, balance and
cognitive problems.

2. Behavioral medicine approach to physical illness considers:
a. The psychological factors that may predispose an individual to physical illness
b. The ways in which the negative effects of stress can be reduced or buffered by personal resources
c. The biological mechanisms by which human physiology is altered by stressors
d. The psychological processes involved in health choices individuals make
e. The factors that determine compliance with sound medical advice
f. The effectiveness of psychological measures in altering unhealthy lifestyles

Use it or Lose it

This question can be answered in either the negative or the affirmative. Key factors include the extent of the child's symptoms, whether or not they have responded to behavioral or other techniques, and whether they experience side effects from the medication.

CRISS-CROSS ANSWERS
Across
7. behavioral medicine
10. psychoneuroimmunology

Down
1. cytokines
2. essential hypertension
3. placebo effect
4. T cells
5. health psychology
6. biofeedback
8. immunosuppression
9. antigen

Chapter 11: Personality Disorders

BEFORE YOU READ

Personality disorders differ from other mental health diagnoses because they are ingrained "lifestyles" or characteristic patterns that are maladaptive and persist throughout the individual's lifetime. These Axis-II disorders are grouped into three clusters on the basis of similarities of features among the disorders. Cluster A includes paranoid, schizoid, and schizotypal personality disorders, which are all characterized by odd or eccentric behavior. Cluster B is made up of disorders which tend to be dramatic and emotional, and includes histrionic, narcissistic, antisocial, and borderline personality disorder. Cluster C is made up of disorders which involve anxiety and fearfulness such as avoidant, dependent, and obsessive-compulsive personality disorders. Unfortunately, there is still disagreement about how best to define these disorders, and they can co-occur with Axis I disorders as well as with each other, further complicating diagnosis. Nevertheless, new treatment approaches are emerging, and showing some success with specific personality disorders. Antisocial Personality Disorder is given extra attention in the chapter, since it is perhaps the best understood, and most socially disruptive of the disorders.

- **CLINICAL FEATURES OF PERSONALITY DISORDERS**
    DSM-IV-TR's Five Criteria
- **DIFFICULTIES DOING RESEARCH ON PERSONALITY DISORDERS**
    Difficulties in Diagnosing Personality Disorders
    Difficulties in Studying the Causes of Personality Disorders
- **CATEGORIES OF PERSONALITY DISORDERS**
    Paranoid Personality Disorder
    Schizoid Personality Disorder
    Schizotypal Personality Disorder
    Histrionic Personality Disorder
    Narcissistic Personality Disorder

Antisocial Personality Disorder

Borderline Personality Disorder

Avoidant Personality Disorder

Dependent Personality Disorder

Obsessive-Compulsive Personality Disorder

Provisional Categories of Personality Disorder in DSM-IV-TR

General Sociocultural Causal Factors for Personality Disorders

- **TREATMENTS AND OUTCOMES**

Adapting Therapeutic Techniques to Specific Personality Disorders

Treating Borderline Personality Disorder

Treating Other Personality Disorders

- **ANTISOCIAL PERSONALITY AND PSYCHOPATHY**

Psychopathy and ASPD

The Clinical Picture in Psychopathy and Antisocial Personality

A Developmental Perspective on Psychopathy and Antisocial Personality

Treatments and Outcomes in Psychopathic and Antisocial Personality

- **UNRESOLVED ISSUES:**

Axis II of DSM-IV

OBJECTIVES

After reading this chapter, you should be able to:

1. List the clinical features of the personality disorders and the problems associated with diagnosis.

2. Compare and contrast the different types of personality disorders and identify the three clusters into which most personality disorders are grouped.

3. Summarize what is known about the biological, psychological, and sociocultural causal factors of personality disorders.

4. Discuss the difficulties of treating individuals with personality disorders and describe the approaches to treatment that have been tried.

5. Compare and contrast the DSM-IV concept of antisocial personality and Cleckley's concept of psychopathy.

6. List the clinical features of psychopathy and antisocial personality.

7. Summarize the biological, psychosocial, and sociocultural causal factors in psychopathy and antisocial personality and the integrated developmental perspective.

8. Explain why it is difficult to treat psychopathy and antisocial personality and describe the most promising of the as yet unproven approaches to treatment.

9. Discuss some of the new treatment options for Bipolar Disorder.

AS YOU READ

Answers can be found in the Answer Key at the end of the chapter.

KEY WORDS

Each of the words below is important in understanding the concepts presented in this Chapter. Write the definition next to each of the words.

Term	Page	Definition
antisocial personality disorder (ASPD)		
borderline personality disorder (BPD)		
avoidant personality disorder		
dependent personality disorder		
depressive personality disorder		
histrionic personality disorder		
narcissistic personality disorder		

obsessive-compulsive personality disorder (OCPD)		
paranoid personality disorder		
passive-aggressive personality disorder		
psychopathy or sociopathy		
personality disorder or character disorder		
schizoid personality disorder		
schizotypal personality disorder		
temperament		

WHO'S WHO AND WHAT'S WHAT—MATCHING

Match the following personality disorders with the appropriate description.

Personality Disorder

_____ Paranoid

_____ Schizoid

_____ Schizotypal

_____ Histrionic

_____ Narcissistic

_____ Antisocial

_____ Borderline

_____ Avoidant

_____ Dependent

_____ Obsessive-Compulsive

_____ Passive Aggressive

_____ Depressive

Description

A. hypersensitivity to rejection, shyness, insecurity

B. overconcern with attractiveness; self-dramatization

C. impulsive, drastic mood shifts, self-mutilation

D. suspicious and mistrustful; blames others

E. persistent unhappiness or dejection; feelings of inadequacy, guilt, and self-criticism

F. lacks desire to form attachments; poor relationships

G. negative attitudes, passive resistance; complaining, sullen, and argumentative

H. grand preoccupation with self, lack of empathy

I. excessive concern with order, rules; perfectionistic

J. peculiar thought patterns; odd perception & speech

K. lacking morals or ethics, deceitful, manipulative

L. discomfort being alone, indecisive, difficulty ending relationships

SHORT ANSWERS

Provide brief answers to the following questions.

1. List the 5 criteria used in DSM-IV-TR to define personality disorders.

2. Discuss the possible biological and psychological causal factors for personality disorders.

PERSONALITY DISORDER

Personality disorders discussed in the text cover a lot of ground and can leave you confused. As you discover items while studying jot down facts and descriptive words for later reference.

CLUSTER A

Characteristics of Cluster A disorders:

Paranoid personality disorder

Characteristics:

Causal Factors:

Treatment or hope for treatment:

Miscellaneous points or terms:

Schizoid personality disorder

Characteristics:

Causal Factors:

Treatment or hope for treatment:

Miscellaneous points or terms:

Schizotypal personality disorder

Characteristics:

Causal Factors:

Treatment or hope for treatment:

Miscellaneous points or terms

CLUSTER B

Characteristics of Cluster B disorders:

Histrionic personality disorder

Characteristics:

Causal Factors:

Treatment or hope for treatment:

Miscellaneous points or terms:

Narcissistic personality disorder

Characteristics:

Causal Factors:

Treatment or hope for treatment:

Miscellaneous points or terms:

Antisocial personality disorder

Characteristics:

Causal Factors:

Treatment or hope for treatment:

Miscellaneous points or terms:

Borderline personality disorder

Characteristics:

Causal Factors:

Treatment or hope for treatment:

Miscellaneous points or terms:

CLUSTER C

Characteristics of Cluster C disorders:

Avoidant personality disorder

Characteristics:

Causal Factors:

Treatment or hope for treatment:

Miscellaneous points or terms:

Dependent personality disorder

Characteristics:

Causal Factors:

Treatment or hope for treatment:

Miscellaneous points or terms:

Obsessive-compulsive personality disorder

Characteristics:

Causal Factors:

Treatment or hope for treatment:

Miscellaneous points or terms:

PROVISIONAL CATEGORY

Passive-aggressive personality disorder

Characteristics:

Causal Factors:

Treatment or hope for treatment:

Miscellaneous points or terms:

Depressive personality disorder

Characteristics:

Causal Factors:

Treatment or hope for treatment:

Miscellaneous points or terms:

ANTISOCIAL PERSONALITY AND PSYCHOPATHY

Antisocial personality

Characteristics:

Causal Factors:

Treatment or hope for treatment:

Miscellaneous points or terms:

Psychopathy

Characteristics:

Causal Factors:

Treatment or hope for treatment:

Miscellaneous points or terms:

3. Many studies have found that people with borderline personality disorder report a large number of negative, even traumatic, events in childhood, including abuse and neglect, separation and loss, and parental psychopathology. However, it is difficult to say childhood trauma plays a causal role. Why?

4. Discuss the difference between a loner with schizoid personality disorder and the loner who is avoidant.)

THE DOCTOR IS IN...PSYCHIATRIC HELP—5¢

Read the following scenarios and diagnose the client. Remember to look carefully at the criteria for the disorder before you make a decision as to the diagnosis. Make a list of other information you might need to help you understand the causal factors.

Helen, a 31-year-old waitress, comes to the office of a male therapist, seeking help trying to understand why she doesn't have a relationship. She tells him about her life in a very dramatic and lively manner and makes flirtatious comments like, "I can't understand why no one likes me— what I wouldn't do to have some cute guy like you just sweep me off my feet." How would Helen be diagnosed and why?

2. Jack, a computer software engineer, comes to your office because he is having problems at work and may lose his job if things don't change. When you ask him what has happened, he looks at you suspiciously, and asks you who else you have been talking to. You assure him you haven't talked to anyone. He tells you that others at work are talking about him behind his back, and he knows they are responsible for his having to see a therapist. Jack tells you he has no friends at work or any place else. How would you diagnose Jack and why?

3. Pam sits in your office not saying much and having a difficulty talking about herself. She manages to tell you that she is alone much of the time—something she doesn't like—and would like to feel comfortable meeting people. She is extremely self–conscious and

avoids situations in which she might be criticized or rejected. How would you diagnose Pam and why?

4. As a therapist, what issues will you face in treating the three patients above?

AFTER YOU READ

Answers can be found in the Answer Key at the end of the chapter.

PRACTICE TESTS

Take the following three multiple-choice tests to see how much you have comprehended from the chapter. Each represents roughly one-third of the chapter. As you study the chapter, use these to check your progress.

PRACTICE TEST NUMBER 1

1. Personality disorders were formerly known as (p. 373)

a. fatal flaws.

b. character disorders.

c. personality patterns.

d. none of the above.

2. Studies estimate that _____ people meet criteria for at least one personality disorder at some point in their lifetime. (p. 373)

a. about 9 out of 10

b. fewer than 1% of

c. about 13% of

d. 42%

3. Most personality traits have been found to be (p. 375)

a. difficult to maintain.

b. moderately heritable.

c. difficult to explain.

d. all of the above.

4. Many studies suggest that _____ may be an important causes for several different personality disorders. (p. 376)

a. genes

b. private schooling

c. early emotional, physical, and sexual abuse

d. understanding the psychobiological substrate

5. People with _____ personality disorder often bear grudges, are unwilling to forgive perceived insults and slightest, and are quick to react with anger. (p. 376)

a. schizoid

b. paranoid

c. narcissistic

d. antisocial

6. People with _____ personality disorder rarely experience strong positive or negative emotions, are unable to express their feelings, appear cold and distant, and can be classified as loners or introverts. (p. 377)

a. schizoid

b. paranoid

c. narcissistic

d. antisocial

7. People with _____ personality disorder are excessively introverted and show cognitive and perceptual distortions and eccentricities in their

communication and behavior. (p. 379)

a. schizoid

b. schizotypal

c. borderline

d. antisocial

8. People with _____ personality disorder exhibit excessive attention-seeking behavior, are dramatic and extraverted, and tend to feel unappreciated if they are not the center of attention. (p. 380).

a. histrionic

b. narcissistic

c. borderline

d. antisocial

9. People with _____ personality disorder show an exaggerated sense of self-importance, a preoccupation with being admired, and a lack of empathy for the feelings of others. (p. 383)

a. histrionic

b. narcissistic

c. borderline

d. schizoid

10. Narcissistic personality disorder may be more frequently observed in (p. 384)

a. older persons.

b. men than in women.

c. women than in men.

d. television news anchors.

PRACTICE TEST NUMBER 2

1. People with _____ personality disorder continually violate the rights of others through deceitful, aggressive, or antisocial behavior, without remorse. (p. 395)

a. schizoid

b. schizotypal

c. borderline

d. antisocial

2. _____ personality disorder is characterized by impulsivity and instability in interpersonal relationships, self-image, and moods. (p. 385)

a. Schizoid

b. Schizotypal

c. Borderline

d. Histrionic

3. People with _____ personality disorder display extreme affective instability, and self-destructive behaviors, such as gambling, sexual promiscuity, and suicide attempts. (p. 385)

a. schizoid

b. schizotypal

c. borderline

d. histrionic

4. Overall, about _____ of patients with borderline personality disorder reported some type of childhood abuse or neglect. (p. 387)

a. 1.732%

b. 20%

c. half

d. 90%

5. A study (Paris, 1999) suggests that borderline personality disorder may be more prevalent in our society today than in the past and in many other cultures, because of (p. 388)

a. marital discord.

b. the weakening of the family structure in our society.

c. the increase of violence in entertainment and the media.

d. all of the above.

6. People with _____ personality disorder have a pattern of extreme social inhibition and introversion, leading to lifelong patterns of limited social relationships. (p. 388)

a. avoidant

b. schizotypal

c. borderline

d. antisocial

7. People with _____ personality disorder show an extreme need to be taken care of, which leads to clinging and submissive behavior. (p. 390)

a. avoidant

b. dependent

c. borderline

d. obsessive-compulsive

8. Dependent personality disorder occurs in about 2-4% of the population and is (p. 390)

a. usually found east of the Mississippi.

b. found mostly in older men.

c. more common in women than men.

d. a product of domineering grandparents.

9. People with _____ personality disorder are characterized by the need for perfectionism and an excessive concern with maintaining order and control. (p. 391)

a. schizoid

b. schizotypal

c. obsessive-compulsive

d. histrionic

10. People with an obsessive-compulsive personality (p. 391)

a. believe they are helpless.

b. is quite rigid and stubborn.

c. have difficulty delegating tasks to others.

d. b and c.

PRACTICE TEST NUMBER 3

1. People diagnosed with _____ personality disorder show a pervasive pattern of passive resistance to demands in social or work situations, sometimes being highly critical or scornful of authority. (p. 392)

a. schizoid

b. passive-aggressive

c. obsessive-compulsive

d. histrionic

2. People whose usual mood state is characterized by unhappiness, gloominess, or dejection may be given the provisional diagnosis of _____ disorder. (p. 392)

a. avoidant

b. depressive

c. obsessive-compulsive

d. borderline

3. The treatment of borderline personality disorder using drugs is controversial because (p. 394)

a. victims become addicted rapidly.

b. it is so frequently associated with suicidal behavior.

c. drugs tend to cause them to "cross the border" and not return.

d. drugs tend to cause them to develop other disorders.

4. People diagnosed with _____ personality disorder persistently disregard and violate the rights of others through a combination of deceitful, aggressive, or antisocial behavior. (p. 395)

a. psychopathy

b. antisocial

c. obsessive-compulsive

d. borderline

5. The prevalence of antisocial personality disorder in the general population is estimated to be about _____% for males and _____% for females. (p. 396)

a. 3, 1

b. 33, 3

c. 3, 10

d. 50, 0

6. People diagnosed with _____ are characterized by callousness, selfishness, and an exploitative use of others, as well as being antisocial, impulsive, and socially deviant lifestyle. (p. 396)

a. psychopathy

b. antisocial

c. obsessive-compulsive

d. borderline

7. Released prison inmates who were diagnosed as psychopaths were estimated to be _____ than those without a psychopathy diagnosis. (pp. 396-397)

a. three times more likely to reoffend

b. four times more likely to reoffend violently

c. less likely to reoffend

d. a and b.

8. The probability that a child with a genetic or constitutional liability will develop conduct disorder, and later adult psychopathy is increased if their own parents (p. 404)

a. had poor and ineffective parenting skills.

b. exhibited antisocial behavior.

c. got divorced.

d. all of the above.

9. A "burned-out psychopath" is one who (p. 407)

a. died

b. had a bad reaction to electroshock therapy.

c. is an older, wiser person whose criminal activities have lessened after age 40.

d. had a bad reaction to drugs.

10. The best multifaceted cognitive-behaviorally oriented treatment programs (p. 407)

a. can cure 77% of antisocial personalities and 34% of psychopaths.

b. generally produce changes of only modest magnitude.

c. greatly help at least half of the patients.

d. have proven to only make things worse in the long run.

COMPREHENSIVE PRACTICE TEST

The following tests are designed to give you an idea of how well you understood the entire chapter. There are three different types of tests: multiple-choice, true-false, and essay.

MULTIPLE-CHOICE

1. In their study, Widiger and colleagues found that _____ patients who qualified for one personality disorder diagnosis also qualified for at least one more. (p. 375)

a. 45%

b. 22.6% of

c. 85% or

d. only a few

2. Which of the following is a provisional personality disorder in DSM? (p.392)

a. depressive disorder

b. avoidant disorder

c. schizotypal disorder

d. dictatorial disorder

3. Cluster A personality disorders are described as (p. 376)

a. odd/eccentric.

b. anxious/fearful.

c. erratic/dramatic.

d. all of the above.

4. To be considered an antisocial personality disorder, the pattern of behavior must have been occurring since the age of 15, and before age 15, the person must have shown (p.395)

a. destruction of property, deceitfulness or theft.

b. persistent patterns of aggression toward people or animals.

c. serious violation of rules at home or in school.

d. all of the above.

5. Approximately 20-40% of borderline personalities have cognitive symptoms that include (p. 386)

a. relatively short or transient episodes in which they appear to out of contact with reality.

b. experiencing delusions or other psychotic-like symptoms, such as hallucinations, paranoid ideas, body image distortions, or dissociative symptoms.

c. complaints about personal misfortunes or of being misunderstood and unappreciated.

d. a and b.

6. People with avoidant personality disorder (p. 387)

a. do not seek out other people but do not enjoy their aloneness.

b. have great anxiety due to their inability to relate comfortable to other people.

c. tend to be hypersensitive and may see ridicule or disparagement where none was intended.

d. all of the above.

7. A person with dependent personality disorder (p. 387)

a. may remain in an abusive relationship due to a fear that defending herself might cause her to lose her partner.

b. may not function well on his own.

c. has great difficulty making even simple everyday decisions due to a lack of self-confidence.

d. all of the above.

8. A person with the provisional diagnosis of passive-aggressive personality disorder (p. 392)

a. may not function well on her own.

b. often alternates between defiance and submission

c. believes that "I am completely helpless."

d. views himself as nearly perfect and in no need of change.

9. Personality disorders are generally very difficult to treat, in part, because (p. 393)

a. people suffering from these disorders view themselves as nearly perfect and in no need of change.

b. these are, by definition, enduring, pervasive, and inflexible patterns of behavior.

c. it is very difficult to get and keep the attention of persons suffering these disorders.

d. all of the above.

10. People who suffer from _____ personality disorder may experience transient psychotic symptoms, believe that they have magical powers, and may engage in magical rituals. (p. 377)

a. schizoid

b. paranoid

c. schizotypal

d. antisocial

11. Psychopaths are (p.398)

a. often charming, spontaneous, and likeable on first acquaintance.

b. deceitful and manipulative, callously using others to achieve their own ends.

c. prone to acting out impulses in remorseless and often senseless violence.

d. all of the above.

12. Psychopaths (p. 398)

a. seem to have good insight into other people's needs and weaknesses and are adept at exploiting them.

b. are irresponsible and unfaithful mates, being manipulative and exploitative in sexual relationships.

c. have learned to take, rather than earn, what they want and seldom forgo immediate pleasure for future gains and long-range goals.

d. all of the above.

13. _____ in childhood is the single best predictor of who develops an adult diagnosis of psychopathy or antisocial personality. (p. 403)

a. An absorption in computer games

b. Excess access to television, particularly violent television

c. The number of antisocial behaviors exhibited

d. Heavy metal and other violent and antisocial forms of music

14. The criminal activities of many people with ASPD declines after the age of _____, but the egocentric, callous, and exploitative dimension does not. (p. 407)

a. 25

b. 40

c. 60

d. 92

TRUE – FALSE

1 T / F   Personality disorder seems to stem from the development of inflexible and distorted personality and behavioral patterns. (p. 373)

2. T / F People with mild personality disorders generally function adequately, but may be seen by others as troublesome or eccentric. (p. 373)

3. T / F Personality disorders are easily changed. (p. 393)

4 T / F Personality disorders rarely overlap. (p. 409)

5. T / F Histrionic personality disorder is estimated at 20-30% and never occurs in women. (p. 387)

6. T / F In a sense, all children begin life as narcissists and only gradually acquire a perspective-taking ability. (p. 384)

7. T / F Self-mutilation is one of the most characteristic features of borderline personality. (p. 385)

8. T / F Approximately 75% of individuals diagnosed as borderline personalities are women. (p. 386)

9. T / F There are cases of generalized social phobia without avoidant personality disorder, but very few cases of avoidant personality disorder without generalized social phobia. (p. 389)

10. T / F A person with dependent personality disorder may fail to get appropriately angry with others because of a fear of losing their support. (p. 390)

11. T / F People with obsessive-compulsive personality disorder have lifestyles characterized by over-conscientiousness, inflexibility, and perfectionism. (p.391)

12. T / F No systematic studies of treating people yet exist for paranoid, schizoid, narcissistic, or histrionic disorders.   (p. 395)

13. T / F The psychopath's conscience seems to be severely retarded

or nonexistent. (p. 398)

ESSAY QUESTIONS

1. Why do more misdiagnoses occur in diagnosing personality disorders than any other category? Explain. (pp. 351-52)

2. Antisocial personality disorder can be an extremely serious affliction, and persons suffering from it can be a danger to society. Name and explain the criteria that need to be met before a diagnosis can be made. (p. 368)

3. People with psychopathic and antisocial personalities are extremely difficult to treat. Why is this so? (pp. 376-77)

WEB LINKS TO ITEMS OR CONCEPTS DISCUSSED IN CHAPTER11

Antisocial Personality Disorder

       www.mentalhealth.com/dis/p20-pe04.html

       www.geocities.com/ptypes/antisocialpd.html

Borderline Personality Disorder

       www.bpdcentral.com/

       www.mentalhealth.com/dis/p20-pe05.html

       www.psycom.net/depression.central.borderline

       .html

Narcissistic Personality Disorder

       www.mentalhealth.com/dis/p20-pe07.html

       www.mental-health-today.com/narcissistic/

www.geocities.com/ptypes/narcissisticpd.html

Paranoid Personality Disorder

www.geocities.com/ptypes/paranoidpd.html

USE IT OR LOSE IT

Provide an answer to the thought question below, knowing that there is more than one way to respond. Possible answers are presented in the Answer Key.

You suspect that your boss has Narcissistic Personality Disorder. What characteristics would you need to observe to confirm this diagnosis?

CRISS-CROSS

Now that you know all there is to know about this chapter, here's your opportunity to put that knowledge to work.

CRISS-CROSS CLUES

Across
3. mistrust of others, sees self as blameless
10. perfectionist, excessive concern with order, rules

Down
1. peculiar; oddities of perception and speech
2. self-dramatization, overconcern with attractiveness
4. grandiosity, self-promoting
5. disregards and violates the rights of others
6. impulsiveness, mood shifts
7. hypersensitivity to rejection
8. antisocial, impulsive, socially deviant lifestyle
9. subordination of needs to keep others involved in relationships
11. impaired social relationships, no desire for relationships

Puzzle created with Puzzlemaker at DiscoverySchool.com

ANSWERS TO TEST QUESTIONS - CHAPTER 11

MATCHING

Personality Disorder
D. Paranoid
F. Schizoid
J. Schizotypal
B. Histrionic
H. Narcissistic
K. Antisocial
C. Borderline
A. Avoidant
L. Dependent
I. Obsessive-Compulsive
G. Passive Aggressive
E. Depressive

SHORT ANSWERS

(Your answer should contain the following points.)

1. The 5 criteria used in DSM-IV-TR to define personality disorders are that the
    pattern:
    A. must be manifested in at least two areas.
    B. must be inflexible and pervasive.
    C. leads to clinically significant distress or impairment in functioning.
    D. is stable and of long duration.
    E. is not better accounted for as another mental disorder.

2. a. Biological factors
    • Infants' temperament may predispose them to develop certain disorders
    • Increasing evidence for genetic contributions to certain disorders
   b. Psychological factors
    • Learning-based habit patterns and maladaptive cognitive styles
    • May originate in disturbed parent-child attachment relationships
    • Role of parental psychopathology and ineffective parenting practices
    • Early emotional, physical, and sexual abuse

3. It difficult to say childhood trauma plays a causal role in
    developing borderline personality disorder because
    a. most children who experienced early abuse and neglect do
    not end up with any serious personality disorders.
    b. the studies that suggested this has serious shortcomings.
    c. childhood abuse is not a specific risk factor, because it also
    is reported at relatively high rates with other personality

disorders.
d. childhood abuse nearly always occurs in families with other pathological dynamics that actually may be more important than the abuse per se.

4. The difference between a loner with schizoid personality disorder and the loner who is avoidant is
   a. a schizoid's primary focus is on avoiding humiliation and rejection
   b. dependent primary focus is on being taken care of

THE DOCTOR IS IN...PSYCHIATRIC HELP—5¢

1. **Histrionic personality disorder**—very dramatic, is flirtatious, wants approval, moves to be closer to therapist than would be considered healthy

2. **Paranoid personality disorder**—pervasive suspiciousness and distrust, interpersonal difficulties, others are to blame for his problems, is not psychotic

3. **Avoidant personality disorder**—extreme social inhibition and introversion. Hypersenstivity to criticism. She is aware of a problem but is afraid of rejection if she were to get involved socially, and is self-conscious.

4. As a therapist, what issues will you face in treating the three patients above?
   a. Personality disorders are difficult to treat because these are enduring, pervasive, and inflexible patterns of behavior.
   b. There are many different goals of treatment, such as reducing subjective distress and enhancing well-being, changing specific dysfunctional behaviors, changing whole patterns of behavior, and changing the entire structure of the personality.
   c. Therapeutic techniques must be modified.
   d. Possible hospitalization or partial hospitalization
   e. Use of new cognitive approach, which assumes that the dysfunctional feelings and behavior associated with the personality disorder are the result of schema that produce biased judgments and the tendency to make cognitive errors in many situations

MULTIPLE-CHOICE PRACTICE TESTS

PRACTICE TESTS

Q#	TEST 1	TEST 2	TEST 3
1	B	D	B
2	C	C	B
3	B	C	B
4	C	D	B
5	B	B	A
6	A	A	A
7	B	B	D
8	A	C	D
9	B	C	C
10	B	D	B

COMPREHENSIVE PRACTICE TEST

Q#	MULTIPLE CHOICE	T/F
1	C	T
2	A	T
3	A	F
4	D	F
5	D	F
6	D	T
7	D	T
8	B	T
9	B	T
10	C	T
11	D	T
12	D	T
13	C	T
14	B	

ESSAY QUESTIONS

(Your answer should contain the following points.)

1. More misdiagnoses occur in diagnosing personality disorders than any other category because
   a. the criteria are not as sharply defined.
   b. the categories are not mutually exclusive.

c. personality characteristics are dimensional in nature—that is, these can range from normal to severe, which can lead to unreliable diagnoses.

2. Antisocial personality disorder can be an extremely serious affliction, and persons suffering from it can be a danger to society. The criteria that need to be met before a diagnosis can be made are
   a. At least three behavioral problems occurring after age 15
   b. At least three instances of deviant behavior before age 15
   c. The antisocial behavior is not a symptom of another mental disorder

3. People with psychopathic and antisocial personalities are extremely difficult to treat because
   a. biological treatments (drugs) do not seem to have any substantial impact on the disorder as a whole
   b. individuals have little motivation to take their medications
   c. of inherent factors in the psychopath's personality—the inability to trust, to learn from experience, to accept responsibility for one's actions
   d. information given by psychopaths is not reliable

USE IT OR LOSE IT

Narcissists tend to be grandiose and self-absorbed. They may demand that employees constantly agree with them, but will also blame the people around them when things go wrong. In order to deal with a Narcissistic boss you would need to understand why they behave as they do, and learn to stand up for yourself, ignore unreasonable behavior, and document your own actions in order to make sure that you get credit for the things you do, and avoid blame for things that are not your fault.

CRISS-CROSS ANSWERS

Across
3. paranoid
10. obsessive-compulsive

Down
1. schizotypal
2. histrionic
4. narcissistic
5. antisocial
6. borderline
7. avoidant
8. psychopathy
9. dependent
11. schizoid

Chapter 12: Substance-Related Disorders

BEFORE YOU READ

Although we know that the use of alcohol, tobacco, and other drugs date back thousands of years, our understanding of their negative impact on health and behavior has grown exponentially in the past fifty years. When individuals have difficulty controlling their use of such substances, or of other behaviors, the term addiction is used. This chapter will explore alcohol abuse and dependence, and will explain the differences between these two conditions. The effects of drugs such as narcotics, stimulants, sedatives, and hallucinogens will also be explored. Possible causes for addictions are discussed, along with differences in substance use as a function of cultural factors. An evaluation of treatment options for specific types of addictive disorders is also provided.

• ALCOHOL ABUSE AND DEPENDENCE

The Prevalence, Comorbidity, and Demographics of Alcohol Abuse and
     Dependence

The Clinical Picture of Alcohol Abuse and Dependence

Biological Factors in the Abuse of and Dependence on Alcohol and Other
     Substances

Psychosocial Causal Factors in Alcohol Abuse and Dependence

Sociocultural Factors

Treatment of Alcohol Abuse Disorders

• DRUG ABUSE AND DEPENDENCE

Opium and its Derivatives (Narcotics)

Cocaine and Amphetamines (Stimulants)

Barbiturates (Sedatives)

LSD and Related Drugs (Hallucinogens)

Ecstasy; Marijuana

• UNRESOLVED ISSUES

Exchanging addictions: Is This an Effective Approach?

OBJECTIVES

After reading this chapter, you should be able to:

1. Outline the major divisions of psychoactive substance-related disorders, define alcohol abuse and alcohol dependence, summarize the many negative consequences of alcohol use for both the individual and society, and indicate the prevalence and gender ratio of excessive drinking.

2. Describe the clinical picture of alcohol abuse, including the biological and psychological effects of chronic consumption of alcohol.

3. Review the biological, psychosocial, and sociocultural contributors to alcohol abuse and dependence.

4. Summarize the research findings on the results of treatment and relapse prevention for alcohol-dependent persons.

5. List the specific drugs and their effects, summarize theories of causal factors, and review treatments for the following drugs of abuse: opium and its derivatives, cocaine and amphetamines, barbiturates, LSD and other hallucinogens, marijuana, and caffeine and nicotine.

6. Discuss the controversy surrounding controlled drinking versus abstinence.

AS YOU READ

Answers can be found in the Answer Key at the end of the chapter.

KEY WORDS

Each of the words below is important in understanding the concepts presented in this chapter. Write the definition next to each of the words.

Term	Page	Definition
Addictive behavior	412	
Alcoholic	413	
Alcoholism	413	
Amphetamine	437	
Barbiturates	412	
Caffeine	431	
Cocaine	431	
Ecstasy	443	
Endorphins	436	
Hallucinogens	441	
Hashish	443	
Heroin	412	
LSD	431	
Marijuana	412	
Mescaline	441	
Mesocorticolimbic dopamine pathway	448	
Methadone	434	
Morphine	433	
Nicotine	412	
Opium	414	
Pathological gambling	445	
Psilocybin	434	
Psychoactive drugs	412	
Substance abuse	412	
Substance	412	

dependence		
Tolerance	412	
Toxicity	412	
Withdrawal symptoms	412	

WHO'S WHO AND WHAT'S WHAT—MATCHING

Match the following drugs with their effects.

Drug

_____ Alcohol

_____ Caffeine

_____ Nicotine

_____ Ecstasy

_____ Opium

_____ Morphine

_____ Heroin

_____ Methadone

_____ Cocaine

_____ Amphetamine

_____ Barbiturates

_____ LSD

_____ Mescaline

_____ Marijuana

Effects

A. intoxicant found in coffee and chocolate

B. mild hallucinogen from a plant; can produce mild euphoria or unpleasant experiences depending upon the mood of the user

C. synthesized drug first used in inhalant for stuffy noses; recalled when discovered that customers were chewing the wicks for "kicks;" newer, more powerful preparation is methedrine, also known as speed

D. a hallucinogen and a stimulant; popular among young adults

E. poisonous alkaloid associated with 14% of all deaths in the U.S.

F. hallucinogen distorts sensory images, causing users to see or hear things differently and unusually

G. the major problem drug in the U.S.; associated with over half of highway deaths, 50% of all rapes, 40-50% of murders, 40% of all assaults

H. drug from a plant, costly, a "high" for the affluent

I. a mixture of about 18 alkaloids; morphine and heroin made from this

J. derived from peyote cactus; hallucinogen used for centuries

K. derived from opium; was used during Civil War as pain killer; legal as prescription only

L. derived from opium; first used in cough syrup around 1900; highly addictive; illegal in U.S.

M. addictive drug used as substitute for heroin during treatment

N. sedatives, depressants that slow down the nervous system; large doses produce immediate sleep or death

SHORT ANSWERS
Provide brief answers to the following questions.

1. Discuss the relationship between being pregnant and drinking alcohol.

2. Discuss the two factors apparently involved in the overpowering addiction to drugs such as opium, cocaine and alcohol.

3. Discuss the neurochemical process underlying addiction and the role the drug plays in activating the "pleasure pathway."

4. Discuss how environmental factors promote substance abuse.

5. Is there an "alcoholic personality"—a type of character organization that predisposes a person to use alcohol, rather than some other defensive pattern of coping with stress? Explain.

6. Discuss the immediate effects of mainlined or snorted heroin.

7. The view that cocaine users did not develop physiological dependence has changed over the past 20 years. Explore this change of view.

THE DOCTOR IS IN...PSYCHIATRIC HELP—5¢

Read the following scenarios and diagnose the client. Remember to look carefully at the criteria for the disorder before you make a decision as to the diagnosis. Make a list of other information you might need to help you understand the causal factors.

1. You have been working with Tony, who is dependent on alcohol. He has had several problems with the law and has lost his job as a result of his drinking. His wife has told him that if he doesn't get help, she is going to leave. As Tony's therapist, how would you treat him? Be sure to look at relapse prevention.

2. Lupe brings her father, Martin, into to see you. Recently, she found him asleep on the kitchen table, a bottle of pills and an alcoholic drink sitting near by. He is an older gentleman who lost his wife to cancer about a year ago. As you are talking, he tells you that he had been having difficulty sleeping until his doctor had given him something. These helped, but he found that having a drink made these work faster, and, since he was on a fixed income, the pills lasted longer even though the label said not to drink. Lupe tells you that her father has become very sluggish and is having sudden mood shifts. Lately, it seems that she is finding him this state more often.

AFTER YOU READ

Answers can be found in the Answer Key at the end of the chapter.

PRACTICE TESTS

Take the following three multiple-choice tests to see how much you have comprehended from the chapter. Each represents roughly one-third of the chapter. As you study the chapter, use these to check your progress.

PRACTICE TEST NUMBER 1

1. As a problem facing our society today, addictive behavior is (p. 412)

a. just beginning to be understood and controlled.

b. one of the most pervasive and intransigent mental health problems.

c. overrated and over blown.

d. a severe problem only in lower income neighborhoods.

2. Substance abuse generally involves (p. 412)

a. use of a substance, resulting in potentially hazardous behavior.

b. a continued use, despite persistent social, psychological, occupational, or health problems.

c. a marked psychological need for increasing amounts of a substance to achieve the desired effects.

d. a and b.

3. Substance dependence involves (p. 412)

a. use of a substance, resulting in potentially hazardous behavior.

b. a continued use, despite persistent social, psychological, occupational, or health problems.

c. a marked psychological need for increasing amounts of a substance to achieve the desired effects.

d. b and c.

4. The need for increased amounts of a substance to achieve the desired effects is called (p. 412)

a. abuse.

b. dependence.

c. tolerance.

d. withdrawal.

5. Depression and alcoholism frequently occur together since alcohol (p. 413)

a. is excitatory.

b. activates the dancing gene.

c. is a depressant.

d. causes many problems, which is depressing.

6. When the blood-alcohol level reaches approximately 0.5 percent, the individual passes out, which is a good thing, because (p. 415)

a. any more drinking would just be a waste of money.

b. both dancing and driving at that level are pretty much out of the question.

c. concentrations above 0.55 percent are usually lethal.

d. all of the above

7. The effects of alcohol vary for different drinkers, depending on (p. 415)

a. their physical condition.

b. the amount of food in their stomach.

c. the duration of their drinking.

d. all of the above.

8. A physiological effect of alcohol is (p. 414)

a. a tendency toward decreased sexual inhibition, but lowered sexual performance.

b. a lapse of memory—a blackout.

c. headache, nausea, and fatigue of a hangover.

d. all of the above.

9. Researchers believe that genetics contribute to one's susceptibility to alcoholism because (p..420)

a. almost one-third of alcoholics in a study had at least one parent with an alcohol problem.

b. females in a study were five times more likely to be alcoholic if both of their parents were alcoholic.

c. children of alcoholic parents who had been adopted by nonalcoholic foster parents had nearly twice the number of alcohol problems by their late 20s as did a control group.

d. all of the above.

10. Certain ethnic groups, particularly Asians and Native Americans, have abnormal physiological reactions to alcohol, known as "_____," including flushing of the skin, a drop in blood pressure, heart palpitations, and nausea. (p. 421)

a. the fatal flaw

b. alcohol flush reaction

c. hypnotic effect

d. pressure-and-palpitation flush reaction

PRACTICE TEST NUMBER 2

1. Stable family relationships and parental guidance are often _____ in families of substance abusers. (p. 421-422)

a. lacking

b. very strong

c. inconsistent

d. not discussed

2. About _____% of persons with schizophrenia have either abuse alcohol or drugs as well. (p. 422)

a. 10

b. 25

c. 50

d. 99.44

3. According to recent survey, what percentage of college students identified themselves as binge drinkers? (p. 424)

a. 21%

b. 30%

c. 44%

d. 85%

4. In cultures whose religious values restrict or prohibit the use of alcohol, the incidence of alcoholism is (p. 425)

a. about the same as other groups.

b. minimal.

c. actually higher.

d. unknown, as they refuse to discuss it.

5. In the Alcoholics Anonymous (AA) view (p. 428)

a. one's alcoholism can be cured through group meetings and the understanding of peers.

b. one is never cured but an alcoholic for life, whether or not one is drinking.

c. the alcoholic is weak-willed and lacking in moral strength.

d. having a drink or occasionally "falling off the wagon" is nothing to worry about.

6. Drug abuse and dependence are most common during (p. 432)

a. adolescence and young adulthood.

b. childhood.

c. retirement age individuals.

d. all of the above

7. Factors which contribute to binge drinking on college campuses include (p. 424)

a. experiencing independence from parents

b. appearing macho

c. the belief that alcohol is a crucial component of celebrations

d. all of the above

8. Because morphine is so addictive, a chemical, called acetic anhydride was added to it around the turn of the 20th century in hopes of converting it into a more controllable substance. This new mix was called (p. 433)

a. aspirin.

b. heroin.

c. acetydride.

d. the Whopper.

9. Opium and its derivatives, morphine, codeine, and heroin were outlawed in 1914 by (p. 433)

a. President Woodrow Wilson.

b. World War I.

c. the Harrison Act.

d. the Mann Act.

10.Withdrawl from nicotine is characterized by (p. 423)

a. craving for nicotine

b. irritability and frustration

c. anger

d. all of the above

PRACTICE TEST NUMBER 3

1. The desire to obtain narcotics can (p. 435)

a. lead to socially maladaptive behavior.

b. force the addict to lie, steal, and associate with undesirable contacts.

c. cause females to turn to prostitution as a means to finance their addiction.

d. all of the above.

2. The most frequently cited reason for beginning to use heroin was (p.436)

a. pleasure.

b. curiosity.

c. peer pressure.

d. all of the above.

3. Cocaine, _____ the action of the central nervous system (p. 437)

a. increases

b. decreases

c. equalizes

d. negates

4. In 2000 about _____% of emergency room visits were cocaine related. (p. 437)

a. 1.732

b. 4

c. 13

d. 29

5. Many life problems experienced by cocaine abusers result, in part, from (p. 438)

a. the low quality of people they are forced to deal with.

b. the considerable amounts of money required to support their habits.

c. disfunction and disinterest in sexual performance.

d. fetal crack syndrome.

6. The earliest amphetamine—benzedrine—was first synthesized in as an inhalant to relieve stuffy noses. However, it was soon withdrawn because (p. 438)

a. it was so powerful that stuffy noses ceased to be a problem.

b. some customers were chewing the wicks in the inhalers for "kicks."

c. it didn't work.

d. it was discovered that nutmeg worked just as well.

7. Curiously, amphetamines have _____ effect on many youngsters. (p. 439)

a. a stimulating

b. a calming

c. an invigorating

d. no

8. Methedrine, used in large amounts, can raise blood pressure (p.439)

a. enough to cause immediate death.

b. slightly.

c. over a period of time.

d. none of the above. It does not raise blood pressure in any amount.

9. A common effect of barbiturates is (p. 439)

a. slow speech.

b. impaired decision making and problem solving.

c. sudden mood shifts.

d. all of the above.

10. Psychedelic drugs do not, in fact, "create" sensory images, but (p. 441)

a. increase the effects.

b. distort thm, so that a person sees or hears things in different and unusual ways.

c. categorizes odd events.

d. none of the above.

COMPREHENSIVE PRACTICE TEST

The following tests are designed to give you an idea of how well you understood the entire chapter. There are three different types of tests: multiple-choice, true-false, and essay.

MULTIPLE-CHOICE

1. Alcohol abuse and dependency are _____ in the United States. (p. 413)

a. not a serious problem

b. a major problem

c. required at some Fraternities

d. easily cured

2. The life expectancy with alcohol dependency is about _____ than that of the average citizen. (p. 413)

a. 12 years shorter

b. 12 years longer

c. a couple of years shorter

d. about the same, but it seems longer

3. Excessive drinkers often suffer from (p. 413-414)

a. chronic fatigue, oversensitivity, and depression.

b. lowered feelings of adequacy and worth, impaired reasoning and judgment, and gradual personality deterioration.

c. coarse and inappropriate behavior, lowered pride and personal appearance, and becoming generally touchy and irritable,

d. all of the above.

4. A number of investigators have pointed out that the typical alcohol abuser is (p. 423)

a. unable or unwilling to tolerate tension and stress.

b. discontented with his or her life.

c. misunderstood and just looking for a good time.

d. a and b.

5. Many young people begin to use alcohol because they expect that it will (p.423)

a. lower tension and anxiety.

b. increase their popularity.

c. increase sexual desire and pleasure in life.

d. all of the above.

6. Alcohol abuse and dependence are difficult to treat because (p. 426)

a. many alcoholics refuse to admit they have a problem.

b. they refuse to seek assistance before they "hit bottom."

c. many leave treatment before therapy is completed.

d. all of the above.

7. A multidisciplinary approach to the treatment of drinking problems appears to be most effective because (p.426))

a. the problems are often complex.

b. researchers really aren't sure what works yet.

c. a substance abuser's needs change as treatment progresses.

d. a and b.

8. Caffeine and nicotine are (p. 431)

a. drugs of dependence.

b. mild stimulants.

c. mild depressants.

d. harmless pastimes.

9. Factors which predispose an individual to substance abuse probably include (p.425)

a. the presence of an alcoholic father

b. marital accord

c. feelings of inadequacy

d. a & c

10. The use of opium derivatives over a period of time usually results in a physiological craving for the drug. The time required varies, but it has been estimated that continual use over a period of _____ is sufficient. (p. 435)

a. 3 days

b. two weeks

c. 30 days

d. a year

11. Strong doses of barbiturates cause sleep almost immediately. Excessive doses (p. 439)

a. are lethal.

b. are extremely enlightening.

c. cause the dance gene to take control, and the user will not be able to sit still.

d. none of the above.

12. When people quit using cocaine they (p.436)

a. do not develop any physiological signs of dependence

b. develop transient depressive symptoms

c. feel better within a few weeks of therapy

d. b and c.

13. Ecstasy users have been found to be more likely to (p. 443)

a. use marijuana.

b. engage in binge drinking.

c. have multiple sexual partners.

d. all of the above.

14. Until the late 1960s, marijuana use in the United States was confined largely to (p. 443)

a. members of lower socioeconomic minority groups.

b. people in the entertainment and related fields.

c. British rock groups.

d. a and b.

15. Continued use of high dosages of marijuana over time tends to produce (p. 416)

a. increased energy.

b. clear and concise thinking.

c. lethargy and passivity.

d. none of the above.

TRUE – FALSE

1. T / F Tolerance for a substance is the need for less and less to achieve the desired effect. (p. 412)

2. T / F Substance dependence means that an individual will show tolerance for a drug and/or withdrawal symptoms when the drug is unavailable. (p. 412)

3. T / F One in seven deaths are associated with cigarette consumption. (p. 431)

4. T / F Men are about five times more likely to have an alcohol problem then women. (p. 414)

5. T / F In a study, college freshmen from families with alcohol abusing parents viewed their families as less healthy and had more problematic family relationships than those with nonalcohol abusing parents. (p. 422)

6. T / F There is a strong association between antisocial personality disorder and alcohol, aggression, and high rates of substance abuse. (p. 422)

7. T / F Excessive use of alcohol is one of the most frequent causes of divorce in the United States.   (p. 424)

8. T / F Users of opium derivatives gradually build up a tolerance to the drug, so that increasingly larger amounts are needed to achieve the desired effects. (p. 435)

9. T / F   The efficacy of Alcoholics Anonymous has been carefully tested clinically. (p. 429)

10. T / F Planning for relapse actually helps people to cope with a substance abuse problem. (p. 430)

11. T / F Addicts often dread the discomfort of withdrawal, but in a hospital setting, it is less abrupt and usually involves the administration of a medication that eases the distress. (p. 436)

12. T / F Amphetamines were initially considered to be "wonder pills" that helped people stay alert, and were used by both the Allied and German soldiers to ward off fatigue during World War II. (p. 438)

ESSAY QUESTIONS

1. Alcohol has complex and seemingly contradictory effects on the brain from the activation of the brain's "pleasure areas" to the health risks and degradation that can result from heavy and long-term usage. Discuss this, particularly in relation to the items below.

a. physiological effects

b. abilities

c. pregnancy

d. chronic use

e. dependence

f. organic damage

g. physical and mental decline

2. Discuss the controversy about whether alcoholics need to give up drinking altogether or can learn to drink moderately.

3. Discuss heroin withdrawal.

WEB LINKS TO ITEMS OR CONCEPTS DISCUSSED IN CHAPTER 12

Substance abuse

www.samhsa.gov/centers/csap/csap.html

www.niaaa.nih.gov/

USE IT OR LOSE IT

Provide an answer to the thought question below, knowing that there is more than one way to respond. Possible answers are presented in the Answer Key.

Do you think that people can be addicted to positive behaviors such as exercise in much the same way they can become addicted to various substances?

CRISS-CROSS

Now that you know all there is to know about this chapter, here's your opportunity to put that knowledge to work.

CRISS-CROSS CLUES

Across

1. hallucinogen and stimulant popular as a party drug currently

5. the poisonous nature of a substance

6. a person with a serious drinking problem

7. involves marked physiological need for a substance and produces withdrawal symptoms, if unavailable

8. the need for increasing amounts of a substance

9. widely used poisonous alkaloid; very addictive; difficult withdrawal; causes many deaths annually

10. grows as a plant, highly addictive; morphine and heroin are derived from it

11. opium derivative; removed from medical practice

12. thought to be a mild pick-me-up, has intoxicating and/or withdrawal potential

Down

2. pathological use resulting in potentially hazardous behavior, or persistent social or health problems

3. behavior based on the pathological need for a substance

4. drug used as replacement for heroin during treatment

Puzzle created with Puzzlemaker at DiscoverySchool.com

ANSWERS TO TEST QUESTIONS - CHAPTER 12

MATCHING
Drug
G. Alcohol
A. Caffeine
E. Nicotine
D. Ecstasy
I. Opium
K. Morphine
L. Heroin
M. Methadone
H. Cocaine
C. Amphetamine
N. Barbiturates
F. LSD
J. Mescaline
B. Marijuana

SHORT ANSWERS

(Your answer should contain the following points.)

1. With reference to drinking any alcohol during pregnancy:
   a. even moderate amounts of alcohol believed dangerous.
   b. fetal alcohol syndrome (FAS) may occur.
   c. birth defects, such as mental retardation, may also occur.

2. The two factors apparently involved in the overpowering hold that occurs in some people after only a few uses of a drug, such as opium, cocaine, or alcohol are,
   a. some drugs activate areas of the brain that produce pleasure
   b. a person's genetic and biological make-up

3. The neurochemical process underlying addiction and the role the drug plays in activating the "pleasure pathway" includes a discussion of:
   a. the mesocorticolumbic dopamine pathway (MCLP)
   b. alcohol and other drugs produces euphoria by stimulating this area in the brain

4. Alcohol-related problems may result from living in an environment that promotes use of the substance:
   a. lack of stability in family relationships and parental guidance
   b. children witness parents using alcohol or drugs
   c. negative parental models have long-range negative consequences
   d. role models and media promote alcohol as stress reducer
   e. alcohol promoted to increase popularity and acceptance in younger

persons

5. An "alcoholic personality
    a. self-medicates with alcohol to reduce discomfort
    b. is emotionally immature, expect a great deal of the world, require praise, feel inferior, low frustration for tolerance, unsure of abilities to fulfill expected male or female roles.
    c. tends to be impulsive and aggressive

6. The immediate effects of mainlined or snorted heroin are:
    a. euphoric spasm (60 seconds or so)
    b. followed by a high; lethargic, withdrawn (typically four to six hours)
    c. negative phase that produces a desire for more

7. The view that cocaine users did not develop physiological dependence has changed over the past 20 years because:
    a. acute tolerance has now been demonstrated
    b. a significant increase in knowledge of cocaine's addictive properties
    c. a new disorder is described—cocaine withdrawal
    d. the psychological and life problems experienced by cocaine users are often great—often related to the considerable amount of money required to support their habits

THE DOCTOR IS IN...PSYCHIATRIC HELP—5¢
(Your answer should include the following points)

1. a. Possible use of medications to reduce cravings and ease detoxification process
    b. Group therapy—peers who will provide a confrontational give-and-take atmosphere; possibly have Tony's wife take part in a group for spouses of alcohol abusers
    c. Family therapy/treatment—to work out the family dynamics
    d. Behavioral therapy—aversive conditioning, behavioral couples therapy
    e. Cognitive-behavioral approach recommended by Marlatt—combines cognitive-behavioral strategies of intervention with social-learning and modeling of behavior
    f. Possibly look at controlled drinking or AA meetings
    g. Be sure to look at relapse prevention

2. Martin is taking barbiturates. His behavior, not sleeping, then being able to do so with the pill, sluggishness; impaired cognition and mood swings, all indicate the use of sedatives. Potential danger is death, since he is taking the barbiturates and drinking.

MULTIPLE-CHOICE PRACTICE TESTS

PRACTICE TESTS

Q#	TEST 1	TEST 2	TEST 3
1	B	A	D
2	D	C	D
3	D	C	A
4	C	B	D
5	C	B	B
6	C	A	B
7	D	D	B
8	D	B	A
9	D	C	D
10	B	D	B

COMPREHENSIVE PRACTICE TEST

Q#	MULTIPLE CHOICE	T/F
1	B	F
2	A	T
3	D	T
4	D	T
5	D	T
6	D	T
7	D	T
8	A	T
9	D	F
10	C	F
11	A	T
12	B	T
13	D	
14	D	
15	C	

ESSAY QUESTIONS
(Your answer should contain the following points.)

1. a. physiological effects—depresses brain functioning, inhibiting glutamate, affects higher brain center, impairing judgment and other rational processes and lowering self control.
   b. abilities—decreased sexual performance, blackouts (lapses of memory), hangover

c. pregnancy—possible fetal alcohol syndrome, producing birth defects, such as mental retardation

d. chronic use—suffers chronic fatigue, oversensitivity, and depression

e. dependence—can produce lowered feelings of adequacy and worth

f. organic damage—alcohol must be assimilated by the liver, which may suffer irreversible damage; 26,000 annual cirrhosis deaths from alcohol

g. physical and mental decline—impaired reasoning and judgment, and gradual personality deterioration

2. a. controlled drinking, the ability to start drinking after drying out, is possible, it seems, in some cases of less severe situations

b. AA view is that once a person is an alcoholic, that person is always at risk and always in recovery, one day at a time.

3. a. addicted users find they feel physically ill when they do not take it

b. after approximately eight hours withdrawal symptoms begin
   • severity depends on many factors: amount used, duration of addiction, addict's health and personality

c. can be agonizing with symptoms, including runny nose, tearing eyes, perspiration, restlessness
   • symptoms get worse as time rolls on: chilliness alternates with flushing and excessive sweating, vomiting, diarrhea, abdominal cramps, pains, dehydration
   • occasionally, symptoms include delirium, hallucinations, manic activity
   • cardiovascular collapse and death is a possibility

d. symptoms are usually on the decline by the third or fourth day, gone by seventh or eighth

USE IT OR LOSE IT

The correct answer to this question is a matter of opinion. Some people believe that the term *addiction* should only be used to refer to negative behaviors. However, others argue that people can be addicted to things like exercise, if they are unable to discontinue the behavior even when it is causing problems in their health or personal life.

CRISS-CROSS ANSWERS
Across
1. ecstasy
5. toxicity

6. alcoholic
7. dependence
8. tolerance
9. nicotine
10. opium
11. heroin
12. caffeine

Down
2. substance abuse
3. addictive behavior
4. methadone

Chapter Thirteen: Sexual Variants, Abuse, and Dysfunctions

BEFORE YOU READ

Paradoxically, sex is a common topic in the movies, on television, and in music, yet we rarely talk about it openly in our own lives, and often wonder about other people's sexuality, whether we are normal, and how to manage sexual problems. This chapter emphasizes the variability in sexual attitudes and behaviors across cultures. It also focuses on a particularly timely topic, homosexuality, which is not considered a sexual deviation in the current version of the DSM-IV. Sexual issues which do cause psychological difficulty for individuals can be classified as either sexual variants, sexual abuse, or sexual dysfunctions. Sexual variants include paraphilias in which individuals seek sexual arousal via nonhuman subjects, hurting others or being hurt, or interacting with nonconsenting partners. For example people with a shoe fetish become excited by touching or fondling shoes, masochists and sadists are people who are sexually aroused by suffering humiliation or hurting others respectively, and pedophiles respond sexually to minors. Gender identity disorders, characterized by strong discomfort with one's own sex are also classified as sexual variants. Sexual abuse, or sexual behavior characterized by coercion and lack of consent is discussed in terms of its negative psychological impact on the victim, and its adverse impact on society. The third section concerns sexual dysfunctions— problems that may interfere with an individual's full enjoyment of sexual relations, but fortunately are the most and treatable disorders discussed.

- **SOCIOCULTURAL INFLUENCES ON SEXUAL PRACTICES AND STANDARDS**
    Case 1: Degeneracy and Abstinence Theory
    Case 2: Ritualized Homosexuality in Melanesia
    Case 3: Homosexuality and American Psychiatry
- **SEXUAL AND GENDER VARIANTS**
    The Paraphilias Causal Factors and Treatments for Paraphilias

Gender Identity Disorders

• SEXUAL ABUSE

Childhood Sexual Abuse

Pedophilia

Incest

Rape

Treatment and Recidivism of Sex Offenders

• SEXUAL DYSFUNCTIONS

Dysfunctions of Sexual Desire

Dysfunctions of Sexual Arousal

Orgasmic Disorders Dysfunctions Involving Sexual Pain

• UNRESOLVED ISSUES

How Harmful is Child Sexual Abuse?

OBJECTIVES

After reading this chapter, you should be able to:

1. Provide a number of examples of sociocultural influences on sexual practices.

2. Describe the clinical features of the following paraphilias: fetishism, transvestic fetishism, voyeurism, exhibitionism, sadism, and masochism.

3. Discuss the most effective treatments for paraphilias, and summarize causal factors implicated in their etiology.

4. Define and describe the clinical features and treatment of the gender identity disorders (gender identity disorder of childhood, transsexualism).

5. Review what is known about the frequency and nature of childhood sexual abuse. Discuss the controversies surrounding childhood testimony regarding sexual abuse and adult "recovered memories" of childhood sexual abuse.

6. Define pedophilia and summarize what is known about pedophiles.

7. Review what is known about the frequency and nature of incest.

8. Summarize what is known about rape and rapists, and discuss the issues regarding the frequency of rape and the motivation of rapists.

9. Describe attempts to treat sex offenders.

10. Define the sexual dysfunctions, describe their general features, review etiological theories, and summarize the major approaches to treatment.

11. Knowledgeably discuss the difficulty of deciding the extent of the harm caused by childhood sexual abuse.

AS YOU READ

Answers can be found in the Answer Key at the end of the chapter.

KEY WORDS

Each of the words below is important in understanding the concepts presented in this Chapter. Write the definition next to each of the words.

Term	Page	Definition
Cross-gender identification	463	
Desire phase	478	
Dyspareunia	480	
Excitement phase	478	
Exhibitionism	457	
Female orgasmic disorder	480	
Female sexual arousal disorder	480	
Fetishism	456	

Gender dysphoria	463	
Gender identity disorder	463	
Hypoactive sexual desire disorder	479	
Incest	485	
Male erectile disorder	480	
Male orgasmic disorder	480	
Masochism	457	
Orgasm	478	
Paraphila	456	
Pedophilia	457	
Premature ejaculation	457	
Rape	472	
Resolution	478	
Sadism	457	
Sexual abuse	467	
Sexual aversion disorder	479	
Sexual dysfunction	478	
Transsexualism	486	
Transvestic	457	

fetishism		
Vaginismus	480	
Voyeurism	457	

MATCHING

WHO'S WHO AND WHAT'S WHAT

Match the following person or term with the appropriate answer.

Answer

A. sexual activity with a person who is legally defined to be under the age of consent

B. dangerous form of masochism that involves self-strangulation to the point of oxygen deprivation

C. anonymously published book in London that started the hypothesis that masturbation caused insanity

D. advocated the abstinence theory during the 1830s

E. said, during the late nineteenth and early twentieth centuries, that homosexuality was natural and nonpathological

F. erectile problem in young men where erection will not diminish, even after a couple of hours

G. Swiss physician who developed the "degeneracy theory"

H. wrote about the 39 signs of the "secret vice" (masturbation) and made a fortune publishing books discouraging masturbation; also urged people to eat more cereal

I. demonstrated that psychologists could not tell the difference between psychological test results of homosexuals and heterosexuals

Person/Term

_____ Simon Tissot

_____ Reverend Sylvester Graham

_____ Dr. John Harvey Kellogg

_____ Onania, or the Heinous Sin of Self-Pollution

_____ Havelock Ellis and Magnus Hirschfeld

_____ Evelyn Hooker

_____ autoerotic asphyxia

_____ statutory rape

_____ priapism

Match the dysfunction with its characteristic.

Dysfunction

of Sexual Desire

_____ Hypoactive sexual desire disorder

_____ Sexual aversion disorder

of Sexual Arousal

_____ Male erectile disorder

_____ Female sexual arousal disorder

of Orgasm

_____ Premature ejaculation

_____ Male orgasmic disorder

_____ Female orgasmic disorder

Sexual Pain Disorders

_____ Vaginismus

_____ Dyspareunia

Characteristics

A. inability to achieve or maintain an erection

B. difficulty in achieving orgasm, either manually or during sexual intercourse

C. painful coitus; may have either organic or psychological basis

D. little or no sexual drive or interest

E. nonresponsiveness to erotic stimulation, physically and emotionally

F. inability to ejaculate during intercourse

G. involuntary muscle spasm at the entrance to the vagina preventing penetration

H. total lack of interest in sex and avoidance of sexual contact

I. unsatisfactorily brief period between the beginning of sexual stimulation and ejaculation

SHORT ANSWERS

Provide brief answers to the following questions.

1. Why has research about childhood sexual abuse increased in the past decade?

2. What are the differences between intrafamilial and extrafamilial child molesters?

THE DOCTOR IS IN...PSYCHIATRIC HELP—5¢

Read the following scenarios and diagnose the client. Remember to look carefully at the criteria for the disorder before you make a decision as to the diagnosis. Make a list of other information you might need to help you understand the causal factors.

1. Jim was referred to you by the courts. He was caught after breaking into a woman's house to steal her underwear. Jim says that he is almost relieved at being caught as his problem was getting worse. He used the underwear to fantasize while he masturbates. You ask him how long this behavior has been going on and he tells you that he has had these feelings since as an adolescent, he found one of his sister's girlfriend's underwear in the bathroom (he had a crush on her).

How would you diagnosis Jim and why?

2. Darla comes to your office. She is an attractive female in her late 40s. She begins by telling you that she was born a boy but always felt like a girl. She never wanted to play boy games, preferred to be with girls, and often wished she would wake up in the morning and find that she had become a girl. She began cross-dressing almost 20 years ago and has lived full-time as a female for the last 10 years. Darla has been on hormones for several years and is planning to have surgery. She is employed as a secretary and has passed as a woman for many years.

How would you diagnose Darla? Why and what would you recommend as treatment?

3. Susan and Ben come to your office seeking couple's counseling. They are both frustrated with their sexual relations. Susan experiences involuntary spasms around her vagina when they attempt to have intercourse. It is very painful and she can't go on. This has begun to affect Ben and he has started to have erectile dysfunctions. They love each other very much and want to work this out.

How would diagnose the problem and what else would you want to know about the couple?

AFTER YOU READ

PRACTICE TESTS
Take the following three multiple-choice tests to see how much you have

comprehended from the chapter. Each represents roughly one-third of the chapter. As you study the chapter, use these to check your progress.

PRACTICE TEST NUMBER 1

1. This society in the South Pacific holds two beliefs that are reflected in their sexual practices: semen conservation and female pollution. (p 453)

a. Bali

b. Melanesia

c. Samba

d. Jamaica

2. Homosexuality was removed as a sexual deviation from the DSM in (p. 453)

a. 1966.

b. 1973.

c. 1981.

d. 1977.

3. Glenn is a 35-year-old married man who cross-dresses. He becomes sexually aroused while looking at himself dressed as a woman. His wife is aware of his cross-dressing and doesn't have a problem with it. Glenn is considered to have a (p. 457)

a. transvestic fetish.

a. exhibitionistic fetish.

c. voyeuristic fetish.

d. fetish fetish.

4. A Peeping Tom is another name for someone who is a(n) (p.459)

a. exhibitionist.

b. transvestite.

c. erotophilia.

d. voyeur.

5. The legal term for _____ is "indecent exposure." (p. 460.)

a. exhibitionism

b. transvestism

c. erotophilism

d. voyeurism

6. Steve finds great sexual pleasure in being bound by his lover and humiliated—and sometimes whipped. He has participated in this behavior for over two years now. Steve would be considered a(n) (p. 461.)

a. sadist.

b. transvestite.

c. exhibitionist.

d. masochist.

7. Voyeurs tend to be (p. 460.)

a. violent

b. otherwise non-criminal in their behavior

c. egocentric

d. rapists

8. _____ appears in genetic males and is a paraphilia characterized by sexual arousal at the thought or fantasy of being a woman. (p. 465)

a. Autoeroticism

b. Autogynephilic

c. Gynoplasticism

d. None of the above

9. The accuracy of children's testimony is an issue, because children (p. 467)

a. are susceptible to the influence of others.

b. can't always distinguish fact from fantasy.

c. are not called on to testify all that often.

d. a and b.

10. Recovered memories are considered (p. 467)

a. controversial

b. absolutely true

c. totally false

d. b and c

PRACTICE TEST NUMBER 2

1. _____ is diagnosed when an adult has recurrent, intense sexual urges or fantasies about sexual activity with a prepubescent child. (p.470)

a. Paraphilia

b. Pedophilia

c. Erotophilia

d. Fetishism

2. The typical victim of a pedophile is a girl between the ages of (p 470)

a. 5 and 8.

b. 15 and 18.

c. 12 and 15.

d. 8 and 11.

3. _____ is sexual activity that occurs under actual or threatened forcible coercion of one person by another. (p. 472)

a. Incest

b. Rape

c. Sadism

d. Masochism

4. In most societies incest is

a. promoted

b. forbidden

c. tolerated

d. forgiven

5. What percentage of rapes are committed in the rapist's neighborhood? (p. 442.)

a. 50

b. 80

c. 45

d. 38

6. About how many rapes are single-offender rapes in which the victim may know the offender? (p. 473)

a. one-third

b. one-half

c. two-thirds

d. one-quarter

7. The psychological impact of rape used to be called (p. 473)

a. post-traumatic stress disorder.

b. rape stress disorder.

c. acute trauma syndrome.

d. rape trauma syndrome.

8. The psychological impact of rape is now called (p.473)

a. post-traumatic stress disorder.

b. rape stress disorder.

c. acute trauma syndrome.

d. rape trauma syndrome.

9. _____ rape is a favorite tactic of defense attorneys, which some police and court jurisdictions still believe, even though it is a myth. (p. 474)

a. Victim-credibility

b. Victim-consent

c. Victim-precipitated

d. None of the above

10. Rapists show some deficits in their cognitive appraisals of women's (p. 475)

a. feelings.

b. intentions.

c. boundaries.

d. a and b.

PRACTICE TEST NUMBER 3

1. Recently, both explanations and treatments of sexual dysfunction have become increasingly (p.478)

a. psychological.

b. behavioral.

c. biological

d. less obvious.

2. The DSM-IV-TR says that sexual dysfunction can occur in which phase? (p. 478)
a. desire
b. excitement
c. orgasm
d. all of the above

3. Hypoactive sexual desire disorder seems to have a very strong _____ component, especially for women. (p. 479.)

a. psychological

b. physiological

c. behavioral

d. none of the above

4. In this type of sexual desire dysfunction, the person shows extreme avoidance of all genital sexual contact with a partner. (p. 479)

a. hypoactive sexual desire disorder

b. sexual aversion disorder

c. erectile insufficiency

d. sexual repulsion disorder

5. Sexual interest in men and women depends on (p. 479)

a. estrogen.

b. dopamine.

c. serotonin.

d. testosterone.

6. The general neglect of research and treatment of female sexual dysfunction is an implicit attitude that women don't care about (p. 479)

a. their bodies.

b. their relationships.

c. sex.

d. the NFL.

7. _____ was formerly called impotence. (p. 481)

a. Erectile contraction disorder

b. Male erectile disorder

c. Priapism

d. all of the above

8. Masters, Johnson and Kaplan, believed that erectile dysfunction was primarily a function of _____ about sexual performance. (p. 481)

a. excitement

b. interest

c. anxiety

e. fantasizing

9. Viagra will promote an erection only if _____ is present. (p.482)

a. a partner

b. sexual desire

c. an opportunity

d. all of the above

10. Premature ejaculation is most likely to occur in

a. young men

b. after abstinence

c. men over 60

d. a & b

COMPREHENSIVE PRACTICE TEST

The following tests are designed to give you an idea of how well you understood the entire chapter. There are three different types of tests: multiple-choice, true-false, and essay.

MULTIPLE-CHOICE

1. The major reason that there are fewer sex researchers than other researchers is (p. 450)

a. sexual taboos.

b. sexual issues are controversial.

c. nobody is interested in sexual issues.

CHAPTER 13: ABNORMAL PSYCHOLOGY, 13e

d. a and b.

2. The _____ theory, developed in the 1750s, had the central belief that semen was necessary for masculine characteristics and physical and sexual vigor in men, thus masturbation and patronizing prostitutes were considered harmful. (p. 452)

a. degeneracy

b. abstinence

c. onanistic

d. semen conservation

3. During what decade did the American Medical Association declare that masturbation was a normal part of adolescent behavior, and the Boy Scouts do away with their antimasturbation warnings? (p. 452.)

a. 1960s

b. 1950s

c. 1980s

d. 1970s

4. The DSM-IV-TR criteria for this group of disorders is a persistent pattern, lasting at least six months, that causes significant distress or impairment, in which unusual objects, rituals, or situations are required for full sexual satisfaction. (p. 456.)

a. pedophilias

b. paraphilias

c. erotophilias

d. all of the above

5. Ted Bundy and Jeffrey Dahmer were cited in your textbook as extreme examples of this paraphilia. (p. 461.)

a. masochism

b. sadism

c. voyeurism

d. frotteurism

6. Sexual abuse includes (p. 467.)

a. pedophilia.

b. rape.

c. incest.

d. All of the above.

7. Although short-term consequences of childhood sexual abuse include fears, PTSD, sexual inappropriateness, and poor self-esteem, approximately _____ of sexually abused children show no symptoms. (p.)

a. one-half

b. a quarter

c. two-thirds

d. one-third

8. Long-term consequences of childhood sexual abuse may include (p. 467)

a. dissociative symptoms.

b. somatization disorder.

c. borderline personality disorder.

d. all of the above.

9. Culturally prohibited relations between family members, such as brother and sister or a parent and child, are known as (p. 471)

a. rape.

b. acquaintance rape.

c. incest.

d. paraphilia.

10. This is the most common form of incest but it is rarely reported. (p. 472)

a. father-daughter

b. mother-son

c. uncle-niece

d. brother-sister

11. According to the FBI Uniform Crime Reports, the greatest concentration of rapists arrested are between _____ years old. (p. 474.)

a. 18 and 24

b. 25 and 35

c. 15 and 20

d. 16 and 23

12. It is difficult to establish the prevalence rates for rape, because studies may (p. 472.)

a. vary in the definitions used.

b. vary in the way information is gathered.

c. not have enough subjects.

d. a and b.

13. Studies done by Raymond Knight and Robert Prentky have shown that all rapists actually have _____ motives. (p. 473.)

a. empathetic

b. aggressive

c. sexual

d. b and c

14. _____ is most likely to occur after a lengthy abstinence and is the most common male sexual dysfunction. (p. 483)

a. impotence

b. male erectile disorder

c. male orgasmic disorder

d. premature ejaculation

15. When treating female orgasmic disorder, it is important to distinguish between a _____ and a _____ dysfunction. (p. 484.)

a. past, present

b. subjective, objective

c. lifelong, situational

d. interest, disinterest

16. _____ in women is more likely to have an obvious organic basis. (p. 480 .)

a. Female orgasmic disorder

b. Female sexual arousal disorder

c. Vaginismus

d. Dyspareunia

TRUE – FALSE

    1. T / F Special caution must be taken when classifying sexual practices as "abnormal" or "deviant." (p. 451)

    2 T / F   The belief that homosexuality is a mental illness has been associated with people's discomfort concerning the sexual behaviors of homosexual people. (p. 453)

    3. T / F Nearly all of the people with paraphilias are female. (p.456-457)

    4.   T / F Fetishes only cause overt harm to others when accompanied by illegal acts like theft or destruction of property. (p. 457)

    5. T / F Voyeurism is the most common sexual offense reported to the police in the United States, Canada, and Europe. (p. 460)

    6. T / F The vast majority of the studies concerning paraphilias have been with men who have not committed any offense, but have come

into clinics to participate in research. (chapter)

7 T / F   Sexual abuse is sexual contact that involves physical or psychological coercion or at least one individual who cannot reasonably consent to the contact. (p. 450)

8. T / F Research has shown that the use of anatomically correct dolls greatly increases the accuracy of three- or four-year olds' reports of what happened to them. (p. 469)

9. T / F The incest taboo is virtually universal among human societies. (p.471)

 10. T / F If the partner is under 18, but consents, it can't be considered statutory rape. (p. 472)

11. T / F Most rapes involve more than one rapist. (p. 474)

12. T / F Conviction rates for rape are low. (p. 475)

13. T / F Megan's Law, intended to protect potential victims, has also encouraged harassment of sex offenders. (p. 476)

14. T / F A high percentage of people will never experience a sexual dysfunction in their life time.

ESSAY QUESTIONS

1. Discuss the types of treatment that are used with sex offenders (psychological, biological, surgical), the goals and effectiveness.

2. What were some of the conclusions of Bruce Rind's research on the association between early sexual experiences and mental health in young adulthood?

WEB LINKS TO ITEMS OR CONCEPTS DISCUSSED IN CHAPTER 13

Pedophilia

www.geocities.com/ericw_970/

www.usnews.com/usnews/issue/020422/opinion/22jo

hn.htm

Gender identity disorder

www.athealth.com/Consumer/disorders/GenderIden.

html www.mental-health-today.com/gender/

www.behavenet.com/capsules/disorders/genderiddis.htm

USE IT OR LOSE IT

Provide an answer to the thought question below, knowing that there is more than one way to respond. Possible answers are presented in the Answer Key.

Do you believe that people should be allowed to surgically change gender if they feel that their body is the wrong sex?

CRISS-CROSS

Now that you know all there is to know about this chapter, here's your opportunity

to put that knowledge to work.

CRISS-CROSS CLUES

Across
1. when an adult has sexual urges, fantasies, or activity with a prepubescent child
4. sexual arousal by the thought of being a woman (males only)
5. receiving sexual fantasies and behavior while observing unsuspecting females undressing or couples having sex
7. behaviors involving exposure of genitals to others in inappropriate circumstances
8. third sexual phase, resulting in the release of sexual tension and peak of sexual pleasure
9. obtaining sexual gratification involving the use of some inanimate object (shoes, for instance)
10. persons with gender identity disorder wishing to change their sex
11. sexual contact that involves physical or psychological coercion

Down
2. culturally prohibited sexual relations between family members
3. experiencing sexual gratification by inflicting pain and cruelty
5. involuntary spasm of the muscles at the entrance to the vagina, preventing penetration
6. experiencing sexual stimulation from pain and degradation

Puzzle created with Puzzlemaker at Discoveryschool.com

ANSWERS TO TEST QUESTIONS - CHAPTER 13

MATCHING
Person / Term
    G. Simon Tissot
    D. Reverend Sylvester Graham
    H. Dr. John Harvey Kellogg
    C. Onania, or the Heinous Sin of Self Pollution
    E. Havelock Ellis and Magnus Hirschfeld
    I. Evelyn Hooker
    B. autoerotic asphyxia
    A. statutory rape
    F. priapism

Dysfunction

of Sexual Desire
    D. Hypoactive sexual desire disorder
    H. Sexual aversion disorder
of Sexual Arousal
    A. Male erectile disorder
    E. Female sexual arousal disorder
of Orgasm
    I. Premature ejaculation
    F. Male orgasmic disorder
    B. Female orgasmic disorder
    G. Vaginismus
    C. Dyspareunia

SHORT ANSWERS
(Your answer should contain the following points.)

1.   a. much more common than once was assumed
    b. possible links between childhood sexual abuse and some mental disorders
    c. some dramatic and well-publicized cases involving allegations of childhood sexual abuse have raised issues concerning validity of children's testimony and accuracy of recovered memories

2.   **Intrafamilial:** tend to have some pedophiliac arousal patterns suggesting they are partly motivated by sexual arousal to children and adult women; majority of offenses are against girls; will offend with one or a few children in the family
   Extrafamilial: victims are more equally distributed between boys and girls (more likely to be victims)

THE DOCTOR IS IN...PSYCHIATRIC HELP—5¢

1.   Jim has a fetish. He uses an inanimate (women's underwear) to obtain sexual gratification and has had the problem for over six months. Also, it is causing him distress, and he seems to be concerned that it is getting worse.

2.   a. Gender identity disorder/Transsexualism: Darla meets the criteria for gender identity disorder. She has had a strong cross-gender identification (desire and insistence on being the opposite sex) and gender dysphoria (discomfort about her biological sex). She is now an adult and considered a transsexual.
b. Treatment: Psychotherapy is not effective in resolving gender dysphoria, so the best treatment would be to help Darla obtain sexual reassignment surgery.

3.   a. Diagnosis: Vaginismus for Susan and situational erectile dysfunction for Ben
b. What else to know: Any past traumatic sexual experience for Susan, when did the problem start and how have they handled the problem so far

MULTIPLE-CHOICE PRACTICE TESTS

PRACTICE TESTS

Q#	TEST 1	TEST 2	TEST 3
1	C	B	C
2	B	D	D
3	A	B	A
4	D	B	B
5	A	B	D
6	D	C	C
7	B	D	B
8	B	A	C
9	D	C	B
10	A	D	B

COMPREHENSIVE PRACTICE TEST

Q#	MULTIPLE CHOICE	T/F
1	D	T
2	A	T
3	D	F
4	B	T
5	B	F

6	D	F
7	D	T
8	D	F
9	C	T
10	D	F
11	A	T
12	D	T
13	D	T
14	D	F
15	C	
16	D	

ESSAY QUESTIONS
(Your answer should contain the following points.)

1. **Goals**:
   - modify patterns of sexual arousal
   - modify cognitions and social skills
   - change habits or behaviors that increase the chance of reoffending
   - reduce sexual drive

   Therapies:
   - Aversion therapy—growing skepticism about its efficacy as sole form of treatment *aversion therapy can involve these methods* covert sensitization assisted covert sensitization satiation
   - Cognitive restructuring—attempts to eliminate cognitive distortions *often involves* social-skills training—learning to process information from women more effectively relapse prevention—helps offender to understand the antecedents of his decision to offend Cognitive behavioral techniques appear more effective than aversion therapy
   - Surgical and chemical castration—lower the testosterone level, which lowers the sex drive, allowing the offender to resist any inappropriate impulses relapse rates when the drugs/chemicals are discontinued are very high recidivism rates of castrated offenders are typically less than three percent

2. a. Correlations between childhood sexual abuse and later problems were of surprisingly small magnitude, suggesting that such experiences are not typically very harmful
   b. After statistically controlling for general family problems, the small association between CSA and adult problems were reduced to essentially zero—suggesting family problems might play a greater problem
   c. Incest and forced sex both associated with more problems than sex between nominally consenting nonrelated individuals
   d. Age at which CSA was experienced was unrelated to adult outcome

USE IT OR LOSE IT

This is a complex question which depends on your personal beliefs about gender, sexual behaviors, and values. As more people speak out about transgender issues, and medical treatments advance, individual and societal approaches to changing ones gender may change as well.

CRISS-CROSS ANSWERS
Across
1. pedophilia
4. autogynephilia
5. voyeurism
7. exhibitionism
8. orgasm
9. fetishism
10. transsexualism
11. sexual abuse

Down
2. incest
3. masochism
5. vaginismus
6. sadism

Chapter 14: Schizophrenia and Other Psychotic Disorders

BEFORE YOU READ

Schizophrenia has been termed the most human of mental illnesses, because it so profoundly impacts the very things that set us apart from animals, our reason, thought and language. As if that weren't enough, it also affects motor behaviors, perception, emotion, and social interactions. This debilitating disorder affects one out of every hundred people. However, its distribution varies as a function of ethnicity, father's age, mother's condition during pregnancy, and even where in the world, and what time of the year a person is born.

Schizophrenic behavior patterns can be classified into different subtypes including paranoid, catatonic, and disorganized patterns. Additionally, abnormal behaviors, such as delusions and hallucinations, are called positive symptoms, while those characterized by the absence of normal behaviors are called negative symptoms. Given this complex pattern of behaviors, it is not surprising that there are a variety of possible causes of schizophrenia, most of which are thought to interact. These include genetic and organic factors, variations in transmitter activity, family and social interactions, and even developmental experiences. The treatment of schizophrenia was revolutionized by the advent of psychotropic medications which alter transmitters, such as dopamine and GABA, and can dramatically improve symptoms in some individuals. Despite the amount of research devoted to understanding schizophrenia, many questions still remain about the causes, prevention and treatment of the disorder, and whether in fact, it is really a collection of disorders rather than a single disease.

- **SCHIZOPHRENIA**
  The Epidemiology of Schizophrenia
  Origins of the Schizophrenia Construct

- **THE CLINICAL PICTURE IN SCHIZOPHRENIA**
  Delusions
  Hallucinations

Disorganized Speech

Disorganized and Catatonic Behavior

Negative Symptoms

• **SUBTYPES OF SCHIZOPHRENIA**

Paranoid Type

Disorganized Type

Catatonic Type

Undifferentiated Type

Residual Type

Other Psychotic Disorders

• **WHAT CAUSES SCHIZOPHRENIA?**

Genetic Aspects

Prenatal Exposures

Genes and Environment in Schizophrenia: A

Synthesis

A Neurodevelopmental Perspective

Biological Aspects; Neurocognition

Psychosocial and Cultural Aspects

• **TREATMENT AND CLINICAL OUTCOME**

Pharmacological Approaches

Psychosocial Approaches

• **UNSOLVED ISSUES:**

Can Schizophrenia Be Prevented?

OBJECTIVES

After reading this chapter, you should be able to:

1. Explain the epidemiology of schizophrenia, as well as the origins of its construct.

2. Describe the clinical picture of schizophrenia, including the diagnostic signs of the positive and negative symptoms.

3. Compare and contrast the subtypes of schizophrenia.

4. Describe the clinical features of other psychotic disorders.

5. Summarize the biological, psychosocial, and sociocultural causal influences in schizophrenia.

6. Evaluate the various biological and psychosocial treatments for schizophrenia.

7. Discuss current issues in treating schizophrenia, including limitations of antipsychotics and the need for expanded psychosocial intervention.

8. Explain the difficulties associated with trying to prevent schizophrenia.

AS YOU READ

Answers and page numbers can be found in the Answer Key at the end of the chapter.

KEY WORDS

Each of the words below is important in understanding the concepts presented in this Chapter. Write the definition next to each of the words.

Term	Page	Definition
antipsychotics (neuroleptics)	522	
brief psychotic disorder	500	
catatonic schizophrenia	497	
cognitive remediation	525	
candidate genes	507	

Delusion	493	
delusional disorder	499	
disorganized schizophrenia	497	
Dopamine	515	
endophenotypes	510	
expressed emotion	519	
Glutamate	519	
Hallucination	493	
linkage analysis	507	
negative symptoms	495	
paranoid schizophrenia	507	
positive symptoms	496	
Psychosis	490	
residual schizophrenia	498	
schizoaffective disorders	499	
schizophreniform disorders	499	
shared psychotic disorder (folie a deux)	500	
undifferentiated schizophrenia	498	

WHO'S WHO AND WHAT'S WHAT—MATCHING

Match the following names and terms with their correct definitions or descriptions.

Description/Definition

A. imitation of the act of others

B. Swiss psychiatrist who in 1911 used the term, "schizophrenia," to characterize a split within the intellect and between the intellect and emotion and external reality

C. completely new made-up words by a patient with schizophrenia

D. studied by David Rosenthal at NIMH in the mid-1950s, because all developed schizophrenia but were discordant with severity

E. theory that schizophrenic individuals find themselves unable to maintain a job or maintaining relationships; thus, they are likely to end up at the lower end of the socioeconomic ladder

F. An apothecary in London who in 1810 gave the first detailed clinical description of schizophrenia

G. theory that the lower the SES, the higher the prevalence of schizophrenia, because the conditions of lower-class existence are stressful, increasing the risk for schizophrenia

H. The first person described in detail in 1810 with schizophrenia

I. measure of how understandable and "easy to follow" the speech of a family member is

J. German psychiatrist who used the term, "dementia praecox," to refer to a group of conditions that feature mental deterioration beginning early in life

K. mimicking of another's phases

L. used the term, "demence precoce," to describe the symptoms of a 13-year-old boy in 1860

Name/Term

_____ Genain quadruplets

_____ John Haslam

_____ John Tilly Matthews

_____ Benedict Morel

_____ Emil Kraepelin

_____ Eugen Bleuler

_____ Neologisms

_____ echopraxia

_____ echolalia

_____ communication deviance

_____ sociogenic hypothesis

_____ social drift hypothesis

WHO'S WHO AND WHAT'S WHAT—MATCHING

Match the following types of schizophrenia with their definitions.

Definition

A. Those persons who are in remission following a schizophrenic episode and show only mild signs of schizophrenia.

B. A form of schizophrenia that occurs at an early age and includes blunting, inappropriate mannerisms, and bizarre behavior.

C. A person in whom symptoms of schizophrenia have existed for six months or less.

D. A person who shows absurd, illogical, changeable delusions and frequent hallucinations.

E. A form of schizophrenia in which all the primary indications of schizophrenia are seen in a rapidly changing pattern.

F. A person who shows some schizophrenic signs, as well as obvious depression or elation.

G. A type of schizophrenia characterized by alternating periods of extreme excitement and extreme withdrawal.

Schizophrenia

_____ Undifferentiated

_____ Paranoid type

_____ Catatonic type

_____ Disorganized type

_____ Residual type

_____ Schizoaffective disorder

_____ Schizophreniform disorder

SHORT ANSWERS

Provide brief answers to the following questions.

1. Describe the types of delusions common in schizophrenia.

2. Discuss the three types of prevention programs with relation to schizophrenia

3. List examples of the positive and negative symptoms of schizophrenia.

THE DOCTOR IS IN...PSYCHIATRIC HELP—5¢

Read the following scenarios and diagnose the client. Remember to look *carefully at the criteria for the disorder before you make a decision as to the diagnosis. Make a list of other information you might need to help you understand the causal factors.*

1. Sharon comes to visit you. She has been referred by her sister after she was picked up by the police outside of Tom Hanks' house. She told the police that she and Tom were getting married and that she was the love of his life. Sharon said that his latest movie was dedicated to her, and that he conveyed it through a secret message on the screen that only she could pick up. With Sharon's permission, you talk to her sister and discover that other than this behavior, Sharon seems normal. How would you diagnosis Sharon and why?

2. You are a family therapist. A family comes to see you, bringing their 23-year-old son who suffers from schizophrenia. How would you treat this family, and, based on studies, what would you expect the son's outcome to be?

AFTER YOU READ

Answers can be found in the Answer Key at the end of the chapter.

PRACTICE TESTS

Take the following three multiple-choice tests to see how much you have comprehended from the chapter. Each represents roughly one-third of the chapter. As you study the chapter, use these to check your progress.

PRACTICE TEST NUMBER 1

1. The hallmark of schizophrenia is a significant loss of contact with reality, referred to as (p. 490)

a. hallucinations.

a. delusions.

b. psychosis.

c. manic reaction.

2. Symptoms of schizophrenia include oddities in (p. 490)

a. perception.

b. thinking.

c. sense of self.

d. all of the above.

3. Schizophrenia is about as prevalent as (p. 490)

a. epilepsy.

b. heart disease.

c. stroke.

d. none of the above.

4. Schizophrenia tends to develop earlier in _____ than in _____. (p. 491)

a. women, men

b. men, women

c. old age, adulthood

d. pre-schoolers, elementary-age children

5. Schizophrenia is becoming more common and severe in males than females. This could be a result of female hormones playing a _____ in development (p. 492)

a. destructive role.

b. constructive role.

c. passive role.

d. protective role.

6. Delusions of grandeur are common in _____ schizophrenia. (p. 496).

a. disorganized

b. catatonic

c. residual

d. paranoid

7. In the past, _____ schizophrenia was called hebephrenic. One of its characteristics is flat or inappropriate affect. (p. 497)

a. disorganized

b. catatonic

c. residual

d. paranoid

8. _____ schizophrenia was once common in Europe and North America but has become less prevalent in recent years. It is still found in less industrialized regions of the world. (p. 497)

a. Disorganized

b. Catatonic

c. Residual

d. Paranoid

9. _____ schizophrenia is considered by the authors as something of a wastebasket category, because a patient may meet the criteria for schizophrenia but not fit into one of the other types. (p. 498)

a. Undifferentiated

b. Residual

c. Disorganized

d. Paranoid

10. The category used for people who have suffered at least one episode of schizophrenia, and now don't have positive symptoms but clinically show negative symptoms, is (p. 498)

a. undifferentiated.

b. residual.

c. disorganize.

d. paranoid.

PRACTICE TEST 2

1. Most instances of an acute, schizophrenic breakdown appear to show symptoms of the _____ type, which may later lead to a change in diagnosis to a specific subtype. (p 498)

a. undifferentiated.

b. paranoid.

c. catatonic.

d. disorganized.

2. Late-onset schizophrenia is much more likely to strike women than men around (p. 492)

a. retirement age.

b. menopause.

c. 35-40 years of age.

d. none of the above.

3. A/an _____ is an erroneous belief that is fixed and firmly held despite clear and contradictory evidence. (p. 493)

a. Hallucination

b. Delusion

c. Differentiation

d. Dementia

4. A/an _____ is a sensory experience that occurs in the absence of any external perceptual stimulus. (p. 493)

a. Hallucination

b. Delusion

c. Differentiation

d. Dementia

5. Disorganized speech is the external manifestation of a disorder in thought (p. 494)

a. form.

b. content.

c. interpretation.

d. all of the above.

6. _____ symptoms reflect behavioral excesses or distortions in schizophrenic patients.
(p. 495)

a. Catatonic

b. Negative

c. Positive

d. Alogia

7. _____ symptoms reflect behavioral deficits in schizophrenic patients. (p. 495)

a. Catatonic

b. Negative

c. Positive

d. Alogia

8. Schizoaffective disorder is characterized by the presence of (p. 499)

a. schizophrenia and a mood disorder

b. schizophrenia and a substance addiction

c. schizophrenia and paranoia

d. OCD and a mood disorder

9. Studies by Elaine Walker and her colleagues found what differences between preschizophrenic children and their healthy siblings? (p. 509)

a. motor abnormalities

b. less positive facial emotions

c. more negative facial emotions

d. All of the above.

10. Because the brain normally occupies the skull fully, the enlarged ventricles of some schizophrenics imply a(n) (p. 511)

a. decreased pressure on the brain.

b. loss of brain tissue mass.

c. increased amount of spinal fluid.

d. predisposition to hydrocephaly.

PRACTICE TEST NUMBER 3

1. _____ is an excitatory neurotransmitter that researchers suspect might be involved in schizophrenia. (p.515)

a. GABA

b. Dopamine

c. Glutamate

d. None of the above

2. A significant percentage of patients with schizophrenia are deficient in their ability to track a moving target. The skill required to do this task is called (p. 517)

a. rapid eye movement.

b. smooth-pursuit eye movement.

c. tracking eye movement.

d. following ability eye movement.

3. The central feature of _____ schizophrenia is pronounced motor symptoms. (p. 497)

a. undifferentiated

b. catatonic

c. disorganized

d. paranoid

4. As a genetic researcher, you have decided to move away from the family, twin, and adoption schizophrenia studies you had been focusing on and become involved in a new paradigm. This paradigm shift would probably be a study of (p. 507)

a. behaviors.

b. the unconscious thoughts of schizophrenic.

c. treatment methods.

d. molecular genetics.

5. In addition to prenatal viral infections, researchers are looking at _____ as a factor that could cause or trigger schizophrenia. (p. 507)

a. rhesus incompatibility

b. early nutritional deficiency

c. perinatal birth complications

d. all of the above.

6. Carlos is referred to you with psychotic symptoms that meet the criteria for schizophrenia. However, he also exhibits clear mood changes. What would your diagnosis of Carlos be? (p. 499)

a. schizophreniform

b. catatonic

c. undifferentiated

d. schizoaffective

7. Jennifer comes into your office for an appointment. For the past two months she has been experiencing schizophrenia-like psychoses but really not severe enough yet for her to be diagnosed with schizophrenia. How would you diagnose Jennifer? (p. 499)

a. schizophreniform

b. catatonic

c. undifferentiated

d. schizoaffective

8. A person in whom symptoms of schizophrenia have existed for at least a month and less than six months would be diagnosed as having the (p. 499)

a. undifferentiated type.

b. catatonic type.

c. disorganized type.

d. schizophreniform disorder.

9. Shared psychotic disorder, in which one person passes on or shares a delusion with someone he or she is close to, is also known as (p. 500)

a. sibling rivalry.

b. cyclical psychotic disorder.

c. undifferentiated disorder.

d. folie á deux.

10. An assumption that can create some problems when interpreting the findings of twin studies is (p. 504)

a. twins all have the same genetic make-up.

b. MZ and DZ twins are equally likely to develop schizophrenia.

c. MZ and DZ twins have equally similar environments.

d. all of the above.

COMPREHENSIVE PRACTICE TEST

The following tests are designed to give you an idea of how well you understood the entire chapter. There are three different types of tests: multiple-choice, true-false, and essay.

MULTIPLE-CHOICE

1. The most common form of hallucination is (p. 493)

a. tactile.

b. visual.

c. auditory.

d. olfactory.

2. Modern research has found support for the idea that auditory hallucinations are really misperceived (p. 494)

a. external stimuli.

b. radio signals.

c. thought insertions.

d. sub-vocal speech.

3. Which of the following choices is NOT a subtype of schizophrenia? (p.498)

a. paranoid

b. disorganized

c. depressed

d. catatonic

4. This disorder is characterized by a duration of days, not weeks or months, usually presents both positive and negative schizophrenic symptoms, and often goes untreated and/or unrepeated. (p. 500)

a. acute onsest schizophrenia

b. sub-chronic schizophrenia

c. acquired schizophrenia

d. brief psychotic disorder

5. The prevalence of schizophrenia in the first-degree relatives of a proband with schizophrenia is about what percent? (p. 501)

a. 25

b. 10

c. 3

d. 2

6. Wahlberg and colleagues found that children who were at genetic risk and lived with families that had high _____ showed high levels of thought disorder. (p.505).

a. levels of affection

b. communication deviance

c. number of siblings

d. a and c

7. The Finnish Adoption Study has provided strong confirmation of what model for the origins of schizophrenia? (p. 507)

a. psychoanalytical

b. cognitive

c. diathesis-stress

d. behavioral

8. Focusing on MZ concordance rates has perhaps caused an overestimation of the heritability of schizophrenia because MZ and DZ twins do not have equally similar

_____ environments. (p. 508)

a. prenatal

b. home

c. community

d. none of the above

9. Schizophreniform disorder is characterized by schizophrenic like psychosis that (p.499)

a. lasts at least a month, but not more than 6 months.

b. lasts less than a year, but not more than 6 years.

c. are exclusively visual in nature.

d. are undetectable.

10. Negative symptoms of schizophrenia seem to be linked to which part of the brain? (p. 513)

a. frontal lobe

b. temporal lobe

c. medial

d. amygdala

11. Positive symptoms of schizophrenia seem to be linked to which part of the brain, especially on the left side? (p. 513)

a. temporal lobe

b. hippocampus

c. amygdala

d. all of the above.

12. The overall organization of the cells in the brain is called the brain's (p. 514)

a. wave.

b. structure.

c. cytoarchitecture.

d. pattern.

13. Some evidence points to patients with schizophrenia as missing particular types of neurons known as (p. 514)

a. inhibitory interneurons.

b. micro neurons.

c. macro neurons.

d. excitatory neurons.

14. The first antipsychotics, developed over 50 years ago to treat schizophrenia, are called (pp. 523-524)

a. conventional antipsychotics.

b. neuroleptics.

c. unconventional antipsychotics.

d. a and b.

15. Which of the following symptoms/side effects are NOT likely to be encountered when taking second generation anti-psychotics? (p. 524)

a. weight gain

b. re-hospitalization

c. .agitation

d. diabetes.

16. Betty, who is schizophrenic, goes to a group everyday where she learns employment skills, relationship skills, and skills in managing medication. This type of training is referred to as (p. 525)

a. real life.

b. case management.

c. social-skills.

d. family.

17. The goal of cognitive-behavioral therapy when treating schizophrenia is to (p. 525)

a. decrease the intensity of positive symptoms.

b. reduce relapse.

c. decrease social disability.

d. all of the above.

18. _____ therapy is staged, which means that it comprises different components that are administered at different points in the patient's recovery. (p. 525)

a. Personal therapy

b. Cognitive therapy

c. Psychodynamic

d. Behavioral

TRUE – FALSE

1. T / F Schizophrenia is a single, discrete illness. (p. 492)

2. T / F People who have a parent with schizophrenia have a statistically higher risk of developing the disorder than those who do not. (p. 508)

3. T / F Delusions reflect a disorder of thought content. (p. 494)

4. T / F A preponderance of negative symptoms in the clinical picture is considered a good sign for the patient's future outcome. (p. 495)

5. T / F The prognosis for someone diagnosed with schizophreniform disorder is better than for established forms of schizophrenia. (p.499)

6. T / F The terms, "familial" and "genetic," are synonymous. (p. 501)

7. T / F Schizophrenia probably involves several, or perhaps many, genes working together to make a person susceptible. (p. 507)

8. T / F The first signs of schizophrenia may be found in the way that children move. (p. 509)

9. T / F Schizophrenics are very sensitive to pain. (p. 512)

10. T / F Schizophrenia manifests itself more in defective cognition than in defective biology. (p. 517)

11. T / F Patients living in more industrialized countries do better than patients living in less industrialized countries. (p. 523)

12. T / F Dopamine is the only neurotransmitter involved in schizophrenia. (p. 529)

ESSAY QUESTIONS

1. Discuss how dopamine became implicated in schizophrenia.

2. Define and explain expressed emotion (EE) and its connection to patient relapse.

3. Compare the conventional antipsychotics with the newer, novel ones in terms of effectiveness and side effects.

WEB LINKS TO ITEMS OR CONCEPTS DISCUSSED IN CHAPTER 14

Psychosis

www.eppic.org.au/

Schizophrenia

www.schizophrenia.com/

www.narsad.org/

www.mentalhealth.com/dis/p20-ps01.html

USE IT OR LOSE IT
Provide an answer to the thought question below, knowing that there is more than one way to respond. Possible answers are presented in the Answer Key.

Do you think people with schizophrenia should be institutionalized against their will in order to insure that they take their medications correctly, and receive treatment for their illness?

Now that you know all there is to know about this chapter, here's your opportunity to put that knowledge to work.

CRISS-CROSS CLUES

Across

3. the most important neurotransmitter implicated in schizophrenia
6. an excitatory neurotransmitter that is widespread in the brain
7. pronounced motor signs, either of an excited or stuporous type of schizophrenia
8. an erroneous belief that is fixed and firmly held
9. the hallmark of schizophrenia, a significant loss of contact with reality
10. a wide variety of disordered processes of varied etiology, developmental pattern, and outcome

Down

1. a measure of the family environment
2. an absence or deficit of behaviors normally present in schizophrenia
4. a sensory experience occurring without any external perceptual stimulus
5. a class of drugs introduced in the mid-1950s that transformed the environment in mental hospital

Puzzle created with Puzzlemaker at DiscoverySchool.com

ANSWERS TO TEST QUESTIONS - CHAPTER FOURTEEN

MATCHING

Name/Term

    D. Genain quadruplets
    F. John Haslam
    K. John Tilly Matthews
    L. Benedict Morel
    J. Emil Kraepelin
    B. Eugen Bleuler
    C. Neologisms
    A. echopraxia
    K. echolalia
    I. communication deviance
    G. sociogenic hypothesis
    E. social drift hypothesis

Match the following types of schizophrenia with its definition

    E. Undifferentiated
    D. Paranoid type
    G. Catatonic type
    B. Disorganized type
    A. Residual type
    F. Schizoaffective disorder
    C. Schizophreniform disorder

SHORT ANSWERS
(Your answer should contain the following points.)

    1. delusions common in schizophrenia:
    a. mad feelings or impulses: thoughts, feelings, or actions are being controlled by external agents
    b. thought insertion: thoughts are being inserted into one's brain by some external agency
    c. thought withdrawal: some external agency has robbed one of one's thoughts
    d. delusions of reference: neutral environmental event (television program or song) is believed to have special and personal meaning intended only for the patient
    e. delusions of bodily changes: (e.g., bowels don't work) or removal of organs

    2. Examples of prenatal factors that could trigger or cause schizophrenia.
    a. **Prenatal viral infection:** More people with schizophrenia are born between January and March, in a study done in Finland after a flu epidemic. It was found that there was a higher rate of schizophrenia in children born to mothers who had

the flu in the second trimester of pregnancy.

b. **Rhesus incompatibility:** A study done by Hollister, Laing and Mednick showed that the rate of schizophrenia is about 2.1 percent in males who are Rh-incompatible with their mothers, as opposed to 0.8 percent of males who were compatible.

c. **Birth complications:** Research has shown that mothers of patients with schizophrenia were more likely to have had some sort of problems with pregnancy or delivery. One possibility is the problem might have caused oxygen deprivation.

d. **Nutritional deficiency:** The results of Dutch Hunger Winter's study, in which people suffered severe famine as a result of a Nazi blockade, found that children who were conceived at the height of the famine had a two-fold increase in their risk of later developing schizophrenia.

3. The positive and negative symptoms of schizophrenia.

Positive:
a. delusions
b. hallucinations
c. disorganized speech
d. grossly disorganized behavior
e. sudden onset
f. derailment of associations

Negative:
a. flat or blunted emotional expressiveness
b. alogia
c. avolition
d. asociality
e. significant cognitive impairment

4. Three types of prevention programs with relation to schizophrenia:
   a. **primary prevention:** to prevent new cases; improve obstetric care for women with schizophrenia and first-degree relatives of schizophrenic patients
   b. **secondary prevention:** early intervention with people at risk; possible screening of at-risk people; problem with how to identify people and how harmful to tell someone they might develop schizophrenia
   c. **tertiary prevention:** early treatment for those who already have the illness; vocational rehabilitation, family support and cognitive therapy

THE DOCTOR IS IN...PSYCHIATRIC HELP—5¢

1. **Delusional disorder with erotomania subtype.** Sharon's actions and beliefs are completely false and absurd. She seems normal outside of the belief that she and Tom Hanks are getting married. Sharon also seems to be stalking him.

2. **Treatment:**
   a. work to change the patient-relative relationship
   b. educate the patient and family about schizophrenia

c. help to improve coping and problem-solving skills

d. enhance communication skills especially the clarity of family communications.

3. **Outcome:** would expect the patient to do better clinically and have a low relapse rate

MULTIPLE-CHOICE PRACTICE TESTS

PRACTICE TESTS

Q#	TEST 1	TEST 2	TEST 3
1	B	A	B
2	D	B	B
3	A	B	B
4	B	A	D
5	D	B	D
6	D	C	D
7	A	B	A
8	B	A	D
9	A	D	D
10	B	B	D

Q#	MULTIPLE CHOICE	T/F
1	C	F
2	D	T
3	C	T
4	D	F
5	B	T
6	B	F
7	C	T
8	A	T
9	A	F
10	A	T
11	D	F
12	C	F
13	A	
14	D	
15	B	
16	C	
17	D	
18	A	

ESSAY QUESTIONS
(Your answer should contain the following points.)

1. Dopamine became implicated in schizophrenia because:
    a. mental changes associated with LSD had scientists interested in schizophrenia consider a possible biochemical basis for the disorder
    b. the observation that chlorpromazine's therapeutic benefits were linked to its ability to block dopamine receptors
    c. the abuse of amphetamines in the 50s and 60s lead to the discovery that, if too much dopamine is produced, a form of psychosis that includes paranoia and auditory hallucinations occurs that looks a lot like schizophrenia
    d. actual clinical studies that treated patients by giving them drugs, which increased the availability of dopamine

2. Expressed emotion (EE) and its connection to patient relapse:
    a. EE is a measure of the family environment which is based on how the family member speaks about the patient during a private interview with a researcher. There are three main elements: criticism, hostility, and emotional over involvement (EOI).
    b. Criticism, the most important, reflects dislike or disapproval; hostility, dislike, or rejection of patient as a person; EOI dramatic or over concerned attitude with illness.
    c. It predicts relapse in patients.
    d. When EE levels in families are lowered, rates of patient relapse rates decrease.
    e. High EE behaviors exhibited by family members are perceived as stressful by patients and possibly triggering the release of cortisol, which triggers dopamine activity.
    f. Studies show that an increase in patients' unusual thinking occurred immediately after the patient was criticized by a family member.

3. **Conventional:** Haldol and Thorazine
    a. work because these are dopamine antagonists
    b. benefits appear within 1-3 weeks, with maximum results in 6-8 weeks
    c. work best for positive symptoms
    d. side effects: drowsiness, dry mouth, weight gain, extra-pyramidal side effects, tardive dyskinesia, and neuroleptic malignant syndrome

Novel: Clozal, Risperday, Zyprexa, Seroquel, Geodon
    a. cause fewer extrapyramidal symptoms
    b. don't block D2 receptors well but block a much broader range of receptors, including D4 dopamine receptor
    c. relieve positive and negative symptoms
    d. patients less likely to be rehospitalized

e. side effects: drowsiness and weight gain, diabetes, and, rarely, agranulocytosis

USE IT OR LOSE IT

When people are psychotic, they frequently make choices which are dangerous to themselves and others. Therefore, most mental health professionals believe that there are instances when people should be involuntarily committed for mental health treatment, in order to stabilize their behavior. Such commitments are typically time sensitive, and subject to legal controls which vary by state.

CRISS-CROSS ANSWERS

Across
3. dopamine
6. glutamate
7. catatonic
8. delusion
9. psychosis
10. schizophrenia

Down
1. expressed emotion
2. negative symptoms
4. hallucination
5. antipsychotics

Chapter 15: Cognitive Disorders

BEFORE YOU READ

The brain is essential for all things organisms do, including the most basic of functions such as breathing and temperature regulation, and the most complex interactions of thought and feeling. However, many things can go wrong. Chapter 15 covers several types of brain impairments. The first part of the chapter discusses diagnostic issues, clinical signs of brain damage, and neuropsychological brain disorders. Then follows a more in-depth look at delirium, dementia (with particular attention paid to Alzheimer's disease), dementia from HIV infection, vascular dementia, and amnestic syndrome. Cognitive disorders can also stem from traumatic head injuries following car accidents, falls, sports accidents, and violence. Temporary loss of consciousness and post impact confusion are common following mild head injuries, while more severe injuries can cause long lasting impairment. Innovations in the treatment of head injuries including the use of medication, dietary supplements, and therapy offer hope for patients, but much remains to be learned about the process of rehabilitation and recovery.

- ## BRAIN IMPAIRMENT IN ADULTS
    Diagnostic Issues
    Clinical Signs of Brain Damage
    Diffuse Versus Focal Damage
    The Neuropsychology/Psychopathology Interaction

- ## DELIRIUM
    Clinical Presentation
    Treatment and Outcome

- ## DEMENTIA
    Alzheimer's Disease
    Dementia from HIV-1 Infection; Vascular Dementia

• **AMNESTIC SYNDROME**

• **DISORDERS INVOLVING HEAD INJURY**

The Clinical Picture

Treatments and Outcomes

• **UNRESOLVED ISSUES:**

Can Dietary Supplements Enhance Brain Functioning?

OBJECTIVES

After reading this chapter, you should be able to:

1. Explain why the DSM-IV dropped the terms, "functional mental disorders" and "organic mental disorders."

2. Discuss diagnostic issues and clinical signs of brain damage.

3. Explain the diffuse versus focal damage as it relates to brain impairment.

4. Describe how neuropsychology and psychopathology interact with each other.

5. Define delirium in terms of clinical presentation and discuss clinical treatments and outcomes.

6. Define dementia and describe the three disorders presented, Alzheimer's, dementia from HIV-1 infection, and vascular dementia, in terms of clinical picture, prevalence, any genetic or environmental aspects, treatment outcomes and effects on caregivers.

7. Explain amnestic syndrome.

8. Explain traumatic brain injury (TBI), describe the clinical picture and discuss treatment outcomes.

9. Discuss the research on the benefits of dietary supplements on the brain

AS YOU READ

Answers can be found in the Answer Key at the end of the chapter.

KEY WORDS

Each of the words below is important in understanding the concepts presented in this Chapter. Write the definition next to each of the words.

Term	Page	Definition
AIDS-related dementia	548	
Amnestic syndrome	549	
Amyloidal plaques	556	
Anterograde amnesia	552	
APOE-E4	545	
Delirium	552	
Dementia	532	
Early-onset Alzheimer's disease	544	
Functional mental disorders	533	
Late-onset Alzheimer's disease	544	
Neurofibrillary tangles	541	
Organic mental	533	

disorders		
Retrograde amnesia	552	
Traumatic brain injury (TBI)	550	
Vascular dementia (VAD)	549	

WHO'S WHO AND WHAT'S WHAT—MATCHING

Name the brain structures using the terms in bold in the top of the box. Match the term with its proper answer.

Corpus callosum	Limbic system	Reticular formation	Sensory strip	Motor strip
Cerebellum	Frontal lobe	Hypothalamus	Parietal lobe	Thalamus
Medulla	Temporal lobe	Occipital lobe		

_____ Integration of sensory information from various parts of the body

_____ Somaesthetic and motor discriminations and functions

_____ Major relay station for messages from all parts of the body, important in sensations of pain

_____ Visual discrimination and some aspects of visual memory

_____ Fine motor coordination, posture, and balance

_____ Breathing, blood pressure, other vital functions

_____ Arousal reactions, information screening

_____ Communication between the brain's right and left hemispheres

_____ Attention, emotions, "fight or flight," memory

_____ Regulation of voluntary movement

_____ Learning, abstracting, reasoning, inhibiting

_____ Regulation of metabolism, temperature, emotions

_____ Discrimination of sounds, verbal and speech behavior

SHORT ANSWERS

Provide brief answers to the following questions.

1. Why are cognitive disorders discussed in the textbook?

2. What determines the extent and magnitude of behavioral deficits or psychological impairments in persons with damage to brain tissue?

THE DOCTOR IS IN...PSYCHIATRIC HELP—5¢

Read the following scenarios and diagnose the client. Remember to look carefully at the criteria for the disorder before you make a decision as to the diagnosis. Make a list of other information you might need to help you understand the causal factors.

1. Glen is an 82-year-old man who suddenly became very confused, unable to remember things and very agitated—. In addition, he was unable to stay on tasks long enough to even complete dressing himself. Glen had been taking several medications and was recently given another.

   How would you diagnose Glen and why? Also, what treatment would you recommend?

2. Terry is a 44-year-old man who has a long history of alcohol abuse. He has come to see you at the insistence of his sister with whom he is staying. In your interview with Terry, he is very capable of telling you about his life and past experiences working on oil rigs around the world. You had asked him to look a picture in a magazine and tell you what he saw. He was able to do this as he looked at the picture. However, when you asked him to recall what the picture was about a few minutes later, he had no idea what you were talking about and made up a story that seemed to him a reasonable explanation as to why he didn't recall the picture.

How would you diagnose Terry and why?

3. What six factors in the case below suggest that your patient has an unfavorable prognosis?

"An 18-year-old male who had several run-ins with the law during high school received a serious head injury in a motorcycle accident. He was in a coma for almost a month. He is currently suffering some paralysis, and is very angry and depressed. He refuses to cooperate with his physical therapist. His parents, who live in a remote rural area where no rehabilitation facilities are available, will take him back home, but are rather unenthusiastic about the prospect."

a.

b.

c.

d.

e.

f.

AFTER YOU READ

Answers can be found in the Answer Key at the end of the chapter.

PRACTICE TESTS

Take the following three multiple-choice tests to see how much you have comprehended from the chapter. Each represents roughly one-third of the chapter. As you study the chapter, use these to check your progress.

PRACTICE TEST NUMBER 1

1. Before the DSM-IV was published, delirium, dementia, and other amnestic and cognitive disorders, were considered (p. 533)
a. functional mental disorders.
b. dysfunctional mental disorders.
c. organic mental disorders.
d. brain injury disorders.

2. When structural defects in the brain occur before birth or at a very early age, the typical result is (p.532)
a. mental retardation.
b. delirium.
c. dementia.
d. progressive.

3. To distinguish the possibility of a brain disorder from mood disorder, the clinician will look to see if the client has (p. 533)

a. headaches.

b. a major change in behavior.

c. a prior history of psychopathology.

d. all of the above.

4. In the past, organic mental disorders were thought to have a _____ cause while functional mental disorders were thought to have a _____ cause. (p. 533)

a. physiological; psychological

b. psychological; physiological

c. internal; external

d. overt; covert

5. The screening test that clinicians often use to determine the possibility of cognitive impairment is (p. 534)

a. MMPI.

b. TAT.

c. MMSE.

d. MAAPT.

6. The _____ hemisphere of the brain is mostly responsible for language and solving mathematical equations. (p. 536)

a. right

b. left

c. center

d. remote

7. The study by LoSasso et. al. (2001) found that nail salon technicians had

significantly more cognitive and neurological impairments, probably due to an exposure to (p. 535)

a. so many people.

b. long work hours.

c. neurotoxic substances.

d. dietary restrictions.

8. After a traumatic brain injury caused by an accident or a fall, for example, around _____ percent of patients make a suicide attempt. (p. 537)

a. 10

b. 18

c. 8

d. 5

9. Which of the following doesn't effect the development of behavioral deficits after a head injury? (p. 534)

a. the nature and location of the injury

b. the individual's prior competence and personality

c. the amount of time since the injury

d. the person's life situation

10. A rapid and widespread disorganization of complex mental processes caused by a generalized disturbance in brain metabolism is called (p. 538)

a. amnestis syndrome.

b. hallucinosis.

c. dementia.

d. delirium.

PRACTICE TEST NUMBER 2

1. Delirium is treated with (p. 539)

a. neuroleptic medications.

b. benzodiazines.

c. Aricept.

d. a and b.

2. What is the correct order for the continuum of level of consciousness? (p.539)

a. coma, delirium, stupor, alert awake

b. alert awake, stupor, delirium, coma

c. alert awake, delirium, stupor, coma

d. stupor, delirium, coma, alert awake

3. Children are at high risk of delirium, because their brains are not yet fully (p. 554)

a. organized.

b. developed.

c. integrated.

d. active.

4. The prevalence of AIDS related dementia has decreased because of (p. 548)

a. the use of antiretroviral therapy

b. psychoimmuinity

c. the use of CBT

d. high death rates from AIDS

5. Alzheimer's cannot be absolutely confirmed until the patient's (p. 541)

a. complete physical exam.

b. complete neurological exam.

c. behavior has deteriorated sufficiently.

d. death.

6. Which of the following is the most common behavioral manifestation of Alzheimer's disease? (p. 546)

a. slow mental deterioration

b. jealousy delusions

c. paranoid delusions

d. psychopathological symptoms

7. Since there is no cure for Alzheimer's, _____ care seems to help with diminishing the patient's and caregiver's distress and some of the complications that come with the disorder. (p. 546)

a. family

b. palliative

c. hospital

d. nursing home

8. These drugs have been shown to slow the rate at which patients with Alzheimer's deteriorate. (p. 546)

a. placebos

b. tacrine

c. donepezil

d. b and c

9. Environmental factors that could contribute to Alzheimer's include (p. 545)

a. diet.

b. aluminum.

c. head trauma.

d. all of the above.

10. Most people with Alzheimer's live (p. 547)

a. with family members in the community.

b. in nursing homes

c. on the streets

d. on their own

PRACTICE TEST NUMBER 3

1. Vascular dementia involves a(n) (p. 549)

a. dementia as a result of repeated injury

b. continuing recurrence of small strokes.

c. breakdown of veins and arteries.

d. b and c

2. Laura has been diagnosed with VAD and AD. As a clinician you would refer to this condition as (p. 549)

a. varied dementia.

b. mixed dementia.

c. undifferentiated dementia

d. multi dementia.

3. Patients with VAD are more likely to suffer from _____ disorders than patients with Alzheimer's. (p. 549)

a. anxiety

b. cognitive

c. stress

d. mood

4. A person with VAD is vulnerable to sudden death from a

a. stroke.

b. cardiovascular disease.

c. blood disorder.

d. a and b.

5. Traumatic brain injury affects more than _____ people each year in the United States. (p. 550)

a. 1 million

b. 2 million

c. 100,000

d. 500,000

6. The general types of TBI recognized by clinicians are (p. 551)

a. closed-head injuries.

b. penetrating head injuries.

c. skull fractures.

d. all of the above.

7. If a head injury is sufficiently severe to result in unconsciousness, the person may experience retrograde amnesia or an inability to recall (p. 552)

a. events immediately following the injury.

b. concrete facts, such as names and dates.

c. events immediately preceding the injury.

d. long past events.

8. In a study of TBI in boxers, it was found that the presence of the _____ genetic-risk factor was associated with more chronic neurological deficits. (p. 552)

a. 23rd allele

b. APOE-4

c. Alzheimer's

d. neurofibrillary

9. A recent study has shown that older individuals and individuals who have TBI share several changes in (p.552)

a. cognitive deterioration

b. motor-skills.

c. information-processing speed.

d. tactile performance

10. Common after effects of moderate brain injury are (p. 554)

a. chronic headaches.

b. anxiety.

c. impaired memory.

d. all of the above.

COMPREHENSIVE PRACTICE TEST

The following tests are designed to give you an idea of how well you understood the entire chapter. There are three different types of tests: multiple-choice, true/false, and essay.

MULTIPLE-CHOICE

1. The thick outer membrane that protects the brain and literally means "hard mother" is called the (p. 532)

a. corpus callosum.

b. medulla.

c. cerebellum.

d. dura mater.

2. People with amnesia can have trouble (p. 549)

a. remembering new information.

b. remembering events that took place very recently.

c. only personal information.

d. In virtually all areas of working and short term memory.

3. The _____ hemisphere of the brain is mostly responsible for grasping overall meanings in novel situations, reasoning on a nonverbal, intuitive level, and appreciation of spatial relations. (p. 536)

a. right

b. left

c. center

d. remote

5. Twenty four percent f TBI cases overall develop post – traumatic epilepsy, thought to be caused by (p. 554)

a. scar tissue

b. low neurotransmitter levels

c. temperature changes

d. none of the above

6. The general types of TBI recognized by clinicians are (p. 551)

a. closed-head injuries.

b. penetrating head injuries.

c. skull fractures.

d. all of the above.

7. If a head injury is sufficiently severe to result in unconsciousness, the person may experience retrograde amnesia or an inability to recall (p. 552)

a. events immediately following the injury.

b. events immediately preceding and following the injury.

c. events immediately preceding the injury.

d. names or faces of friends.

8. In a study of TBI in boxers, it was found that the presence of the _____ genetic-risk factor was associated with more chronic neurological deficits. (p. 552)

a. granulovacuoles

b. APOE-4

c. PS1

d. PS2

9. In contrast to diffuse damage that results in dementia, focal lesions are _____areas of abnormal change in brain structure. (p. 534)

a. deep

b. circumscribed

c. large

d. progressive

10. The most common cause of delirium is (p. 538)

a. stroke.

b. HIV/AIDS.

c. drug intoxication.

d. syphilis.

11. The herb Ginko Biloba has been shown to (p. 555)

a. increase dementia

b. decrease dementia

c. increase delirium

d. decrease delirium

12. Cases of early onset AD appear to be caused by rare (p. 544)

a. brain cell mutations.

b. environmental factors.

c. genetic mutations.

d. neurological mutations.

13. Chronic alcoholism combined with vitamin B1 deficiency can cause

a. amnestic syndrome (p. 549)

b. Alzheimer's disease

c. epilepsy

d. depression

14. Cerebral arteriosclerosis can be medically managed by decreasing the
   likelihood of further (p. 549)

a. contact with hazardous waste.

b. medical problems

c. strokes

d. none of the above.

15. Post-trauma epilepsy is common (p. 551)

a. closed-head injuries.

b. penetrating head injuries.

c. skull fractures.

d. b and c.

16. The TBI that could result from a roller coaster ride (p. 551)

a. closed-head injury.

b. penetrating head injury.

c. skull fracture.

d. subdural hematomas.

17. The _____ a child, who has a significant traumatic brain injury, the
   more likely to be adversely affected they are (p. 554)

a. older

b. younger

c. more mature

d. a and c

TRUE – FALSE

1. T / F Alzheimer's disease is the most common cause of dementia. (p. 556)

2. T / F Alzheimer's disease usually begins after about age 65. (p. 544)

3. T / F AD is not an inevitable consequence of aging. (p. 544)

4. T / F People who are the caregivers for Alzheimer's patients are at high risk for depression. (p. 548)

5. T / F Brain damage is the root cause of amnestic disorders. (p. 559)

6. T / F Sports injuries are the most common cause of TBI. (p. 550)

7. T / F In a majority of brain injury cases, notable personality changes occur. (p. 554)

8. T/F Both environmental and genetic influences determine an individual's reaction to brain damage. (p. 556)

9. T/F Treating TBI most often focuses on recovery, rather than teaching compensatory strategies. (p. 555)

10. T/F Anterograde amnesia involves the inability to store in memory events that happen after a brain injury. (p. 552)

ESSAY QUESTIONS

1. Discuss the progressively diffuse damage that may occur when a brain disorder has a mainly focal origin but gradually spreads over a greater area to become diffuse.

WEB LINKS TO ITEMS OR CONCEPTS DISCUSSED IN CHAPTER 15

Dementia

dementia.ion.ucl.ac.uk/

Delirium

www.alzheimers.org

www.alzheimers.org/pubs/adfact.html www.ninds.nih.gov/health_and_medical/

www.nlm.nih.gov/medlineplus/alzheimersdisease.html

USE IT OR LOSE IT

Provide an answer to the thought question below, knowing that there is more than one way to respond. Possible answers are presented in the Answer Key.

As the population ages more and more families will find themselves dealing with a member with Alzheimer's disease. What sorts of support should we be providing for these individuals and their caregivers?

CRISS-CROSS

Now that you know all there is to know about this chapter, here's your opportunity to put that knowledge to work.

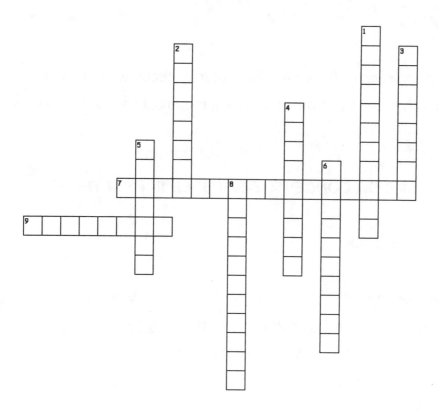

CRISS-CROSS CLUES

Across
7. similar to progressive, but caused by a series of circumscribed cerebral infarcts
9. an acute confusional state lying between normal wakefulness and stupor

Down
1. dementia producing general deterioration of the brain; observed in AIDS patients
2. a syndrome in which short-term memory is so impaired that the person is unable to recall events from a few minutes previously
3. gradual, permanent decline from a previously attained level of functioning
4. the man who first described Alzheimer s disease
5. brain abnormalities characteristic of Alzheimer's disease
6. a form of amnesia where person cannot recall the events preceding the injury
8. a form of amnesia in which a person cannot recall events after an injury

Puzzle created with Puzzlemaker at DiscoverySchool.com

ANSWERS TO TEST QUESTIONS - CHAPTER 15

MATCHING

Frontal lobe -Learning, abstracting, reasoning, inhibiting
Sensory strip -Integration of sensory information from various parts of the body
Parietal lobe - Somaesthetic and motor discriminations and functions
Thalamus -Major relay station for messages from all parts of the body, important in sensations of pain
Occipital lobe -Visual discrimination and some aspects of visual memory
Cerebellum -Fine motor coordination, posture, and balance
Corpus callosum -Communication between the brain's right and left hemispheres
Limbic system -Attention, emotions, "fight or flight," memory
Motor strip- Regulation of voluntary movement
Hypothalamus -Regulation of metabolism, temperature, emotions
Temporal lobe- Discrimination of sounds, verbal and speech behavior
Reticular formation -Arousal reactions, information screening
Medulla- Breathing, blood pressure, other vital functions

Term/Name
D. Anosognosia
C. Alois Alzheimer
A. Presenilin 1 and presenilin 2
E. Apolipoprotein (APOE)
B. Phineas Gage

SHORT ANSWERS

(Your answer should contain the following points.)

1. a. These disorders are regarded as psychopathological conditions.
   b. Some brain disorders cause symptoms that look remarkably like other abnormal psychology disorders.
   c. Brain damage can cause changes in behavior, mood, and personality.
   d. Many people who suffer from brain disorders react to the news with depression or anxiety.
   e. Cognitive disorders take a heavy toll on family members in the form of depression and anxiety.

2. a. the nature, location, and extent of neural damage
   b. the premorbid competence and personality of the individual
   c. the individual's life situation
   d. the amount of time since the first appearance of the condition

THE DOCTOR IS IN...PSYCHIATRIC HELP—5¢

1. **Glen suffers from delirium**. The sudden onset, age considerations, and behaviors point to this diagnosis. He has also been given another medication, so the delirium may be brought on by the interactions of the medicines. For treatment: neuroleptics, environmental manipulations, family support, and orienting techniques.

2. **Amnestic syndrome**. Terry had a long history of alcohol abuse and his memory for remote events is intact as is immediate recall. However, his short-term memory is impaired as he can't remember events that took place a few minutes before.

3. a. in a coma for a month
b. cognition impairment
c. only graduated from high school (he is young)
d. didn't have well-functioning, promising personality
e. refuses to cooperate with physical therapist
f. not returning to favorable situation

MULTIPLE-CHOICE PRACTICE TESTS

PRACTICE TESTS

Q#	TEST 1	TEST 2	TEST 3
1	C	A	B
2	A	C	B
3	D	B	D
4	A	A	D
5	C	D	B
6	B	A	D
7	C	B	C
8	B	D	B
9	D	D	C
10	D	A	D

COMPREHENSIVE PRACTICE TEST

Q#	MULTIPLE CHOICE	T/F
1	D	T
2	B	F
3	A	T
4	A	T
5	A	T

6	D	F
7	C	F
8	B	T
9	B	F
10	C	T
11	B	
12	D	
13	A	
14	C	
15	D	
16	D	
17	B	

ESSAY QUESTIONS

(Your answer should contain the following points.)

1   a. Impairment of memory: notable trouble remembering recent events but not necessarily remote past events
b. Impairment of orientation: unable to locate him or herself accurately
c. Impairment of learning, comprehension and judgment: thinking becomes clouded, sluggish, and/or inaccurate
d. Impairment of emotional control or modulation: emotional over reactivity
e. Apathy or emotional blunting: emotional under activity
f. Impairment in the initiation of behavior: lack of self-starting capability and may have to reminded about what to do next
g. Impairment of controls over matters of propriety and ethical conduct: marked lowering of personal standards in appearance, personal hygiene, etc.
h. Impairment of receptive and expressive communication: inability to comprehend written or spoken language or to express his or her own thoughts
i. Impaired visuospatial ability: difficulty coordinating motor activity with the characteristics of the visual environment

2.   a. Senile plaques: made of deformed nerve cell terminals that, at their core, contain beta amyloid, which has been shown to be neurotoxic, causing cell death
b. Neurofibrillary tangles: webs of abnormal filaments within a nerve cell that contain protein called tau, thought to be caused by increasing burden of amyloid, thus the presence of tau indicates the disease is progressing

c. Abnormal appearance of small holes in the neuronal tissue: called granulovacuoles and caused from cell degeneration—the earliest and most severely affected structures are a cluster of cell bodies located in the basal forebrain and involved in reducing the release of ACh, a neurotransmitter involved in mediation of memory

USE IT OR LOSE IT

As Alzheimer's disease rates rise we will need to find ways to provide safe, secure care for patients which is affordable, and more support services for their caregivers who are at risk for poor physical and mental health themselves.

CRISS-CROSS ANSWERS

Across
7. vascular
9. delirium

Down
1. AIDS-related
2. amnestic
3. dementia
4. Alzheimer
5. plaques
6. retrograde
8. anterograde

CHAPTER 16: Disorders of Childhood and Adolescence

BEFORE YOU READ

Many of the mental disorders described in previous chapters do not develop until early or middle adulthood. There are some problems, though that develop in childhood and adolescence. However, children are not simply small versions of adults, but instead are dynamic, developing individuals. Children's symptoms of mental illness may vary from adults, and even differ in the same child over time. This chapter discusses the types of problems seen in children and adolescents, including attention-deficit hyperactivity disorder, oppositional defiant disorder, conduct disorder, anxiety disorders, childhood depression, enuresis, encopresis, sleepwalking, and tics. Three disorders which begin in childhood and can persist into adulthood are also discussed, including depression, autism, and mental retardation. Finally, the chapter concludes with a discussion of the difficulties inherent in developing and testing treatments in children, and how society might better deal with youthful maladaptive and disruptive behaviors.

• MALADPTIVE BEHAVIOR IN DIFFERENT LIFE PERIODS

Varying Clinical Pictures Special Vulnerabilities of Young Children

The Classification of Childhood and Adolescent Disorders

• DISORDERS OF CHILDHOOD

Attention-Deficit/Hyperactivity Disorder

Oppositional Defiant Disorder and Conduct Disorder

Anxiety Disorders of Childhood and Adolescence

Childhood Depression; Symptom Disorders: Enuresis, Encopresis

Sleepwalking, and Tics

Pervasive Developmental Disorders

Autism

• LEARNING DISORDERS AND MENTAL RETARDATION

Learning Disorders

Causal Factors in Learning Disorders

Treatments and Outcomes

Mental Retardation

Brain Defects in Mental Retardation

Organic Retardation Syndromes

Treatment, Outcomes, and Prevention

• PLANNING BETTER PROGRAMS TO HELP CHILDREN AND ADOLESCENTS

Special Factors Associated with Treatment for Children and Adolescents

Child Advocacy Programs

• UNRESOLVED ISSUES

Can Society Deal with Delinquent Behavior?

OBJECTIVES

After reading this chapter, you should be able to:

1. Discuss how childhood disorders are different from adult disorders, and describe how young children are especially vulnerable to psychological problems.

2. Discuss general issues in the classification of childhood and adolescent disorders.

3. Discuss attention-deficit hyperactivity disorder.

4. Describe the clinical features, causal factors, and treatment of conduct disorder and oppositional defiant disorder.

5. Describe the clinical features, causal factors, and treatment of the anxiety disorders of childhood.

6. Describe the clinical features, causal factors, and treatment of childhood depression.

7. Summarize what is known about the symptom disorders of functional enuresis, functional encopresis, sleepwalking, and tics as these occur in children and adolescents.

8. Describe the clinical features, causal factors, and treatment of autism.

9. Review treatments approaches, outcomes and prevention with regard to mental retardation.

10. Describe the clinical features, causal factors, and treatment of learning disorders.

11. Explain the four levels of mental retardation and describe the functioning associated with each level.

12. Discuss the types of brain defects associated with mental retardation.

13. List and explain mental retardation stemming from biological causes, especially Down syndrome, PKU, and cranial anomalies.

14. List and explain six special factors that must be considered in relation to treatment for children.

15. Outline the findings regarding the prevalence of child abuse, list the deficits seen among abused children, discuss potential causal factors in child abuse, and summarize efforts to prevent child abuse.

16. Describe the need for mental health services for children, and review the difficulties with recent efforts to increase the available resources.

17. Discuss delinquency as a major societal problem, summarize the many causal factors involved in delinquency, and describe different ways that society deals with delinquency.

AS YOU READ

Answers can be found in the Answer Key at the end of the chapter.

KEY WORDS

Each of the words below is important in understanding the concepts presented in this chapter. Write the definition next to each of the words.

Term	Page	Definition
Asperger's disorder	575	
Attention-deficit/hyperactivity	560	

disorder		
Autism	575	
Conduct disorder	563	
Developmental psychopathology	558	
Down syndrome	583	
Dyslexia	580	
Echolalia	576	
Juvenile delinquency	594	
Learning disorders	580	
Macrocephaly	587	
Mainstreaming	589	
Mental retardation	582	
Microcephaly	587	
Oppositional defiant disorder	563	
Pemoline	562	
Pervasive developmental disorders	575	
Phenylketonuria	586	
Ritalin	562	
Selective mutism	568	
Separation anxiety disorder	568	
Sleepwalking disorder	573	
Tourette's syndrome	574	

WHO'S WHO AND WHAT'S WHAT—MATCHING

Match the following with the appropriate description.

_____ Imipramine

_____ intranasal hormone replacement

_____ used to treat enuresis

_____ somnambulism

_____ NREM

_____ Asperger's disorder

_____ Tourette's syndrome

_____ Kanner

_____ autistic-savant

_____ Siegel

_____ "Eden Model"

_____ Integrative Strategy Instruction

_____ hypoxia

_____ Langdon Down

_____ Children's Defense Fund

A. the first to describe autism in infancy and childhood

B. author of the book, *The World of the Autistic Child*

C. an approach to assisting people with autism over the course of their lifespan

D. an extreme tic disorder involving multiple motor and vocal patterns

E. a public-interest group based in Washington D.C. that advocates for children

F. sleepwalking

G. medication used to treat enuresis

H. DDAVP

I. a period during sleep when sleepwalking takes place

J. a comprehensive intervention model to facilitate learning in LD children offered by Ellis

K. autistic children who show markedly discrepant and relatively isolated abilities

L. pervasive developmental disorder that appears later than autism

M. lack of sufficient oxygen to the brain

N. the first person to describe the best known clinical conditions associated with moderate and severe mental retardation

SHORT ANSWERS

Provide brief answers to the following questions.

1. What are the three subtypes of ADHD now recognized in the DSM-IV-TR?

2. What are the clinical signs of separation anxiety?

3. Describe the clinical picture of a child with autism.

4. What two groups do children who are institutionalized fall into?

THE DOCTOR IS IN...PSYCHIATRIC HELP—5¢

Read the following scenarios and diagnose the client. Remember to look carefully at the criteria for the disorder before you make a decision as to the diagnosis. Make a list of other information you might need to help you understand the causal factors.

1. Mark, who is seven years old, is referred to your office by his school. He comes to the session with his mother. The school report says that Mark is

defiant, disobedient, and has tried to punch his teacher and the principal on more than one occasion. This behavior has been getting worse for the last year. You note that the mother is also hostile and believes that coming to see you is a waste of time. You find out that the household is in turmoil and the parents are having marital problems.

How would you diagnose Mark, and what treatment would you recommend?

2. Gary is a four-year-old boy who has started wetting the bed after his new sister was born. His parents are troubled and don't know what to do.

How would you diagnose Gary and what would you do to treat him?

AFTER YOU READ

Answers can be found in the Answer Key at the end of the chapter.

PRACTICE TESTS

Take the following three multiple-choice tests to see how much you have comprehended from the chapter. Each represents roughly one-third of the chapter. As you study the chapter, use these to check your progress.

PRACTICE TEST NUMBER 1

1. Until the twentieth century, children were seen as being (p. 558)

a. unique in their psychopathology.

b. miniature adults.

c. unable to have any mental illness.

d. all of the above.

2. Clinicians now realize that to understand childhood disorders, they must take into account (p. 558)

a. developmental processes.

b. play time.

c. siblings.

d. unconscious motivations.

3. Cindy is two years old, has temper tantrums, and puts everything she finds into her mouth. This behavior, for her age, is (p. 558)

a. appropriate.

b. inappropriate.

c. a sign of anxiety.

d. something to watch as it may lead to future psychopathology.

4. There was no formal, specific system available for classifying the emotional or behavioral problems of children and adolescents until the

a. 1850's

b. 1900's

c. 1950's

d. 2000's

5. A problem with the early classification system for childhood disorders is that it was (p. 560)

a. not updated.

b. the same one used for adults.

c. not inclusive of the disorders that were important at the time.

d. Inclusive of too many disorders.

6. Attention-deficit/hyperactivity disorder, conduct disorder, anxiety disorders of childhood, depressive disorders, symptom disorders, and autism are coded on which axis? (p. 560.)

a. Axis I

b. Axis II

c. Axis III

d. Axis IV

7. Learning disabilities and mental retardation are coded on which axis? (p. 560)

a. Axis I

b. Axis II

c. Axis III

d. Axis IV

8. Perhaps because of their behavioral problems, children with ADHD are often lower in intelligence by about _____IQ points. (p. 560)

a. 3 to 5

b. 15 to 20

c. 7 to 15

d. 2 to 8

9. ADHD is thought to occur in about _____ percent of the school-aged children. (p. 560)

a. 3 to 5

b. 15 to 20

c. 7 to 15

d. 20 to 80

10. ADHD is more frequently found in boys before the age of (p. 560)

a. 10.

b. 11.

c. 12.

d. 8.

PRACTICE TEST NUMBER 2

1. Which of the following is not a characteristic of ADHD (p. 560)

a. impulsivity

b. exaggerated motor activity

c. sustained attention

d. decreased IQ

2. Oppositional defiant disorder is apparent by about the age of (p. 563)

a. 8.

b. 9.

c. 15.

d. 18.

3. Conduct disorder is apparent by about the age of (p. 563)

a. 8.

b. 9.

c. 15.

d. 18.

4. Risk factors that oppositional defiant and conduct disorders have in common include (p. 565)

a. family discord.

b. socioeconomic disadvantage.

c. antisocial behavior in parents.

d. all of the above.

5. Conduct disordered children and adolescents are frequently comorbid for (p. 563)

a. depressive symptoms.

b. substance abuse disorder.

c. conversion disorder.

d. a and b.

6. An effective treatment strategy for conduct disorder is the (p. 566)

a. juvenile justice system model.

b. cohesive family model.

c. punitive model.

d. IP model.

7. The goal of teaching behavior therapy techniques to the parent or parents of children with conduct disorder is so they can (p. 566)

a. function as therapists in reinforcing desirable behavior.

b. function as disciplinarians.

c. increase their child's behavior.

d. decrease their interaction with the child.

8. _____ is the most common childhood anxiety disorder. (p. 567)

a. Selective mutism

b. Post-traumatic stress

c. Separation anxiety

d. OCD

9. Selective mutism is rare in clinical populations and is seen most typically at what age? (p. 568)

a. within the first year of life

b. elementary school age

c. kindergarten

d. preschool

10. Although childhood and adult depression essentially use the same DSM diagnostic criteria, a recent modification to the childhood diagnosis is (p. 569)

 a. sadness.

b. loss of appetite.

c. irritability.

d. withdrawal.

PRACTICE TEST NUMBER 3

1. Depression in children has been related to depression in (p. 570)

a. their siblings.

b. their mothers.

c. their fathers.

d. b and c.

2. Andrea is five years old has been diagnosed with childhood depression. She could benefit from what type of therapy? (p. 572)

a. antidepressants

b. play therapy

c. cognitive-behavioral therapy

d. psychoanalytical therapy

3. A tic is a persistent, intermittent muscle twitch or spasm, usually limited to a (p. 574)

a. particular movement.

b. particular time of day.

c. generalized pattern.

d. localized muscle group.

4. A child with Tourette's syndrome (p. 574-575)

a. may be ostracized by friends

b. may exhibit vocal and motor tics

c. may be embarrassed by their own behavior

d. all of the above

5. _____ was a pioneer in the development of behavioral treatment for autistic children. (p. 578)

a. Sigmund Freud

b. Ivar Lovaas

c. Albert Ellis

d. Eric Erikson

6. Many famous and successful people have overcome their learning disabilities. Which of the following people had a learning disability? (p. 580)

a. Sir Winston Churchill

b. Woodrow Wilson

c. Nelson Rockefeller

d. all of the above

7. Ionizing radiation may harm a child by acting directly on the _____ or may damage the sex chromosomes of either parent. (p. 584)

a. fertilized egg

b. womb

c. brain tissue

d. unfertilized egg

8. Research has shown that a person with Down syndrome will have the greatest deficits in
(p. 586)

a. math skills.

b. spatial relationships.

c. verbal and language-related skills.

d. visual-motor coordination.

9. Treatment without parental consent is permitted in all of the following cases, **except**

(p. 589)

a. immature minors.

b. emancipated minors.

c. emergency situations.

d. court-ordered situations.

10. Haney and Gold found that most delinquent acts were committed (p. 595)

a. alone, without any help.

b. in association with one or two other persons.

c. with three or four other persons.

d. as part of a gang of at least a dozen.

COMPREHENSIVE PRACTICE TEST

The following tests are designed to give you an idea of how well you understood the entire chapter. There are three different types of tests: multiple-choice, true/false, and essay.

MULTIPLE-CHOICE

1. Children are vulnerable to psychological problems because they (p. 559)

a. have less self-understanding.

b. haven't developed a stable sense of identity.

c. haven't a clear understanding of what is expected of them.

d. all of the above.

2. _____ is devoted to studying the origins and course of individual maladaptation in the context of normal growth processes. (p. 559)

a. Behavioral psychopathology

b. Cognitive psychopathology

c. Aging psychopathology

d. Developmental psychopathology

3. Recent research, although inconclusive, has pointed to ADHD being a result of (p. 562)

a. biological factors.

b. social environmental factors.

c. cognitive behavioral factors.

d. a and b.

4. Side effects of Ritalin include (p. 562)

a. decreased blood flow to brain.

b. disruption of growth hormone.

c. psychotic symptoms.

d. all of the above.

5. Which of the following is the most common developmental sequence for conduct disorder (CD), antisocial personality (ASP), delinquency, and/or oppositional defiant disorder (ODD)? (p. 563-564)

a. CD, ODD, ASP

b. ODD, CD, ASP

c. CD, ASP, ODD

d. CD, ODD, delinquency

6. Anxiety disorders are more common in which group? (p. 570)

a. boys

b. girls

c. teenagers

d. middle-school children

7. Causal factors for childhood depression are also implicated in (p..570)

a. childhood anxiety disorders.

b. autism.

c. mental retardation.

d. b and c.

8. Children's exposure to early _____ events can increase their risk for developing depression. (p. 571)

a. happy

b. traumatic

c. unplanned

d. all of the above

9. Enuresis and encopresis are known as (p. 572)

a. elimination disorders.

b. anal fixation disorders.

c. anxiety disorders.

d. none of the above.

10. The onset of sleepwalking disorder is usually between the ages of six and 12. It is classified under _____ in the DSM-IV-TR, rather than disorders of infancy, childhood, and adolescence. (p. 573)

a. mood disorders

b. anxiety disorders

c. sleep disorders

d. dissociative disorders, particularly fugue

11. Causal factors in autism include (p. 578)

a. genetic factors.

b. disturbance in the central nervous system.

c. chromosome abnormalities.

d. all of the above.

12. All of the following are true of autism, **except** (p. 578)

a. there have been several effective treatments found, which are awaiting approval by the FDA.

b. it is usually identified before the child is 30 months old.

c. self stimulation is a common symptom in autistic children.

d. most investigators believe that autism beings with an inborn defect which impairs perceptual-cognitive functioning.

13. The drug(s) used most often in autism is/are _____; however, the effects have not been very impressive. (p. 578)

a. haloperidol

b. barbiturates

c. caffeine

d. anti-anxiety

14. Dana has trouble in school. He has difficulty spelling and in word recognition. Often Dana will omit, add, or distort words. Dana probably has (p. 580)

a. autism.

b. dyslexia.

c. mental retardation.

d. ADHD.

15. Mental retardation is coded on (p. 596)

a. Axis I.

b. Axis II.

c. Axis III.

d. Axis IV.

16. Which of the following degrees of retardation is, by far, the most common? (p. 582)

a. profound

b. moderate

c. severe

d. mild

17. One of the factors that should be considered when studying or treating children is the fact that (p. 583)

a. children can always seek help on their own

b. children are dependent on those around them

c. drugs are never warranted to treat children under 12

d. children are small adults.

18. The goal of early intervention programs for children is to (p. 593)

a. reduce the stressors in the child's life.

b. strengthen the child's coping mechanisms.

c. not have the problem repeat itself.

d. a and b.

19. Many habitual delinquents share the traits typical of the _____ personality. (p. 594)

a. antisocial

b. obsessive-compulsive

c. narcissistic

d. passive-aggressive

20. Alienation from family and the broader society causes juveniles to become more vulnerable to (p. 594)

a. incest and related sexual crimes.

b. negative influences of TV and other media.

c. the psychological support afforded by membership in a delinquent gang.

d. solitary acts of violence.

TRUE – FALSE

1. T / F Progress in child psychopathology has caught up with that in adult psychopathology. (p. 558)

2. T / F Young children may attempt suicide without any understanding of the finality of death.   (p. 559)

3. T / F Hyperactive children are not anxious, in general. (p. 560)

4. T / F Pemoline, when used to treat children with ADHD, has as many side effects as Ritalin. (p. 562)

5. T / F Not all children with conduct disorder will go on to become antisocial personalities. (p. 563)

6. T / F Kazdin (1995) said that family and social context factors are not as important causal factors in conduct disorders as genetics. (p. 565)

7. T / F Selective mutism should be diagnosed only if the child actually has the ability to speak and knows the language. (p. 568)

8. T / F Typically, children with anxiety disorders grow up to be adults who don't fit in. (p. 569)

9. T / F Depression in children and adolescents occurs with high frequency. T (p. 570)

10. T / F Children can learn to be depressed. (p. 570)

11. T / F The average age of children with encopresis is three years. (p. 573)

12 T / F If a baby is to inherit PKU, both parents must carry the recessive

gene.   (p. 587)

13. T / F Increasingly, the treatment of children has come to mean family therapy for all members, including both parents, the child, and his or her siblings. (p. 590)

14. T / F Play therapy, when used with children, is an effective tool that can be used to reduce problems and promote adjustment. (p. 591)

ESSAY QUESTIONS

1. Explain the causal factors in childhood anxiety disorders.

2. Discuss the causal effects of mental retardation.

WEB LINKS TO ITEMS OR CONCEPTS DISCUSSED IN CHAPTER 16

Autism

www.autism-resources.com/

Dyslexia

www.dyslexia.com/

www.interdys.org/

Down Syndrome

www.ndss.org/

www.ndsccenter.org/

USE IT OR LOSE IT

Provide an answer to the thought question below, knowing that there is more than one way to respond. Possible answers are presented in the Answer Key.

Psychologically, why do you think that membership in a gang appeals to young men from impoverished background?

CRISS-CROSS

Now that you know all there is to know about this chapter, here's your opportunity to put that knowledge to work.

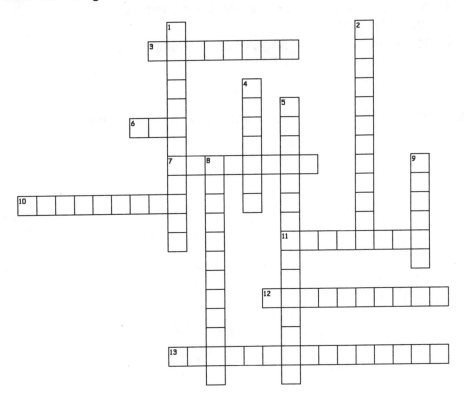

Puzzle created with Puzzlemaker at DiscoverySchool.com

CRISS-CROSS CLUES

Across

3. problems in word recognition and reading comprehension; routinely omit, add, and distort words; often resulting in slow reading

6. a persistent, intermittent muscle twitch

7. another medication used in the treatment of ADHD

10. the parrot-like repetition of a few words

11. habitual, involuntary discharge of urine after the age of expected continence
12. a symptom disorder of children who have not learned appropriate toileting
13. anxiety-based condition involving persistent failure to speak in certain situations

Down

1. damage caused by accumulation of an abnormal amount of cerebrospinal fluid in the cranium
2. irreversible limitations on survivability, achievement, and competence; 1 in every 1,000 babies
4. medication most administered by school nurses
5. a liver-based disorder, leading to brain damage if not diagnosed early
8. failure of cranium to achieve full size
9. a developmental disorder involving a wide range of problematic behaviors

Puzzle created with Puzzlemaker at DiscoverySchool.com

ANSWERS TO TEST QUESTIONS - CHAPTER 16

MATCHING

G. Imipramine
H. intranasal hormone replacement used to treat enuresis
F. somnambulism
I. NREM
L. Asperger's disorder
D. Tourette's syndrome
A. Kanner
K. autistic-savant
B. Siegel
C. "Eden Model"
J. Integrative Strategy Instruction
M. hypoxia
N. Langdon Down
E. Children's Defense Fund

SHORT ANSWERS
(Your answer should contain the following points.)

1. a. **Attention:** Deficit/Hyperactivity Disorder, Combined Type
   b. **Attention:** Deficit/Hyperactivity Disorder, Predominantly Inattentive Type
   c. **Attention:** Deficit/Hyperactivity Disorder, Hyperactive/Impulsive Type

2. a. excessive anxiety about separation from major attachment figure
   b. lack of self-confidence
   c. unrealistic fears
   d. oversensitive
   e. self-conscious
   f. nightmares
   g. chronic anxiety

3. a. difficulties in relating to others
   b. problems with perceptual-cognitive functioning
   c. absence of speech
   d. lack of development of sense of identity
   e. engage in bizarre and repetitive activities
   f. fascinations with unusual objects
   g. obsession with maintaining environmental sameness

4. a. those who in infancy and childhood, manifest severe mental retardation

and associated physical impairment and are institutionalized at an early age

  b. those who have no physical impairments but show relatively mild mental retardation and a failure to adjust socially in adolescence and are institutionalized because of behavior problems

THE DOCTOR IS IN...PSYCHIATRIC HELP—5¢

1. **Diagnosis:** Oppositional defiant disorder
   Treatment: Work on getting the family in for therapy; use the cohesive family model as a treatment strategy, along with behavioral therapy techniques, and possibly remove Mark from his home as a last resort.
2. **Diagnosis:** secondary functional enuresis **Treatment:** use medication, such as imipramine; also conditioning procedures, but the incidence of enuresis tends to decrease significantly with age and as he comes to accept his baby sister.

MULTIPLE-CHOICE PRACTICE TESTS

PRACTICE TESTS

1	B	C	C
2	A	A	B
3	A	B	D
4	C	D	D
5	B	B	B
6	A	B	D
7	B	A	A
8	C	C	C
9	A	D	A
10	D	C	B

COMPREHENSIVE PRACTICE TEST

Q#	MULTIPLE CHOICE	T/F
1	D	F
2	D	T
3	D	T
4	D	F
5	B	T
6	B	F
7	A	T
8	B	F
9	A	T

10	C	T
11	D	F
12	A	T
13	A	T
14	B	T
15	B	
16	D	
17	B	
18	D	
19	A	
20	C	

ESSAY QUESTIONS
(Your answer should contain the following points.)

1. • early illnesses, accidents, or losses that involved pain and discomfort
    • modeling effect of an overanxious and protective parent who sensitizes a child to the dangers and threats of the outside world
    • indifferent, detached, or rejecting parents
    • possibly cultures that favor inhibition, compliance, and obedience
    • exposure to violence leading to a reduced sense of security and psychological well-being

2. a. Genetic—chromosomal factors; mental retardation tends to run in families and is in the moderate to severe categories
    b. Infections and toxic agents
    c. Trauma (physical injury)—physical injuries at birth
    d. Ionizing radiation—radiation acting on fertilized egg or parents' eggs and sperm
    e. Malnutrition and other biological factors—may affect child more indirectly by altering child's responsiveness, curiosity and motivation

USE IT OR LOSE IT

It is believed that young people join gangs when they feel inadequate and rejected by the larger society. Belonging to a gang gives them a sense of belonging and a means of gaining status and approval from others.

CRISS-CROSS ANSWERS

Across
3. dyslexia
6. tic
7. Pemoline
10. echolalia
11. enuresis

12. encopresis
13. selective mutism

Down
1. hydrocephaly
2. down syndrome
4. Ritalin
5. phenylketonuria

8. microcephaly
9. autism

Chapter 17: Therapy

BEFORE YOU READ

Why should people pay for psychological therapy when they could simply talk to a friend or family member? How do we decide whether a therapy is effective, ineffective, or even harmful? How can we determine which treatment should be used for each disorder, or how to combine therapies to the best effect? This chapter summarizes the many therapeutic and pharmacological approaches available for the treatment of mental health issues.

No single approach to psychotherapy has yet proven capable of handling the entire range of problems seen clinically. Consequently, the inclination to identify strongly with one approach or another is decreasing. Today, many therapists are familiar with a variety of techniques chosen from several therapeutic approaches and use these depending on the type of problems the client is having. The chapter closes with discussions on the influences of social values and cultural diversity of psychotherapy.

- **AN OVERVIEW OF TREATMENT**

    Why Do People Seek Therapy?

    Who Provides Psychotherapeutic Services?

    The Therapeutic Relationship

- **MEASURING SUCCESS IN PSYCHOTHERAPY**

    Objectifying and Quantifying Change

    Would Change Occur Anyway?

    Can Therapy Be Harmful?

- **WHAT THERAPEUTIC APPROACH SHOULD BE USED?**

    Empirically Validated Treatments Medication or Psychotherapy?

    Combined Treatments

- **PHARMACOLOGICAL APPROACHES TO TREATMENT**

Antipsychotic Drugs

Antidepressant Drugs

Antianxiety Drugs

Lithium and Other Mood-Stabilizing Drugs

Neurosurgery

• **PSYCHOLOGICAL APPROACHES TO TREATMENT**

Behavior Therapy

Cognitive and Cognitive-Behavioral Therapy

Humanistic-Experiential Therapies

Psychodynamic Therapies

Eclecticism and Integration

• **PSYCHOTHERAPY AND SOCIETY**

Social Values and Psychotherapy

Psychotherapy and Cultural Diversity

• **UNRESOLVED ISSUES**

Is there bias in the reporting of drug trials?

OBJECTIVES

After reading this chapter, you should be able to:

1. Provide a general overview of the

a) the assumptions and goals of psychotherapy,

b) varied types of individuals who receive psychotherapy,

c) various categories of providers of psychotherapeutic services and their specialized training,

d) critical elements of the therapeutic relationship, and

e) qualities that enhance therapy.

2. Discuss the many difficulties associated with attempting to evaluate the effectiveness of psychotherapy.

3. Explain what is meant by negative process, and describe potential

deteriorative effects in psychotherapy.

4. Discuss the methodology, as well as the value and limitations of psychotherapy outcome studies, and the other issues related to determining a therapeutic approach.

5. Summarize the major psychopharmacological treatments currently in use (antipsychotics, antidepressants, antianxiety drugs, and lithium and other mood-stabilizers), discuss their history, major effects, side effects, modes of action, and effectiveness.

6. Outline the issues associated with the widespread possibility of "cosmetic psychopharmacology" drugs, such as Prozac.

7. Describe early attempts at biological intervention, including coma and convulsive therapies and neurosurgery, and indicate which are currently believed to be effective.

8. Discuss the advantages of combining the biological and psychological forms of treatment.

9. List and describe the basic goals and techniques of the behavior therapies. Summarize recent developments in the behavior therapies, and evaluate their effectiveness in the treatment of maladaptive behavior.

10. List and describe the basic goals and techniques of the cognitive and the cognitive-behavior therapies. Summarize recent developments, and evaluate their effectiveness in the treatment of maladaptive behavior.

11. List and describe the basic goals and techniques of the humanistic-experiential therapies. Summarize recent developments in the humanistic-experiential therapies, and evaluate their effectiveness in the treatment of maladaptive behavior.

12. List and describe the basic goals and techniques of psychoanalysis, as well as developments in psychodynamic therapy since Freud. Evaluate the effectiveness of the psychodynamic approach to the treatment of maladaptive behavior.

13. Describe the basic goals and techniques of couples counseling, family therapy, and group therapy. Summarize recent developments in these therapies, and evaluate their effectiveness in the treatment of maladaptive relationships.

14. Review the issues and evidence surrounding the matching or mismatching of ethnicity in client-therapy pairings, and its potential effects on the therapeutic process.

AS YOU READ

Answers and page numbers can be found in the Answer Key at the end of the chapter.

KEY WORDS

Each of the words below is important in understanding the concepts presented in this Chapter. Write the definition next to each of the words.

Term	Page	Defintion
Antianxiety drugs	615	
Antidepressant drugs	611	
Antipsychotic drugs	609	
Behavior therapy	622	
Client-centered therapy	628	
Cognitive/cognitive-behavioral therapy	609	
Counter-transference	623	
Double-blind	606	
Efficacy	606	
Electroconvulsive therapy (ECT)	618	
Family therapy	633	

Free association	630	
Half -life	609	
Imaginal exposure	623	
Integrative behavioral Couple therapy	634	
In vivo exposure	623	
Latent content	631	
Manifest content	631	
Manualized therapy	607	
Marital therapy	633	
Modeling	623	
Neurosurgery	620	
Placebo	603	
Psychodynamic therapy	630	
Psychopharmacology	609	
Psychotherapy	609	
Randomized clinical trials	606	
Rational emotive behavior therapy	625	
Resistance	631	
Response shaping	624	
Structural family therapy	634	
Systematic desensitization	623	
Tardive dyskinesia	610	
Token economy	624	
Traditional behavioral	633	

Couple therapy		
Transference	631	

WHO'S WHO AND WHAT'S WHAT—MATCHING

Match the following psychological tests with the appropriate description of each test s purpose.

Psychological Test

_____ John Cade

_____ Albert Ellis

_____ psychoactive

_____ Carl Rogers

_____ Ugo Cerletti and Lucio Bini

_____ team approach

_____ negative process

_____ working alliance

_____ Aaron Beck

_____ Peter Kramer

_____ Virginia Satir

_____ Antonio Moniz

_____ Ladislas von Meduna

_____ randomized clinical trials

_____ depot neuroleptics

Purpose

A. Involves coordinated efforts of medical, psychological, social work, and other mental health personnel working together as each case warrants.

B. A relationship between client and therapist that is essential to psychotherapeutic gain

C. What Binder and Strupp refer to as a rupture in the therapeutic alliance

D. Efficacy trials

E. Mind-altering

F. Antipsychotic medications administered in a long-acting injectable form

G. Author of *Listening to Prozac*

H. Discovered that lithium salts were effective in treating manic disorders

I. Regarded as the modern originator of inducing convulsions to treat mental disorders

J. Italian physicians who after visiting a slaughter house and seeing electric shock used on animals, passed electric current through a patient's head, a method which became known as ECT

K. Introduced the frontal lobotomy in 1935

L. Founder of REBT

M. His cognitive therapy assumes that client's problems stem from illogical thinking

N. Founder of client-centered therapy

O. Founder of conjoint family therapy

Short Answers

Provide brief answers to the following questions.

1. What are the elements of a therapeutic alliance?

2. When evaluating treatment success, what sources of information are important?

3. Discuss the advantages and disadvantages of Buspirone in treating anxiety.

4. Compared with some other forms of therapy, behavior therapy has some distinct advantages. Briefly explain.

5. According to cognitive therapies, clients' errors in the logic behind their thinking leads them to problems like depression. Briefly explore this.

6. Briefly explain why the humanistic-experiential therapies have been criticized.

THE DOCTOR IS IN...PSYCHIATRIC HELP—5¢

Read the following scenario and diagnose the client. Remember to look carefully at the criteria for the disorder before you make a decision as to the diagnosis. Make a list of other information you might need to help you understand the casual factors.

1. Bernice is a 47-year-old woman who recently lost her job in an auto factory. She is depressed and very concerned about how she is going to make ends meet when her unemployment insurance runs out. She married right out of high school and supported her husband through school by working in a factory. Her husband was killed in an auto accident seven years ago. She has two children, 22 and 15 years old. Bernice tells you that she is concerned about her drinking. Because her father was an alcoholic and her mother was always sad and withdrawn. She also still feels like a bad mother because she can't give her children all the things she sees other kids have, even though the

children tell her they don't care.

After reading the above scenario, pretend that you are a therapist and decide what aspects of the scenario would be emphasized/important for each of the following approaches. Also, discuss one aspect of treatment from each approach you would use with Bernice.

Pharmacological Treatment:

Behavior Treatment:

Cognitive and Cognitive-Behavioral Treatment:

Humanistic—Experiential Treatment:

Psychodynamic Treatment:

AFTER YOU READ

Answers can be found in the Answer Key at the end of the chapter.

PRACTICE TESTS

Take the following three multiple-choice tests to see how much you have comprehended from the chapter. Each represents roughly one-third of the chapter. As you study the chapter, use these to check your progress.

PRACTICE TEST NUMBER 1

1. Which of the following people is the most obvious candidate for psychological treatment? (p. 600)

a. Susan, whose husband left her

b. Andre, who lost his job

c. Carlos, whose wife just died from cancer

d. all of the above

2. A new drug developed by a pharmaceutical company must obtain approval from what agency before it can be marketed? (p. 606)

a. NIMH

b. DEA

c. FDA

d. CCM

3. Which of the following might account for the reluctance of men to seek psychological therapy? (p. 601)

a. men are less able to label their own feelings.

b. they don't want to look weak.

c. they fear that exposing their feelings to others will cause them to lose control.

d. all of the above

4. The unique quality of antipsychotic drugs is their ability to (p. 609)

a. calm patients.

b. put patients to sleep.

c. reduce patients' anxiety.

d. reduce the intensity of delusions and hallucinations.

5. Virtually all of the antipsychotic drugs accomplish the same biochemical effect, which is (p. 609)

a. blocking dopamine receptors.

b. blocking the production of noradrenalin.

c. stimulating the production of endorphins.

d. stimulating the production of glutamic acid.

6. Tardive dyskinesia is a side effect of taking conventional (p. 610)

a. antipsychotic medication.

b. antidepressant medication.

c. ECT.

d. none of the above.

7. In 1988, this became the first SSRI to be released in the United States. (p. 611)

a. Zoloft

b. Haldol

c. Prozac

d. Paxil

8. The immediate short-term effects of the tricyclic antidepressants serve to (p. 611)

a. reduce central nervous system arousal.

b. reduce intracranial pressure by absorbing cerebral spinal fluid.

c. increase the availability of lithium in the central nervous system for absorption.

d. increase the availability of serotonin and norepinephrine in the synapses.

9. The first antidepressant medications to be developed in the 1950s were (p. 614)

a. SSRIs

b. SNRIs

c. MAO inhibitors

d. tricyclics

10. Antidepressants are also being widely used to treat (p. 615)

a. bulimia.

b. panic disorders.

c. GAD.

d. all of the above.

PRACTICE TEST NUMBER 2

1. Benzodiazepines are used to treat (p. 615)

a. depression.

b. anxiety.

c. bipolar.

d. none of the above.

2. Lithium compounds are used in the treatment of (p. 617)

a. anxiety.

b. hyperactivity and specific learning disabilities.

c. bipolar mood disorders.

d. hallucinations and delusions.

3. Which of the following caused an immediate decrease in the widespread use of psychosurgical procedures in this country? (p. 620)

a. a 1951 law banning all such operations

b. the advent of electroconvulsive therapy (ECT)

c. the advent of the major antipsychotic drugs

d. the unusually high mortality rate

4. Psychosurgery is sometimes used for patients with debilitating (p. 620)

a. obsessive-compulsive disorders.

b. severe self-mutilation.

c. schizophrenia.

d. a and b.

5. In _____, positive reinforcement is often used to establish, by gradual approximation, a response that was initially resisted. (p. 624)

a. response shaping

b. token economy.

c. modeling.

d. avoidance therapy.

6. Systematic desensitization is aimed at teaching a person in the presence of an anxiety-producing stimulus to relax, because (p. 623)

a. avoidance therapy makes one extremely tense.

b. it is difficult, if not impossible, to feel pleasant and anxious at the same time.

c. resistance is futile.

d. sooner or later, one will have to confront one's fatal flaw.

7. In systematic desensitization, a patient confronting a feared real stimulus, as opposed to an imaginal one, is called (p. 623)

a. desensitized exposure.

b. unimaginative exposure.

c. in vivo exposure.

d. indecent exposure.

8. Using a form of the old-fashioned method of punishment to modify undesirable behavior is called (p. 623)

a. aversion therapy.

b. avoidance therapy.

c. abhorrence therapy.

d. subversion therapy.

9. Aversion therapy has been used successfully in the treatment of (p. 623)

a. bizarre psychotic behavior.

b. sexual deviance.

c. smoking, drinking, overeating, drug dependence, and gambling.

d. all of the above.

10. Response shaping is an example of   (p. 624)

a. a token economy.

b. systematic use of reinforcement

c. aversion therapy.

d. transference.

PRACTICE TEST NUMBER 3

1. In 1964, Bandura found that the most effective treatment for snake phobia was (p. 624)

a. avoidance therapy.

b. live modeling of fearlessness, combined with instruction and guided exposure.

c. having patients crawl through snake pits.

d. suppressing problematic behavior.

2. Generally, behavioral therapy has been found to be less useful for (p. 625)

a. responses not initially in an individual's behavioral repertoire.

b. the more pervasive and vaguely defined the client's problem is.

c. older female patients.

d. shy, withdrawn adolescents.

3. Behavioral techniques are the backbone of modern approaches to treating (p. 625)

a. sexual dysfunctions.

b. racism.

c. psychopathy.

d. eustice.

4. Albert Ellis' _____ posits that a well-functioning individual behaves rationally and in tune with empirical reality. (p. 625)

a. cognitive therapy

b. rational emotive behavior therapy (REBT)

c. classical psychotherapy

d. response shaping

5. Cognitive and cognitive behavioral therapy are types of self-instructional training focused on (p. 625)

a. avoidance training.

b. altering the self-statements an individual routinely makes in stress-producing situations.

c. reinforcers for socially appropriate behavior.

d. all of the above.

6. During therapy, a gestalt therapist is likely to ask, (p. 629)

a. "What are you aware of in your body now?"

b. "When you close your eyes, do you see the light?"

c. "What does it feel like in your gut when you think of that?"

d. a and c.

7. Therapists must constantly beware of developing mixed feelings toward the client, which is known as (p. 632)

a. negative affect analysis.

b. psychosis psychoanalysis.

c. counter-transference.

d. cognitive transcounterysis.

8. In integrative behavioral couple therapy (IBCT), _____ are integrated with change strategies to provide a form a therapy that is more tailored to individual characteristics and the needs of the couple. (p. 634)

a. acceptance strategies

b. fighting stances

c. "flight-or-fight" strategies

d. kugnitive fu

9. Most family therapists believe that _____—not just the designated "client"—must be directly involved in the therapy if lasting improvement is to be achieved. (p. 634)

a. a teacher

b. the family dog

c. the family

d. a minister

10. The _____ are based on the assumption that we have the freedom and the responsibility to control our own behavior. (p..627)

a. existential therapies

b. humanistic-experiential therapies

c. avoidance technology

d. Democratic Party doctrines

COMPREHENSIVE PRACTICE TEST

The following tests are designed to give you an idea of how well you understood the entire chapter. There are three different types of tests: multiple-choice, true-false, and essay.

MULTIPLE-CHOICE

1. A depot neuroleptics (p. 610)

a. is given in pill form

b. is given as a long-acting injection

c. is given in a liquid ingestible form

d. is used to calm train travelers

2. The half-life of a drug refers to (p. 609)

a. how long it takes to finish half of a prescription

b. time it takes for the level of a drug in the body to be reduced by 50%

c. length of time it is safe to use a drug

d. the sell by date for a drug

3. Which of the following would you see as making substantial gains in personal growth as a result of therapy? (p. 601)

a. Louis, who feels he would like to go back to school to finish his degree.

b. Meagan, who is depressed and suicidal.

c. Tommy, who has a drinking problem that has affected his entire life.

d. Paula, who has severe GAD.

4. Research suggests that about _____ percent of patients show clinically significant change after 21 therapy sessions. (p. 606)

a. 75

b. 50

c. 25

d. 28

5. A particularly harmful unethical behavior on the part of the therapist towards his or her client is (p. 606)

a. going over the allotted hour for the therapy session.

b. canceling an appointment.

c. engaging in a sexual relationship.

d. referring the client when it is apparent that the two of them can't work together.

6. A new drug that seems to be more effective in treating major depression, is (p. 611)

a. Effexor, a SSRI.

b. Effexor, a SNRI.

c. Prozac, a SSRI.

d. Prozac, a SNRI.

7. Carl Rogers client-centered therapy focuses on (p. 628)

a. placing the client at the center of therapy sessions and answering his/her questions.

b. natural power of the organism to heal itself.

c. removing the constraints and restrictions that grow out of unrealistic demands that people tend to place on themselves.

d. b and c.

8. The view of the existential therapist is that human beings, being aware of their own existence, are responsible for (p. 628)

a. deciding what kind of person to become.

b. establishing their own values.

c. actualizing their own potentialities.

d. all of the above.

9. The main two basic forms of psychodynamic therapy are (p. 633)

a. transference and counter-transference.

b. negative affect analysis and manifest analysis.

c. manifest psychosis and latent oriented psychoanalytical.

d. classical psychoanalysis and psychoanalytically oriented psychotherapy.

10. According to psychoanalysis, a dream has two kinds of content: (p. 631)

a. transference and dream transference.

b. cognitive content and dreary content.

c. manifest content and latent content.

d. big, hairy spider content and sexual content.

11. In _____, the therapist is careful to maintain a neutral manner, to allow the client to "work though" the conflict. (p. 632)

a. dreams

b. negative affect analysis

c. psychoanalysis

d. all of the above.

12. The original version of Freud's psychoanalysis is practiced only rarely today, because it (p. 632)

a. is arduous.

b. is costly in time, money, and emotional commitment.

c. may take several years before all major issues have been resolved.

d. all of the above.

13. The interpersonal therapy model developed by Klerman and associates, originally targeted for the problem of depression, has since been shown to be a promising treatment for (p. 633)

a. avoidance recession.

b. bulimia nervosa.

c. avoidable stress.

d. antisocial personality disorder.

14. Structural family therapy's approach is that family members will have altered experiences in the family and behave differently if (p.634)

a. they pack up and move to a different town.

b. they change the organization of the family in such a way that members will behave more supportively and less pathogenically toward each other.

c. the family context can be changed.

d. b and c.

15. Today, clinical practice is characterized by a relaxation of the boundaries previously found between disciplines, and most psychotherapists (p. 634.)

a. do pretty much what they want, striking out in whatever direction seems appropriate.

b. try to borrow and combine concepts and techniques from various schools.

c. don't really want to talk about it.

d. all of the above.

TRUE – FALSE

    1. T / F Therapy can offer magical transformations. (p. 600)

    2. T / F A client's motivation and the seriousness of the problem are important to the outcome of therapy. (p. 603)

    3. T / F Effective therapy depends, to some extent, on a good match between the client and therapist. (p. 603)

    4. T / F   Lithium is most useful for the treatment of anxiety. (p. 616)

    5. T / F Atypical antipsychotics may effectively treat the positive and

negative symptoms of schizophrenia. (p. 611)

6. T/ F SSRIs are chemically related to the older tricyclic antidepressants. (p. 612)

7. T / F A patient is in remission when treatment removes all symptoms. (p. 612)

8. T / F Prozac, Paxil, and Zoloft are now among the drugs most often prescribed by physicians. (p. 613)

9. T / F Benzodiazepines are widely prescribed, because these aren't addictive. (p. 616)

10. T / F A variety of behavioral techniques have developed to help patients unlearn maladaptive behaviors. (p. 622-623)

11. T / F In token economy programs, patients earn tokens good for privileges by demonstrating appropriate ward behavior. (p. 624)

12. T / F Psychoanalysis is not easy to describe, and the problem is complicated because of inaccurate conceptions based on cartoons and other forms of caricature. (p. 631)

13. T / F The greatest contribution of the interpersonal approach may be its role in the developing movement toward "integration" of the various forms of therapy. (p. 632)

14. T / F Although it is quite routine at the start of couples therapy for each partner to secretly harbor the idea that only the other will have to do the changing, it is nearly always necessary for both do so. (p. 633)

15. T / F The criticism has been raised that psychotherapy can be viewed as an attempt to get people adjusted to a "sick" society, rather

than to encourage them to work toward its improvement. (p. 635)

16. T / F Even though there is little or no solid evidence that psychotherapeutic outcomes are diminished when client and therapist differ in race or ethnicity, most members of minority groups state a strong preference for therapists who share their ethnic background. (p. 635)

ESSAY QUESTIONS

1. Explain how ECT is administered, and contrast the public and therapeutic views of its use.

2. Evaluate cognitive-behavioral therapies.

3. Name and discuss the four basic techniques of Freud's psychoanalysis.

USE IT OR LOSE IT

Provide an answer to the thought question below, knowing that there is more than one way to respond. Possible answers are presented in the Answer Key.

Supposing one of your family members needed mental health care, what information would you need to pick a therapist?

CRISS-CROSS

Now that you know all there is to know about this chapter, here's your opportunity to put that knowledge to work.

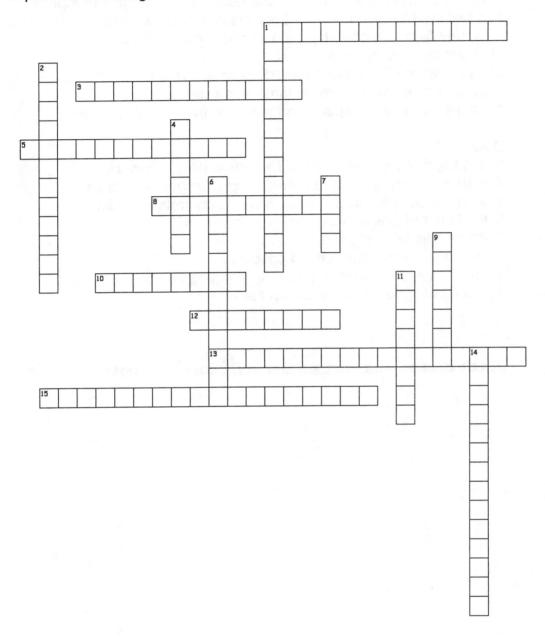

CRISS-CROSS CLUES

Across

1. assisting people with psychological problems to change
3. clients applying their attitudes and feelings toward their therapists
5. a test in which neither patient nor prescriber knows which drug is real
8. an unwillingness or inability to talk about certain things
10. learning skills by imitating
12. a measure of whether a drug does what it is supposed to do
13. passing an electric current through a patient's head
15. trials given by therapists who are following a detailed manual

Down

1. therapy that focuses on individual personality dynamics
2. a 19th-century procedure for relieving pressure in the brain
4. a physiologically inactive drug given to controls in studies
6. the father of classical psychoanalysis
7. Albert Ellis rational emotive therapy
9. therapy designed for married couples
11. a direct and active therapy acknowledging the role of learning
14. confronting real (not imagined) feared stimuli

Puzzle created with Puzzlemaker at DiscoverySchool.com

ANSWERS TO TEST QUESTIONS - CHAPTER 17

MATCHING
Psychological Test
  H. John Cade
  I. Albert Ellis
  E. psychoactive
  N. Carl Rogers
  J. Ugo Cerletti and Lucio Bini
  A. team approach
  C. negative process
  B. working alliance
  M. Aaron Beck
  G. Peter Kramer
  O. Virginia Satir
  K. Antonio Moniz
  I. Ladislas von Meduna
  D. randomized clinical trials
  F. depot neuroleptics

SHORT ANSWERS
(Your answer should contain the following points.)

1. a. agreement between patient and therapist about goals and tasks of
     therapy
   b. an affective bond between patient and therapist
   c. sense of working collaboration on the problem
   d. clear communication

2. a. therapist's impression of changes that have occurred
   b. client's report of change
   c. reports from client's family and friends
   d. comparisons of pre- and post-treatment scores on tests or other
      relevant measures
   e. measure of change in selective overt behaviors

]3. a. acts on serotonergic functioning
   b. as effective as the benzodiazepines in treating GAD
   c. low potential for abuse
   d. no withdrawal effects
   e. not as effective for those who had previously taken benzodiazepines
   f. takes two to four weeks to take effect; therefore, not effective in acute
      situations

4. a. treatment approach is precise

b. explicit learning principles is a sound basis

c. economy of time and costs is quite good

5. a. they selectively perceive the work as harmful while ignoring evidence to the contrary

b. over generalize on the basis of limited examples

c. magnify the significance of undesirable events

d. engage in absolutistic thinking

6. a. lack of highly systematized models of human behavior

b. lack of agreed-upon therapeutic procedures

c. vagueness about what is supposed to happen between client and therapist

THE DOCTOR IS IN...PSYCHIATRIC HELP—5¢

Pharmacological Treatment:
Focus on possible genetic connection with depression and prescribe antidepressants

Behavior Treatment:
Bernice learned her behavior from her family and is modeling the behavior she learned. Treatment focus on modeling the behavior of someone she admires and feels is successful and reinforcing behavior that might be beneficial, e.g., taking a few college classes, looking for a job, etc.

Cognitive and Cognitive-Behavioral Treatment:
Bernice's difficulties are a result of dysfunctional beliefs about herself and her situation. Use Ellis' REBT to restructure her belief system and self-evaluation, e.g., feeling like a bad mother in spite of her children saying otherwise.
Use Beck's cognitive therapy to challenge her illogical thinking about the present and the future, e.g., all she can ever do is factory work or stress-inoculation therapy, changing the way Bernice talks to herself about her current situation and how she is dealing with it.

Humanistic—Experiential Treatment:
Bernice's difficulties stem from problems with alienation, depersonalization, loneliness and failure to find meaning and genuine fulfillment. Using Rogerian therapy you would help Bernice become able to accept and be herself by establishing a psychological climate in which she can feel comfortable and accepted

Psychodynamic Treatment:

Classical psychoanalysis—search for repressed memories, thoughts, fears, and conflicts stemming from Bernice's early psychosexual development that would have to do with her experiences and relationships with her father and mother

Psychoanalytical oriented psychotherapy—attempt would be to help Bernice clarify distortions and gaps in the client's construction of the origins and consequences of her problem, thus challenging her "defenses"

Methods used:

Classical psychoanalysis—free association, resistance, transference, and dream analysis

Psychoanalytically oriented psychotherapy—active conversational style in which you would attempt to clarify distortions, such as her feelings about being family and if she is like her parents, schedule fewer sessions and face Bernice as you talked to her

MULTIPLE-CHOICE PRACTICE TESTS

PRACTICE TESTS

Q#	Test1	Test 2	Test 3
1	D	B	B
2	C	C	B
3	D	C	A
4	D	D	B
5	A	A	B
6	A	B	D
7	C	C	C
8	D	A	A
9	C	D	C
10	D	B	B

COMPREHENSIVE PRACTICE TEST

Q#	MULTIPLE CHOICE	T/F
1	B	F
2	B	T
3	A	T
4	B	F
5	C	T
6	B	F
7	D	T
8	D	T
9	D	F
10	C	T

11	C	T
12	D	T
13	B	T
14	D	T
15	B	T
16		T

ESSAY QUESTIONS
(Your answer should contain the following points.)

1.   a. The public sees ECT as horrific and primitive primarily because of lawsuits where patient consent was not obtained before treatment.
b. may be the only way of dealing with severely depressed and suicidal patients who have not responded to other forms of treatment
c. used as treatment for severely depressed pregnant women or the elderly who cannot take the antidepressant drugs
d. ECT is 80 percent effective with difficult-to-treat patients
e. Types
• bilateral ECT—electrodes are placed on either side of patient's head and brief electrical pulses are passed from one side of head to other for 1.5 seconds; bilateral more effective than unilateral, but has more severe cognitive side effects and memory problems
• unilateral ECT—involves limiting current flow to one side of the brain, typically nondominant side
f. patients are given anthemia and a muscle relaxant
g. patient has amnesia for a period preceding the therapy and is confused for the next hour or so
h. treatment administered three times weekly with patient becoming disoriented, which will clear when treatment terminates
i. recommended to start with unilateral and switch to bilateral if no improvement is seen

2. Evaluate cognitive-behavioral therapies.
a. appears inferior to exposure-based therapies in the treatment of anxiety disorders
b. may be most useful in helping basically healthy people to cope
c. stress-inoculation therapy successfully used with anger, pain, Type A behavior, mild forms of anxiety
d. extremely beneficial in alleviating many types of disorders: depression, panic disorder, generalized anxiety disorder, bulimia

3. a. Free association
• individual says whatever comes into his mind
b. Analysis of dreams

• procedure for uncovering unconscious material
c. Analysis of resistance
• the unwillingness or inability to talk about certain painful or threatening material
d. Analysis of transference
• client brings and unconsciously applies to her therapist, attitudes and feelings

USE IT OR LOSE IT
In order to pick an effective therapist for someone in your family you might want to ask about their specific degree, where they trained, their therapeutic philosophy, how much experience they have, and even personal factors such as their gender, and ethnicity. Finally, you might want to find out whether their services are covered by your insurance policy!

CRISS-CROSS ANSWERS

Across
1. psychotherapy
3. transference
5. double-blind
8. resistance
10. modeling
12. efficacy
13. electroconvulsive
15. manualized research

Down
1. psychodynamic
2. neurosurgery
4. placebo
6. Sigmund Freud
7. REBT
9. marital
11. behavior
14. in vivo exposure

Chapter 18: Contemporary and Legal Issues in Abnormal Psychology

BEFORE YOU READ

This chapter focuses on the ways in which society deals with abnormal behavior and changes which could be made to optimize these efforts. Chief among these are finding ways to prevent, rather than to treat, mental illness. Another topic addresses the availability of mental health care and the state of mental hospitals, and the role of health management organizations in regulating health care services. Finally, a number of legal issues are raised including the voluntary and involuntary commitment of mentally ill individuals for treatment, the assessment of whether a person is dangerous to themselves or others, the use of the insanity defense in criminal proceedings, and the issue of how best to treat mentally ill patients who commit crimes. As a final challenge, the ways in which people can improve mental health in their communities and on an individual level are discussed and detailed.

- **PERSPECTIVES ON PREVENTION**
    - Universal Interventions
    - Selective Interventions
    - Indicated Interventions
    - The Mental Hospital as a Therapeutic Community
    - Deinstitutionalization

- **CONTROVERSIAL LEGAL ISSUES AND THE MENTALLY DISORDERED**
    - The Commitment Process
    - Assessment of "Dangerousness;" The Insanity Defense

- **ORGANIZED EFFORTS FOR MENTAL HEALTH**
    - U.S. Efforts for Mental Health
    - International Efforts for Mental Health

- **CHALLENGES FOR THE FUTURE**

  The Need for Planning

  The Individual's Contribution

- **UNRESOLVED ISSUES**

  The HMOs and Mental Health Care

- **CONTEMPORARY AND LEGAL ISSUES IN ABNORMAL PSYCHOLOGY**

<u>OBJECTIVES</u>

After reading this chapter, you should be able to:

1. Define "universal intervention," and explain how universal intervention includes biological, psychosocial, and sociocultural efforts.

2. Define "selective intervention," and describe and illustrate selective intervention programs, using the example of teen alcohol and drug abuse prevention.

3. Define "indicated intervention," describe two types of crisis intervention, and describe and illustrate three types of indicated intervention, using the example of an airplane crash or other major disaster.

4. Describe efforts to resocialize patients in mental hospitals and aftercare programs, including methods for making a mental hospital a therapeutic community. Compare the effectiveness of these approaches.

5. Outline the procedures involved in civil commitment and the safeguards for patients' rights and due process in involuntary commitment.

6. Discuss the problems of assessing and predicting "dangerousness" and explain the obligations of the clinician under the "duty-to-warn" legal doctrine.

7. Review the various legal rulings relevant to the insanity defense and discuss the problems and controversies associated with this concept.

AS YOU READ

Answers can be found in the Answer Key at the end of the chapter.

KEY WORDS

Each of the words below is important in understanding the concepts presented in this Chapter. Write the definition next to each of the words.

Term	Page	Definition
Deinstitutionalization	649	
Forensic psychology (forensic psychiatry)	652	
Guilty but mentally ill	661	
Health maintenance organization	666	
Indicated interventions	642	
Insanity defense	657	
Managed health care	666	
Milieu therapy	648	
NGRI plea	657	
Selective interventions	642	
Social-learning programs	649	
Tarasoff decision	656	
Universal interventions	642	

WHO'S WHO AND WHAT'S WHAT—MATCHING

Alphabet Soup.

The acronyms in column one are all related to mental health. Name these in the second column and describe what each does in the third.

What it means...

Acronym	Name	What it Means
AABT		
APA		
APA		
APS		
NAMI		
NIMH		
NIOSH		
WHO		

SHORT ANSWERS

Provide brief answers to the following questions.

1. Briefly discuss the three requirements for psychosocial "health."

a.

b.

c.

2. Our government has approached the drug abuse problem with three broad strategies, all of which have proven insufficient. Name these and discuss.

a.

b.

c.

3. Discuss the three general therapeutic principles that guide the "milieu therapy" approach.

a.

b.

c.

4. Compare the relative effectiveness of the following three treatment approaches. Discuss what was discovered.

a. Milieu therapy

b. Social-learning treatment program

c. Traditional mental hospital treatments

5. An overcontrolled hostile person can become dangerous. Explain.

THE DOCTOR IS IN...PSYCHIATRIC HELP—5¢

Read the following scenarios and diagnose the client. Remember to look carefully at the criteria for the disorder before you make a decision as to the diagnosis. Make a list of other information you might need to help you understand the causal factors.

1. Stuart, a 26-year-old man you had been seeing for several years comes, into your office demanding to see you immediately, even though he doesn't have an appointment. He hasn't seen you for more than a month, because he had a job and was trying to go to school. Stuart is diagnosed with schizophrenia and is fine as long as he takes his medications; his behavior indicates he is not taking his medication. You try explaining to him that you have other appointments, but he becomes more and more agitated, talking about the people at work who are out to get him—but that he is going to get them first. Stuart is disheveled and looks like he hasn't bathed in several days. He tells you that you have to help him or he will do something awful.

As Stuart's therapist, what would you do and why?

2. Jack had been friends with Jill for two years. He was madly in love with her although she had made it clear that she liked him only as a friend and didn't want a romantic relationship. About five months ago, Jill met Brian and they dating. Jack felt jealous and left out. He had been through other "boyfriends" and always managed to wait them out until Jill stopped seeing them. This time is different, and Jill is talking about possibly marrying Brian. Jack is beside himself and is consumed with anger and jealousy. He is talking about killing Brian and making it look like an accident. He reasons that Jill will then have to seek him out

again for comfort. When asked how he would make it look like an accident, Jack replies that he would fix the breaks on Brian's car. Jack has the knowledge to do such a thing.

As Jacks' therapist, how would you respond, and what are your legal responsibilities?

<u>AFTER YOU READ</u>

Answers can be found in the Answer Key at the end of the chapter.

<u>PRACTICE TESTS</u>

Take the following three multiple-choice tests to see how much you have comprehended from the chapter. Each represents roughly one-third of the chapter. As you study the chapter, use these to check your progress.

PRACTICE TEST NUMBER 1

1. Universal interventions are concerned with (p. 642)

a. altering conditions that can cause or contribute to mental disorders.

b. establishing conditions that foster positive mental health.

c. early detection and prompt treatment of maladaptive behavior.

d. a and b.

2. Any effort aimed at improving the human condition, at making life more fulfilling and meaningful, may be considered part of _____ prevention of mental or emotional disturbance. (p. 643)

a. universal

b. selective

c. indicated

d. secondary

3. All of the following are sociocultural efforts toward universal intervention of mental disorders, **except** (p. 644)

a. economic planning.

b. penal systems.

c. public education.

d. social security.

4. Teenage drug and alcohol use is still viewed as one of today's (p. 644-5)

a. biggest money makers for organized crime.

b. victories over crime.

c. most significant psychological and community problems.

d. a and c.

5. Through their own drinking or verbalizations about alcohol, parents may (p. 646)

a. encourage use in their children.

b. sanction usage by their children.

c. have little affect in their children's usage.

d. a and b

6. The most powerful influence on whether a teen begins to use drugs seems to be (p. 646)

a. peers.

b. parents.

c. teachers and schools.

d. Pete, the mean kid down the block.

7. Programs designed to help youngsters overcome negative pressures from peers focus on (p. 646)

a. boxing and Kung Fu.

b. teaching social skills and assertiveness.

c. chess.

d. strengthening family bonds.

8. A study in 2000 reported that _____ had had more than a few sips of alcohol. (p. 646)

a. 80.3 percent of twelfth graders

b. 71.4 percent of tenth graders

c. 51.7 percent of eighth graders

d. all of the above.

9. A persistent concern about hospitalization is that (p. 649)

a. the mental hospital may become a permanent refuge from the world.

b. negative feedback is used to encourage appropriate verbalizations and actions by patients.

c. the environment, or milieu, is a crucial aspect of the therapy.

d. b and c.

10. Milieu therapy is (p. 648)

a. the temporary substitution of one treatment mode by another until adequate resources can be acquired to provide the treatment of choice.

b. a general term for any form of preventive treatment.

c. the use of the hospital environment itself as a crucial part of the therapeutic process.

d. the integration of any two distinct forms of treatment.

PRACTICE TEST NUMBER 2

1. The rise of biological therapies has meant that (p. 649)

a. nearly one-third of patients will be ineligible to return to the mental hospital.

b. from 70% to 90% of patients labeled as psychotic and admitted to mental hospitals can now be discharged within a few weeks.

c. all the activities in many mental hospitals can be brought into the total treatment program.

d. many patients are encouraged to take responsibility for their behavior.

2. Studies have shown that in the past, up to _____% of schizophrenic patients have been readmitted to the hospital within the first year after their discharge. (p. 650)

a. 1.732

b. 12.6

c. 45

d. 99.

3. Between 1970 and 1992, the number of state mental hospitals dropped from 310 to 273, and the patient population was reduced by 73 percent due to (p. 650)

a. the AIDS epidemic.

b. fallout from the Vietnam war.

c. the introduction of antipsychotic drugs.

d. deinstitutionalization.

4. Deinstitutionalization has contributed substantially to (p. 652)

a. mental health and general well-being in the U.S.

b. the number of homeless people.

c. the number of mentally ill people in prison.

d. b and c.

5. According to recent Justice Department statistics, _____ of the people in prison in the U.S. (275,000) have a mental disorder. (p. 652)

a. 1.732%

b. more than 16%

c. about half

d. almost all

6. Typically, the first step in committing an individual to a mental hospital involuntarily is (p. 653)

a. appointing a physician and a psychologist to examine the client.

b. filing a petition for a commitment hearing.

c. holding a commitment hearing.

d. notifying the police.

7. Studies have confirmed that individuals acquitted of crimes by reason of insanity typically spend _____ time in psychiatric hospitals as (than) individuals convicted of crimes spend in prison. (p.. 659)

a. less

b. about the same amount of

c. about the same amount or more

d. much more

8. Violent acts are difficult to predict because these are determined as much by _____ circumstances as by the personality traits of the individual. Mental health professionals typically err on the conservative side when assessing violence proneness. (p.. 656)

a. territorial

b. behavioral

c. situational

d. hostile

9. Which of the following groups of mentally ill individuals would be the LEAST likely to commit a violent act? (p. 656)

a. schizophrenic individuals.

b. manic individuals.

c. patients with deeply entrenched delusions.

d. patients in a major depressive state.

10. Congress passed its first comprehensive mental health bill, the National Mental Health Act in (p. 662)

a. 1789.

b. 1865.

c. 1946.

d. 1993.

PRACTICE TEST NUMBER 3

1. The M'Naghten Rule of 1843 established legal defense for a person (p.. 660)

a. if she lacked "substantial capacity" to appreciate the criminal character of her behavior.

b. if he were "unable to appreciate" the criminality of his act and the mental disorder involved must be severe.

c. unless it can be proven that at the time of her act, she did not know what she was doing was wrong, she is assumed to be sane.

d. if an "irresistible impulse" caused him to commit the crime, even though he knew what he was doing was wrong.

2. The Irresistible Impulse Rule of 1887 established legal defense for a person (p. 660)

a. if she lacked "substantial capacity" to appreciate the criminal character of her behavior.

b. if he were "unable to appreciate" the criminality of his act and the mental disorder involved must be severe.

c. unless it can be proven that at the time of her act, she did not know what she was doing was wrong, she is assumed to be sane.

d. if an "irresistible impulse" caused him to commit the crime, even though he knew what he was doing was wrong.

3. The American Law Institute (ALI) Standard of 1962 established legal defense for a person (p. 660)

a. if she lacked "substantial capacity" to appreciate the criminal character of her behavior.

b. if he were "unable to appreciate" the criminality of his act and the mental disorder involved must be severe.

c. unless it can be proven that at the time of her act, she did not know what she was doing was wrong, she is assumed to be sane.

d. if an "irresistible impulse" caused him to commit the crime, even though he knew what he was doing was wrong.

4. The Federal Insanity Defense Reform Act (IDRA) of 1984 redefined legal defense for a person to be such that (p. 660)

a. if she lacked "substantial capacity" to appreciate the criminal character of her behavior.

b. if he were "unable to appreciate" the criminality of his act and the mental disorder involved must be severe.

c. unless it can be proven that at the time of her act, she did not know what she was doing was wrong, she is assumed to be sane.

d. if an "irresistible impulse" caused him to commit the crime, even though he knew what he was doing was wrong.

5. The National Institute of Mental Health (NIMH) was formed in Washington, D.C. in (p. 662)

a. 1812.

b. 1849.

c. 1946.

d. 1984.

6. The National Institute of Mental Health (NIMH) (p. 660)

a. conducts and supports research.

b. supports training in the mental health field.

c. helps communities plan, establish, and maintain effective mental health programs.

d. all of the above.

7. The National Mental Health Association (NMHA) (p. 662)

a. sets and maintains the high professional and ethical standards within the psychological industry.

b. recognizes psychological disorders as one of the 10 leading work-related health problems.

c. works for the improvement of services in community clinics and mental hospitals.

d. works to reduce the incidence of mental retardation and carry on a program of education.

8. The American Psychological Association (APA) (p. 662)

a. sets and maintains the high professional and ethical standards within the psychological industry.

b. recognizes psychological disorders as one of the 10 leading work-related health problems.

c. works for the improvement of services in community clinics and mental hospitals.

d. works to reduce the incidence of mental retardation and carry on a program of education.

9. The National Institute for Occupational Safety and Health (NIOSH) (p. 663)

a. sets and maintains the high professional and ethical standards within the psychological industry.

b. recognizes psychological disorders as one of the 10 leading work-related health problems.

c. works for the improvement of services in community clinics and mental hospitals.

d. works to reduce the incidence of mental retardation and carry on a program of education.

10. The National Association for Retarded Citizens (NARC) (p. 663)

a. sets and maintains the high professional and ethical standards within the psychological industry.

b. recognizes psychological disorders as one of the 10 leading work-related health problems.

c. works for the improvement of services in community clinics and mental hospitals.

d. works to reduce the incidence of mental retardation and carry on a program of education.

COMPREHENSIVE PRACTICE TEST

The following tests are designed to give you an idea of how well you understood the entire chapter. There are three different types of tests: multiple-choice, true-false, and essay.

MULTIPLE-CHOICE

1. At high risk for mental disorders are (p. 642)

a. recently divorced people and the physically disabled.

b. elderly people and physically abused children.

c. persons recently uprooted from their homes and victims of severe trauma.

d. all of the above.

2. Adequate preparation for potential problems likely to be encountered by

anyone during a given life stage is a requirement for _____ health, at

the _____ level of prevention (p. 643)

a. biological, universal

b. psychosocial, universal

c. biological, selective

d. psychosocial, selective

3. In addition to mental illness, grounds for commitment require that a person

must be judged to be _____ and in need of treatment or care in a

hospital. (p. 648)

a. dangerous to themselves or to others

b. incapable of providing for their basic physical needs

c. unable to make responsible decisions about hospitalization

d. any of the above

4. Which of the following patient rights was limited, according to a 1990 U.S.

Supreme Court ruling? (p. 654)

a. right to compensation for work

b. right to refuse ECT and psychosurgery

c. right to receive treatment

d. right to refuse psychotropic medication

5. Violence among psychiatric patients is especially prominent for those who (p.

655)

a. watch television.

b. drink alcohol.

c. do not get enough exercise.

d. all of the above.

6. One dilemma in attempting to rehabilitate previously violent psychiatric

patients is that the mental health workers must exhibit some degree of (p. 655)

a. patience.

b. stability.

c. professionalism.

d. trust.

7. A man's NGRI plea ("not guilty by reason of insanity") in a court case means (p. 657)

a. "he couldn't have done it, because that would be an insane thing to do."

b. "Not Getting Rightful Incarceration."

c. "while he did do it, he lacked moral blameworthiness, because he was insane."

d. whichever reason seems like it might work.

8. Courts have generally not considered _____ sufficient grounds for an insanity defense. (p..659)

a. altered states of consciousness

b. being divorced

c. having more than one personality

d. being married

9. An NGRI pleas was more likely to be found to be successful if the defendant was (p. 661)

a. diagnosed with a major mental disorder, or there had been prior mental hospitalizations.

b. a female.

c. accused of a violent crime other than murder.

d. all of the above.

10. Several states have adopted a different mentally ill plea, known as (p. 661)

a. Please Let Me Go (PLMG).

b. Guilty But Mentally Ill (GBMI).

c. Too Drunk to Know (TDTK).

d. all of the above.

11. During World War II, _____ recruits were rejected for military service for psychiatric reasons. (p. 662)

a. no

b. 50% of

c. two out of seven

d. 55,734

12. Most often, in an HMO, the gatekeeper who determines which mental health treatments will be offered is a (p. 666)

a. psychiatric social worker.

c. medical generalist or business professional.

b. Ph.D. psychologist.

d. psychiatrist.

13. The World Health Organization (WHO) estimates that mental disorders affect at least _____ people worldwide. (p. 663)

a. 42

b. three million

c. 200 million

d. 1.732 billion

14. Serious mental health risk factors, unrecognized as workplace problems, may exist in (p. 663)

a. the work load and pace; machine-paced work in particular.

b. the work schedule; rotating shifts and night work.

c. role ambiguity; who has responsibility for what.

d. all of the above.

15. Other than accepting some measure of responsibility for the mental health of

others through the quality of one's own interpersonal relationships, another constructive course open to each citizen is (p. 665)

a. serving as a volunteer in a mental or other hospital.

b. supporting realistic measures for ensuring comprehensive health services for all age groups.

c. working toward improved public education, responsible government, the alleviation of prejudice, and the establishment of a more sane and harmonious world.

d. All of the above.

TRUE – FALSE

1. T / F For the most part, mental health efforts have been restorative, rather than preventative. (p. 642)

2. T / F . Often the most beneficial aspect of a therapeutic community is the interaction among the patients themselves. (p. 649)

3. T / F Today, in most states, the therapist not only can violate confidentiality with impunity, but may be required by law to take action to protect persons from the threat of imminent violence against them. (p. 656)

4. T / F The new "guilty but mentally ill" (GBMI) plea requires a two-part decision.
(p. 661)

5. T / F Psychological difficulties among employees may result in absenteeism, accident proneness, poor productivity, and high job turnover. (p. 663)

6. T / F The World Federation for Mental Health was established in 1861. (p. 665)

7. T / F The world's mental health problems are so large and so scattered that there is really nothing that an individual can do to help. (p. 664)

8. T / F Most people will have to deal with severely maladaptive behavior during their lives. (p. 665)

9. T / F Economic considerations have drastically altered the machinations of the mental health field. (p. 667)

10. T / F Prevention of mental illness focuses on universal, selective, and indicated interventions (p. 667)

ESSAY QUESTIONS

1.. A relatively new approach in behavioral psychology is in its prevention, as opposed to previous approaches, all aimed at treatment. Name and discuss the three subcategories of these efforts.

2. Deinstitutionalization, the movement to close down mental hospitals and treat persons with severe mental disorder in the community, has been the source of considerable controversy. Discuss the pros and cons of

    a.

    b.

    c.

3. The wake of the Tarasoff decision left many perplexing issues for practitioners. Discuss the decision and its aftermath.

WEB LINKS TO ITEMS OR CONCEPTS DISCUSSED IN CHAPTER 18

Mental Health

www.mentalhealth.org/

www.nmha.org/

www.mental-health-matters.com/

insanity defense

www.psych.org/public_info/insanity.cfm

www.forensic-psychiatrist.com/insanity.html

USE IT OR LOSE IT

Provide an answer to the thought question below, knowing that there is more than one way to respond. Possible answers are presented in the Answer Key.

Should mentally ill people who commit crimes be put in jail or mental institutions?

CRISS-CROSS

Now that you know all there is to know about this chapter, here's your opportunity to put that knowledge to work.

<u>CRISS-CROSS CLUES</u>

Across

1. health services company
4. professional organization for psychologists
7. recognizes psychological disorders as one of the leading work-related health problems
8. NGRI
11. intervention efforts aimed at a specific subgroup
12. professional organization that sets standards for U.S. psychiatric industry
13. professional organization for behavioral therapists
14. intervention efforts aimed at influencing the general population
15. agency serving as central research and training center

Down

2. total treatment program
3. murder victim whose death led to duty-to-warn rule
5. new criminal court plea requiring two-part decision
6. legal status of the mentally ill
8. intervention efforts directed toward high-risk individuals
9. volunteer organization working for improvement of services in community clinics
10. volunteer organization for the mentally ill

Puzzle created with Puzzlemaker at DiscoverySchool.com

ANSWERS TO TEST QUESTIONS - CHAPTER 18

SHORT ANSWERS
(Your answer should contain the following points.)

1.   a. develop the skills needed for effective problem solving, expressing emotions constructively, and engaging in satisfying relationships
   b. an accurate frame of reference on which to build his or her identity
   c. be prepared for the types of problems likely to be encountered during life

2.   a. Interdicting and reducing the supply of drugs available.
   • War on drugs has had little impact on the availability of drugs.
   b. Providing treatment services for those who develop drug problems
   • Perhaps the least effective way to reduce the problem
   c. Encouraging prevention
   • Most desirable; teaching young people ways to avoid use; hasn't worked because efforts have not been powerful enough or been well implemented

3.   a. staff expectations are clearly communicated to patients
   b. patients are encouraged to become involved in all decisions
   c. patients belong to social groups on the ward

4.   a. Milieu therapy
   • more successful releases than traditional
   • 70% of released patients remained in the community
   b. Social-learning treatment program
   • more successful releases than traditional
   • more than 90% of released patients remain out
   c. Traditional mental hospital treatments
   • fewer than 50% released patients remained out

5.   Often exhibits an unusually low level of manifestly aggressive behavior prior to the commission of an aggressive act—very often an extremely violent one.
   • i.e., the high school honor student who kills several of his classmates with a gun.

THE DOCTOR IS IN...PSYCHIATRIC HELP—5¢

1. Have Stuart committed to the hospital as an emergency. There isn't time to get a court order, and Stuart is dangerous to himself or others; incapable of providing for his basic physical needs; unable to make responsible decisions about hospitalization, and is in need of treatment.

2. First, you would discuss the consequences of such behavior and what it could

mean to his life and others. If, as the therapist, you believe that Jack is capable of carrying out his threat, you have a duty-to-warn. This means that client/therapist confidentiality can be broken to inform police and to make "reasonable efforts" to inform the potential victim.

MULTIPLE-CHOICE PRACTICE TESTS

PRACTICE TESTS

Q#	Test1	Test 2	Test 3
1	D	B	C
2	A	C	D
3	B	D	A
4	C	D	B
5	D	B	C
6	A	B	D
7	B	A	C
8	D	C	A
9	A	D	B
10	C	C	D

COMPREHENSIVE PRACTICE TEST

Q#	MULTIPLE CHOICE	T/F
1	D	T
2	B	T
3	D	T
4	D	T
5	B	T
6	D	F
7	C	F
8	A	T
9	D	T
10	B	T
11	C	
12	C	
13	C	
14	D	
15	D	

ESSAY QUESTIONS

(Your answer should contain the following points.)
  1.   a. **Universal Interventions:** General population
   • Biological measures lifestyles, diet, physical exercise, good health habits
   • Psychosocial measures develop physical, intellectual, emotional, and

social competencies
• Sociocultural measures relationship between an individual and his or her community
b. **Selective Interventions:** Specific subgroup
Selective prevention strategies
Education programs for high-risk teens
Parent and family-based intervention
Peer group programs
Increase self-esteem
Mass media
c. **Indicated Interventions:** high-risk individuals
  • Mental hospital as therapeutic community
Aftercare programs
2.   a. Significant improvement versus "abandonment"
b. Seemed a workable plan
c. Problems arose
  • substandard homes and services
  • many became homeless
  • lack of follow-up
3.   a. decision held therapists responsible to warn authorities if a specific threat emerges during a session with a client
b. calls into question the patient confidentiality
c. ethical dilemmas

USE IT OR LOSE IT

This is a complex question, with no clear answer. Most people would agree that the public should be protected from crime and dangerous behavior. However, it is often difficult to determine who constitutes a future threat, or how mental health issues have contributed to a particular crime. In addition, if people are placed in a mental institution instead of prison there are questions about how long they should be held, who will determine their release, and whether this constitutes incarceration without due process of law if they did not receive a trial

CRISS-CROSS ANSWERS

Across
1. HMO
4. APS
7. NIOSH
8. insanity defense
11. selective
12. APA
13. AABT
14. universal
15. NIMH

Down
2. milieu therapy
3. tarasoff
5. GBME
6. forensic psychology
8. indicated
9. NMHA
10. NAMI

CHAPTER NOTES

Use the next few pages for any random notations....

NOTES

NOTES

NOTES